Literacy Theo Digital Age

NEW PERSPECTIVES ON LANGUAGE AND EDUCATION

Series Editor: Professor Viv Edwards, *University of Reading, Reading, Great Britain*

Two decades of research and development in language and literacy education have yielded a broad, multidisciplinary focus. Yet education systems face constant economic and technological change, with attendant issues of identity and power, community and culture. This series will feature critical and interpretive, disciplinary and multidisciplinary perspectives on teaching and learning, language and literacy in new times.

Full details of all the books in this series and of all our other publications can be found on http://www.multilingual-matters.com, or by writing to Multilingual Matters, St Nicholas House, 31–34 High Street, Bristol BS1 2AW, UK.

NEW PERSPECTIVES ON LANGUAGE AND EDUCATION: 45

Literacy Theories for the Digital Age

Social, Critical, Multimodal, Spatial, Material and Sensory Lenses

Kathy A. Mills

MULTILINGUAL MATTERS
Bristol • Buffalo • Toronto

This book is dedicated to Ryan,
Lachlan, Juliette, Marie and Henry

Library of Congress Cataloging in Publication Data
Mills, Kathy, 1974- author.
Literacy Theories for the Digital Age: Social, Critical, Multimodal, Spatial, Material and
Sensory Lenses/Kathy A. Mills.
New Perspectives on Language and Education: 45
Includes bibliographical references and index.
1. Literacy—Study and teaching. 2. Literacy—Technological innovtions. 3. Literacy—
Social aspects. 4. Interactive multimedia. I. Title.
LC159.M55 2015
302.2'244–dc23 2015023398

British Library Cataloguing in Publication Data
A catalogue entry for this book is available from the British Library.

ISBN-13: 978-1-78309-462-2 (hbk)
ISBN-13: 978-1-78309-461-5 (pbk)

Multilingual Matters
UK: St Nicholas House, 31–34 High Street, Bristol BS1 2AW, UK.
USA: UTP, 2250 Military Road, Tonawanda, NY 14150, USA.
Canada: UTP, 5201 Dufferin Street, North York, Ontario M3H 5T8, Canada.

Website: www.multilingual-matters.com
Twitter: Multi_Ling_Mat
Facebook: https://www.facebook.com/multilingualmatters
Blog: www.channelviewpublications.wordpress.com

The policy of Multilingual Matters/Channel View Publications is to use papers that are
natural, renewable and recyclable products, made from wood grown in sustainable for-
ests. In the manufacturing process of our books, and to further support our policy, preference is given to printers that have FSC and PEFC Chain of Custody certification. The FSC
and/or PEFC logos will appear on those books where full certification has been granted
to the printer concerned.

Typeset by Techset Composition India (P) Ltd, Bangalore and Chennai, India.
Printed and bound by CPI Group (UK) Ltd, Croydon, CR0 4YY

Contents

Figures

Acknowledgements

Have you ever wondered about a book that you wanted to read, but it wasn't written yet? This is the book I wrote because I wanted to read it. It is my hope that others, including established and recent scholars and educators from a range of disciplines, will find value and renewed inspiration in the theories and conceptualisation of this work for their own research and practice. To the growing number of graduate students in education around the world, I trust you will find this volume a vital introduction to some of the key theories that are shaping the challenging and ever-relevant field of literacy education in the digital turn.

I acknowledge Professor Len Unsworth for his unfailing encouragement, for supporting our scholarly research collaborations, and for demonstrating how to extend the boundaries of current thinking in multimodality.

I greatly appreciate David Howes, a noted cultural anthropologist, who wrote the brilliantly insightful foreword to the book. He wrote his contribution more than once because he strives for quality.

I thank distinguished Professor Allan Luke, whose critical debate and co-authorship with me has influenced the framing of Chapter 3 on critical scholarship.

I thank Professor Barbara Comber for co-authoring with me since 2010, and for influencing my conceptualisation of Chapter 5, socio-spatial literacies.

Professor Kar-Tin Lee is acknowledged for leading and supporting me, and many other scholars, to continue the vital legacy of educational research for the public good.

I thank Maryam Sandhu for her contribution to the detailed formatting and pagination of the original manuscripts. Finally, I thank the blind peer reviewers and series editor, Viv Edwards, for their encouragement, constructive feedback, and support of this volume.

Foreword

The Sensory Turn in Literacy Theory and Practice

This book charts a range of established and emergent paradigms for literacy research. Classic paradigms include socio-cultural literacies, multimodal literacies and critical approaches to literacy. More recent paradigms include socio-spatial literacies, socio-material literacies, and presented for the first time here, sensory literacies. Kathy Mills lays out the key concepts of each of these approaches, notes their internal tensions, surveys recent developments, and draws out implications for the classroom. In the process, the old definition of literacy as essentially alphabetical is exploded, and replaced by the notion of 'multiliteracies', derived from the work of the New London Group (2000). There is also a strong focus on the extracognitive and extralinguistic dimensions of literacy. This will not sit well with many educational psychologists, who have a vested interest in the restricted definition of literacy. But it will appeal, and appeal strongly, to those who recognise, like Mills, that the digital revolution has put an end to literacy, as we knew it.

Texts are no longer static the way they were in the print era – they are interactive. And why shouldn't a student be allowed to submit a home video alongside or even in place of an essay in English class? In the age of YouTube, it is visual literacy skills that students are most in need of – skills to produce videos themselves, and skills to analyse videos critically. Thus, whereas an earlier generation of educators stirred up lots of anxiety about our 'amusing ourselves to death' and 'the closing of the American mind' (i.e. ignoring the canon), or allowing 'edutainment' to take the place of education proper, Mills' main message in this book is to get over it and get on with the show.

In one research project Mills and her colleagues conducted, upper primary school students were provided with camcorders and invited to make videos of their schoolyard activities. One video included clips of going down a slide – from the perspective of the slider. Carsten Höller would approve. He is the German artist best known for installing a series of gigantic, glass-encased slides in the Tate Modern Turbine Hall gallery. Like many contemporary artists (Jones, 2006), Höller is bent on exploding the conventional understanding of aesthetic experience as one of 'disinterested contemplation'. Art should be sensational, should be thrilling, and it is if you hurtle down one of his slides. In offering museum-goers this opportunity, Höller is also recovering and restoring the original meaning of the term aesthetic, which comes from the Greek *aisthēsis*, which translates as 'perception from the senses' without specification as to modality or limitation to 'the beautiful'.

Mills explodes our understanding of literacy in the same way Höller explodes our conventional understanding of art. She does so through introducing her own theory of 'sensory literacies', which can be broken down into the visual, audio, gestural, tactile, spatial, olfactory, gustatory and various assemblages (e.g. audio-visual), all of which exceed, but also complement, the textual. This move is inspired in part by Mills' reading of recent research in neuroscience and in the anthropology and history of the senses. Briefly, while we live in a society in which much of our knowledge comes to us through our eyes (e.g. the printed text, the computer screen), we now know that the senses work together to promote learning. As Rosalind Charlesworth, a professor of child development puts it: 'We learn best through multisensory experiences' (Charlesworth, 2014: 51). This is confirmed by neuroscientists, such as Jeanette Norden, who states, 'The brain loves diversity' (quoted in Henshaw, 2012: 249). Indigenous societies have long been aware of the importance of integrating the senses in learning experiences. In her article, Other Ways to Wisdom: Learning through the Senses Across Cultures, Constance Classen describes how for Indigenous cultures, '…each of the senses has a vital role to play in the acquisition of knowledge about the world' (Classen, 1999: 269; see further Howes, 2014b). Engaging multiple senses makes events and objects more interesting and memorable in whichever culture one lives.

I had the pleasure of reading Mills' book in manuscript form while on the plane to Toledo to attend the 47th annual meeting of the International Visual Literacy Association (IVLA), which was held at the Toledo Museum of Art (TMA). It enabled me to better comprehend the ground-breaking nature of that conference and its venue. In the words of John Debes (1969: 27), one of the founders of the IVLA, writing in 1969, 'Visual literacy refers to a group of vision competencies a human being can develop by seeing and at the same time having and integrating other sensory experiences'. This definition, with its stress on multisensoriality, resonates with a point made by Brian Kennedy, the visionary Director of the TMA, in a TEDx Dartmouth talk called 'Visual literacy: Why we need it.' In his talk, Kennedy expressed the view that 'visual literacy is the key to sensory literacy', and that creating conditions for sensory literacy should be the goal of the contemporary museum. The TMA accordingly staged a special exhibition entitled InSight: Contemporary Sensory Works, curated by Adam Levine, timed to coincide with the IVLA conference. The exhibition brochure states provocatively:

> Is art meant only for the eyes? The three artists featured in this exhibi-tion don't think so. They [i.e. Pinaree Sanpitak, Aminah Robinson, and Magdalene Odundo] all create works that explicitly or implicitly evoke a multisensory experience. Although each artist's work is highly visual, the art on display in *InSight: Contemporary Sensory Works* also plays with notions of tactility and sound.

The conference itself was entitled The Art of Seeing: From the Ordinary to the Extraordinary. This idea of seeing as an art, as a competency not a given, is a tremendously powerful one. Knowing how to see a painting is seen as equivalent to knowing how to read a book, and therefore, as a skill which requires training. The TMA has taken the promotion of visual literacy to extraordinary lengths, beginning with baby tours, and continuing with the publication of an alphabet book called *The Art of Seeing Art: A, B & See* under the direction of Director of Education, Kathy Dank-McGhee.

> Reading and looking at this alphabet book of works from the Toledo Museum of Art will help children develop important looking skills that contribute to visual literacy. Being literate in the visual arts could give young children an advantage in learning to read and write. (Toledo Museum of Art, 2013: 3)

The extraordinarily rich body of research on the complementarity of visual and alphabetic literacy, and how skill at one not only could, but does, enhance performance in the other (see Dank-McGhee & Slutsky, 2007), as well as the notion of multiliteracies promoted throughout this book by Kathy Mills, gives the lie to phenomenological anthropologist Tim Ingold's suggestion, in his critique of the anthropology of the senses, that 'the eyes and ears should not be understood as separate keyboards for the registration of sensation, but as organs of the body as a whole' (Ingold quoted in Mills, this volume). In his statement, Ingold belittles the differences between seeing and hearing (and completely ignores tasting, smelling and the rest). He is oblivious to the notion of multiple intelligences because of his diminished understanding of the multisensoriality of human experience, and his dismissal of the growing body of research in the history and anthropology of the senses that points to the differential elaboration of the senses in different cultures and historical periods (see Howes & Classen, 2014). Ingold dismisses this vast corpus of work because it fails to cohere with what the philosopher Merleau-Ponty would lead us to expect. But Ingold's work is really just a testimony to the poverty of phenomenology and, in our estimation, only serves to underscore the need to take a sociologically savvy, cross-culturally aware approach to the study of the multimodality of human learning and experience (see Howes & Classen, 2014; Ingold & Howes, 2011). As Classen observes, when we examine the meanings vested in different modalities and sensations across cultures:

We find a cornucopia of potent sensory symbolism. Sight may be linked to reason or to witchcraft, taste may be used as a metaphor for aesthetic discrimination or for sexual experience, an odour may signify sanctity or sin, political power or social exclusion. Together, these sensory meanings and values form the *sensory model* espoused by a society, according to which the members of that society 'make sense' of the world, or translate sensory perceptions and concepts into a particular 'worldview.' There will likely be challenges to this model from within the society – persons and groups who differ on certain sensory values – yet this model will provide the basic perceptual paradigm to be followed or resisted. (Classen, 1997: 402)

In keeping with the spirit of exploding literacies that animates this book, I would like by way of closing, to address one last example of a kind of literacy practice that actually takes us beyond the pale of literacy and enucleates writing from an analphabetical perspective. It comes from the last chapter of *Worlds of Sense* (Classen, 1993b). It is a study of literacy as anti-culture, which has to do with the Andean experience of the written word.

Andean society was traditionally, and remains, a profoundly oral society. For example, according to Andean cosmogony, the world and its peoples were called into being by the creator, Viracocha, and his voice made the corn grow. While most of the empires of the world have depended on some form of writing, the Inca Empire was unique in that it depended on the quipu, described below.

Throughout the Andes today, there is an annual tradition of holding Conquest Plays. Unlike the Conquest Plays of Mexico, which celebrate the coming of the Spanish and the civilising influence of Christianity, these dramas commemorate the destruction of the Inca Empire. A common theme is the disjunction between orality and literacy, sound and silence. In one version, the Spanish move their lips when they speak, but make no sound. The Inca Emperor Atahualpa is handed a written letter. He raises it to his ear in an attempt to listen to its contents, but to no avail. He passes it around among his followers, but the scratches on the paper equally mystify them:

> Seen from this side, it is like a swarm of ants ... Looking at it again, I see stags, upside down and their feet in the air. Who on earth could understand that?

The process is repeated with a Bible, which is handed to the Emperor by a Spanish priest. After examining it, Atahualpa drops it. This is the excuse the Spanish needed. Pizarro's soldiers rush in and seize the Inca for refusing to receive (and submit to) the Word. He will later be beheaded. In another version, the priest sets about beating the Indians with the Bible after Atahualpa drops it. These plays offer 'a graphic portrayal of the Andean experience of [the onslaught of] writing and Christianity as a brutal imposition' (Classen, 1993a: 117).

The beheading of Atahualpa plunged the Andean world into silence. Bereft of the Inca's commanding voice, the empire crumbled. The Inca's voice had used to be relayed by the quipu-makers to the far corners of the empire, just as information, typically used for accounting purposes, flowed back to the capital Cuzco via the same medium.

The quipu is a fascinating technology of communication. It consists of a set of knotted cords of different colours hung on a string. The information is encoded in the differences of colour and the position and size of the knots. The quipu is, then, 'a recording in three dimensions with colour' (Ascher & Ascher, 1981: 62). But unlike writing or photography, or any of the other recording and communications media with which we modern Westerners are familiar, the quipu does not store information independently of the mind or body of the recorder. It is a mnemonic device, nothing more, and each quipu maker had a personal style, a kind of shorthand, as it were. This is why several hundred extant quipu can only bear mute testimony to a vanished civilisation. Every attempt by scholars to decode them has failed.

Can quipu making and telling be considered a form of literacy? On the basis of Kathy Mills' definition, it could be so. It is actually a very sensual medium of communication, engaging touch and rhythm in the tying of the knots, and involving a wide range of colours and patterns (Classen, 1999: 125). Furthermore, the quipu is not flat and linear, as is writing; it is multidimensional – which makes it unlike a two-dimensional computer screen as well. Functioning on several sensory levels and in more than two-dimensions, the quipu is a highly sophisticated form of sensory literacy. As for cracking the code, the quipu scholar Robert Ascher suggests that the problem lies with Western academics being too visualist in their approach. If we could but curb our visuality a little:

> We might understand [quipu] writing as simultaneously tactile and visual, and probably more. Being that we are who we are, it is difficult to internalise this notion so that it becomes a part of us, but I think that it is the next step that must be taken in the study of Inka writing. (Ascher, 2002: 113)

The multisensoriality of the quipu rivals that of any digital device. There is a very real problem with truancy in the Andes. For example, Classen recounts a delightful myth that explains why children keep running away from school. This is not surprising, given the association of the kind of learning that goes on in school (i.e. learning to read and write) with anti-culture. What sort of policy would be needed to attract the children back? Certainly, it would not be a policy based on one copybook per child, however colourful, or even one laptop per child, but perhaps one quipu per child.

Hopefully, these ruminations have revealed something of how stimulating Kathy Mills' theory of sensory literacies can be. It is the same with each of the approaches to literacy she treats: the socio-cultural, the critical, the multimodal, the socio-spatial and the socio-material approaches to literacy. This slim volume is a remarkable compendium, a brilliant work of synthesis – and the book to end all books.

David Howes
Sensory Anthropologist

Preface

Rhizomatic Literacy Theories

... no theorist developed their view of the world in an intellectual vacuum.
(Hubbard & Kitchen, 2011: 14)

Narrow conceptions of literacy in educational research and practice have given way to a number of emerging social and cultural paradigms in recent decades that have reconfigured the field. Currently, researchers can select from an array of tangential or rhizomatic confluences of theory to interpret literacy practices in research. These have included socio-cultural, socio-spatial and socio-material theories, critical pedagogy, theories of multimodality and social semiotic traditions with shared characteristics (e.g. systemic functional linguistics). Taken together, these and other theories have continually repositioned literacy research over recent decades, generating significant scholarship that has continually sought to regenerate and maintain a heritage of literacy research, while continually challenging and extending this legacy to reflect the challenges of the current political, cultural, historical and technological context in which literacy practices occur.

This volume is an attempt to bring together, critique the strengths and weaknesses, and systematise in a single, concise volume, some of the trending theories of literacy research in the 'digital turn' (Mills, 2010b: 246). At the same time, it is acknowledged that in order to theorise each approach in sufficient depth, there is always selectivity, and such an endeavour cannot presume to be comprehensive. This book draws on disciplines within the social sciences, such as critical sociology, applied linguistics, philosophy, cultural geography and cultural anthropology. It is acknowledged that there are also important perspectives of literacy learning from the field of archaeology, literary studies, history, political sciences, psychology, cognitive science and other clinical and behavioural sciences, which are beyond the purview of this volume.

Since the last quarter of the 20th century, there has been a continual move among literacy researchers away from views of a single, universal set of literacies – an 'autonomous model' as Street (1984: 2) advocated in the 1980s – to consider literacies as social practices. This mirrored a significant parallel shift in educational theory more broadly, away from behaviourist perspectives to approaches that were founded on progressive philosophies of education. Skills-based approaches, also known as basic skills approaches, had begun in the 1930s, aligned with psychometric models of skills testing and measurement – an epistemological stance consistent with positivism.

Socio-cultural literacy theory, also known as the New Literacy Studies (Street, 1997a), drew attention to the ideological nature of literacy practices, arguing that dominant Western or colonising powers use the autonomous model of literacy to oppress cultures and communities whose literacy practices are positioned marginally. The redefining of literacy to account for communities of literacy practices was accompanied by the flourishing of naturalistic or ethnographic approaches to literacy research, with methodological roots in cultural anthropology (Grenfell, 2012). Such approaches were applied to the study of language communities, and later of institutions. Literacy researchers around the world amassed detailed, first-hand observations and descriptions of the varieties of literacy that proliferate in many forms across social geographies and cultures. The last decade has seen a digital turn in the socio-cultural literacy research tradition, with a significant number of studies examining sign-making practices in digital contexts of use (Mills, 2010b).

This body of work intersected with the earlier tradition of ethnographies of communication by Gumperz and Hymes (1972: 1) that began in the 1970s. These theorists and others, including Cazden (1988) in the late 1980s, drew attention to the linguistic rights of cultural and linguistic minorities and vernacular speech communities. Waging an ideological battle to honour marginalised language groups, language studies turned to focus on lexico-grammatical descriptions of Black English to generate awareness of the silencing of Native American languages, communities and children (Gumperz & Hymes, 1972). Such research often combined ethnography and linguistics to document the differences between the discourses or available narrative language resources in users' early socialisation (e.g. dialect variation, genre mastery, cultural semantics, discourse strategy), and mainstream institutional discourses (Iyer *et al.*, 2014). Socio-linguists followed in this tradition, analysing how classism and racism functions discursively and often unreflectively in literacy classrooms. Examples include the study of oral and written language in early childhood classrooms by Michaels (1985) and Gee (2012) and my book-length critical ethnographic and socio-linguistic analysis of discourses and power relations in an Australian multiliteracies classroom this century (Mills, 2011c).

Colleagues and I recently recounted the key political shifts in the United States that paved the way for literacy scholars to challenge racial hegemony and white epistemological supremacy, most notably in the landmark case of Brown versus the Board of Education in 1954, which lead to the racial segregation of students being deemed unconstitutional (see Iyer *et al.*, 2014). While arguably, even the Brown decision has ultimately served to advantage whites (see Ladson-Billings, 2009), law in the United States began to express a concern to protect the interests of African American children and to move towards a more socially just education and legal system. It should be acknowledged here that Critical Race Theory emerged in law scholarship and later in education theory, to challenge the incompleteness of the civil rights movement. Critical Race Theory points to both overt and subtle forms of institutional racism that persist in schools, such as through standards-based reform, inequitable property rights (including knowledge capital), and the racial bias of the curriculum in the United States. Marginalisation of minority languages and discourses still persists in schooling, with racism underlying the near-demise of language diversity and the use of English becoming the dominant mode of instruction in many countries.

The need to expose relations of power and inequality was a parallel move to theoretical developments in socio-cultural literacy research and sociolinguistics. Critical literacy scholars challenged the constitution of 'official' knowledge, including who holds the power of curriculum decision-making and text selection. Pedagogies, education, and ultimately the essential processes of institutionalised schooling, became radically repositioned. A central goal of critical applied linguistics was to interrogate and subject to scrutiny the encoding of institutional and ideological power in language, whether of speech, writing or other modes, to identify patterns of oppression and marginalisation (Apple *et al.*, 2009). A critical approach to applied linguistics emerged taking a variety of forms, including critical discourse analysis and critical language studies (Kress, 1990), neo-Marxian social analysis, philosophical post-structuralism, critical linguistics (Fowler & Hodge, 1979) and pedagogical models of critical literacy (Anderson & Irvine, 1993; Lankshear *et al.*, 1993). Building up a persuasive and vigorous account, together, these critical applied linguistic traditions theorised the relations between language use, ideologies and social power, using social semiotics to interrogate language across multiple and diverse social contexts (Iyer *et al.*, 2014).

Multimodal approaches to literacy studies have recently taken centre stage, in step with the global changes to the ease of production and widespread circulation of images and other non-verbal modes in web-based texts

(Kress, 2000b). I pluralise the phrase 'multimodal approaches' here because there are a number of different multimodal approaches, each with a particular understanding and usage of the terms 'modes', 'multimodality', and 'discourses'. For example, O'Halloran (2004: 1) has coined the term multimodal discourse analysis (MDA) in which discourse refers to the micro-textual level analysis of texts. This differs from Hodge and Kress' references to macro-level discourses, and socio-political interests and understandings. O'Halloran also identifies a distinction between MDA and systemic functional multimodal discourse analysis in the Hallidayan tradition (SF-MDA).

Another distinctive approach is multimodal interactional analysis, which is evident in the original theorising of Scollon and Scollon (2003) in the book, *Discourses in Place*. This approach draws in part, on the interactional socio-linguistics of Goffman, such as in *The Presentation of Self in Everyday Life* (1959) and *The Interaction Order* (Goffman, 1993). Our position relative to various interaction orders is indicated through our use of language, which indexes us to the groups to which we belong (or from which we are excluded). For example, even a simple sentence such as, 'Do you work in this building too?' is about locating others socially, spatially, economically and ideologically, indexing those who are within, without, alongside, below or above in the institutional social order.

Each of these approaches to multimodality – and this list is not exhaustive – aims to analyse and systematise a broad repertoire of semiotic resources in human communication. An important caveat is that while extending grammars of spoken and written language, such analyses do not assume that the structure of these language forms dictates the structure of other forms of communication, such as music, gestures, dance, visual arts and so on (Jewitt, 2011a).

The shared rationale for multimodal approaches is to broaden understandings of semiotics or meaning making to address the full range of representational modes used in cultures, such as writing, image (still and moving), sound, spatial meanings, gestures, gaze, speech and posture (Jewitt, 2011a). For example, theorists such as Painter *et al.* (2013) have developed analytic tools for theorising and analysing the intermodal meaning relations in multimodal texts, such as picture books, animated movies and other children's literature, to extend the boundaries of current descriptions of image-word relations. They anticipate that the expansion and development of such grammars will continue across a range of genres and registers with the same fervour as semantically based investigations of words.

More recently, spatial theories that have emerged from social geography have found a place in literacy studies, recognising that the spaces of literacy practices are socially produced (Mills, 2010a). For several decades, social geographers, such as Lefebvre (1991), have acknowledged the implications of the social production of space, while others have begun to theorise how space matters to society, to cities (Soja, 2008) and to global networks (Castells, 2000b). In Soja's (2004: ix) words, the '...transformative and edgy retheorisation...' of the spatiality of society flowed through disciplines, such as history, philosophy, art, anthropology and education. In literacy studies, there have been examinations of the social spaces interrelated with literacy practices, and how those spaces are similarly tied up in power geometries that operate across a range of scales, from the bodies of individuals to global spatiality (Hubbard & Kitchen, 2011). Key edited contributions, such as *Spatialising Literacy Research* (Leander & Sheehy, 2004), have pointed to the potentials of putting space first in literacy practice and research. This move is not to be seen in opposition to historical and social analysis, but rather, as multidimensional approaches that bring these elements together dialectically (Soja, 2004).

A related and more recent turn in educational theory is the clustering of ideas around the materiality of learning – the view that the material technologies, bodies, objects, cultural artefacts and so on are inextricably tied to meaning, rather than assumed to bear little or no relation to it (Fenwick *et al.*, 2011). There has often been a privileging of human intentionality or active agency in educational research, and for some time in theories of social cognition, tools and materials have been recognised as constitutive of learning processes (see Vygotsky, 1978). However, socio-materiality removes the conceptual blinkers that obscure how educational practices are shaped by materials.

Socio-material approaches to literacy are about mapping the webs of relations or collections of things – of actors, curriculum, pedagogies, discourses and assemblages of non-human material forces, such as classrooms, writing materials, buildings, furniture, cultural artefacts and learning resources. It has long been understood that the material resources for writing in homes and early childhood settings play an important role in literacy learning. Children use a plethora of materials – crayons, paper, paint, pencils, chalk, educational toys, alphabet blocks, books, foam bath letters and magnets – to learn concepts of print, and how to represent ideas using various materials. The changing media and technologies of literacy, media production, and communication have perhaps stimulated the renewed interest in the materiality of textual practices.

It is time to examine the role of the senses and experiences in the changing world of digital communication. Extending previous work with colleagues that have foregrounded the sensorial dimensions of filmmaking or digital video production (see Mills *et al.*, 2013; Mills *et al.*, 2014; Ranker &

Mills, 2014), here I outline the beginnings of an approach to sensory literacies. Extending the key principles of sensory or experiential learning, located
in social geography, cultural anthropology and sensory research methodologies, sensory literacies explicitly attends to the senses in literacy practice and
research. This paradigm is about attending to the forgotten sensoriality of
literacies, that is, how literacy practices relate to, influence, and deeply
engage the senses in embodied experiences of the world.

To some extent, the broadening of literacy research to include the multiple clustering of ideas around central themes of importance in literacy
research and practice parallels the postmodern turn across a number of disciplines, where literacies and its theories of analysis have become pluralised,
branching in multiple directions. This is like Deleuze and Guattari's (1987:
21) rhizomes, which are offshoots and multiplicities '...composed... of
dimensions, directions. And when a multiplicity of this kind changes dimension, it necessarily changes in nature as well, undergoes a metamorphosis'.
This is the nature of literacy and literacy research. It is hoped that this
volume will help readers to reflect on the paradigms within which we view
the field, and which have laid the conceptual foundations of literacy studies
for the future.

This book is an attempt to bring together established and new theories
of literacy practices and research to understand their distinctive features,
their strengths and their weaknesses. It is time to trace the multidisciplinary,
theoretical threads currently winding through the fabric of literacy research.

Paradigmatic approaches

The paradigmatic approach, applied here to trace literacy research in the
digital turn, comes with certain clarification. While some of the literacy
studies traditions that are included here have withstood the test of time, new
theoretical approaches have emerged to challenge or extend existing ways of
conceptualising the changing nature of literacy and communication practices. Such transitions in literacy studies and other fields are a by-product of
tectonic shifts in the modes of media of literacy practice, and perhaps the
global time-space pathways of interdisciplinary scholars that intersect to
bring to light new ways of thinking about educational change.

It is acknowledged that there are benefits as well as limitations of paradigmatic approaches to conceptualising any field. Schools of thought never
develop as unified, theoretically tidy and linear narratives. Researchers may
borrow from multiple theoretical perspectives, or fail to recognise the theoretical roots of their own thinking. Literacy studies are never completely
stable, and never completely able to be compartmentalised. The notion of

sequential or historical trajectories of schools of thought, such as of multi-modal approaches or critical approaches, are always contested terrain, and there are many derivations of each theory. Literacy theories are never pure, but are constantly emerging, changing, and becoming and being legitimated in relation to particular social contexts and times.

The paradigms that are traced in this book reflect amalgamations of thought that have perceptible internal consistency to constitute recognised and emerging traditions. Research paradigms in literacy and digital practices often cross-reference one another, drawing from rich legacies of the past, and drawing from theoretical approaches across disciplines, such as sociology, anthropology, psychology, philosophy, linguistics and social geography. Mapping conventional and new approaches to literacy and digital practices needs to be done, particularly when post-graduate theses in the academy are required to draw from distinct theoretical frameworks to approach problems or potential issues of inquiry.

Mapping emerging paradigms of literacy research

Chapter 1 provides an introduction to the digital turn in literacy studies. The opening chapter anticipates the significance of studies of literacy in a digital age, citing some of the social moves that have influenced this shift. It gives an overview of recent significant developments in the field, providing a foundation and context for the reader to navigate the paradigmatic approach to the book, the 'aggregates of intensities' or discernible clustering of ideas, within the broader policy debates about literacy curriculum (Deleuze & Guattari, 1987: 15).

Chapter 2, Socio-cultural Literacies, outlines the scope of one of the most well-cited paradigms of literacy research since late last century. These theorists view literacy as socially constructed through talk and other language exchanges that occur and vary across communicative settings, such as homes and classrooms. Often applying ethnographic methods and interactional socio-linguistics, moment-by-moment social interactions and practices contribute to shaping the use of language in classrooms, communities and cultures. The chapter reviews the recent augmentation of this important work with new developments, including the digital hybridisation of literacy practices, networked alliances of practices in online communities, new epistemologies and user-generated web literacies.

Chapter 3, Critical Literacies, reviews foundational contributions of key critical theorists of schooling and education, such as Giroux (1988), Freire (1985), Gore (1988) on Foucault, McLaren (1993), Apple (1982) and Apple *et al.* (2009), and literacy education more specifically, which have in many ways shaped current understanding of literacy practices in institutions, such as access, power, critical media literacy and control of literate bodies.

Chapter 4, Multimodal Literacies, traces the work of multimodal theory with social semiotics, as put forward by Kress and van Leeuwen (2006), Jewitt (2011b), van Leeuwen (1999), Lemke (1998) and others who have influenced the analysis of the semiotic resources used in multimodal texts and practices. It begins by defining the core concepts of multimodal theory and provocatively explores the burgeoning development of non-verbal communication and multimodal theory from its inception. This is a critical account, and one that brings to light and examines some of the tensions that have arisen in this steadily trending approach, with implications for current classroom practice.

Chapter 5, Socio-spatial Literacies, demonstrates the powerful role of spatial flows in digital literacy research, continuing the spatial turn in the broader social sciences. The chapter highlights studies and theories about 'deterritorialisation' (Deleuze & Guattari, 1987: 319) of literacy practices, border crossing, mapping the circulation and flows of digital literacy practices, creating third spaces in classrooms and spatial justice in digital literacy practices.

Chapter 6, Socio-material Literacies, is based on a topic that is steadily growing in educational research (Fenwick *et al.*, 2011), though its influence on writing research has been regarded since the late 1990s (Haas, 1996). Material approaches demonstrate that matter matters to literacy research, because social practices are always entangled with corporeal objects, and are not merely social and cognitive. At a time when the media of reading and writing are constantly becoming more complex and multiple, socio-material approaches counterbalance views of literacy that ignore the physical dimensions of reading and writing to focus on literacy practices as abstract mental processes.

The final chapter, Sensory Literacies, represents the beginnings of a new paradigm developed here, outlining the potentials of a sensorial approach for literacy practice. I propose new ideas that draw on a sensorial shift in the social sciences and ethnographic research, such as of Howes (2005), Pink (2009), and Ingold and Vergunst (2008), to anticipate potentials for the study of literacy practices and teachers' work in classrooms within the purview of technological change. This approach draws on recent epistemological shifts in the social sciences from cognition and rationality as primary sources of knowledge, to better account for sensorial and experiential forms of knowing and communicating what is known. Such a perspective is needed in the context of the changing hybrid capabilities of digital technologies to respond to human motion, haptics, gestures and other sensory input. However, its truth is also evident in historical forms of writing and communication across cultures and times. This dialogue is begun tentatively here, as an offshoot from its theoretical soil in cultural anthropology and the social sciences, to literacy research in the digital turn.

Personal postscript

This book aims to reflect some of the important lines of flight, a deterritorialisation of the shape of literacy research, always undergoing metamorphosis. Literacy research is more than reproduction – it is like a rhizome that continually expands. While I have attempted to honour many of the key theorists who have shaped the field of literacy as we know it today, I am equally conscious that good literacy theory generation must constitute anteduplication and ante-replication, in order to accommodate the continual changes to the role of literacy in society, in education and in the context of the technological means by which we communicate. It is for this reason that I have included both old and new paradigms, including 'sensory literacies' – something new and relatively unexplored. This book was not written sequentially, but rhizomatically, as a map that was produced from the middle, from the end and then to what is now the beginning. Every map is only partial, even when the desire is to be somewhat comprehensive. To extend Deleuze and Guattari's (1987: 21) analogy to literacy research, I see each literacy theory represented in this book as essentially '...detachable, connectable, reversible, modifiable' and any reading of the book can have '... multiple entryways and exits...' to take you, the reader into your '...own lines of flight'.

1 Globalisation, Mobile Lives and Schooling in the Digital Turn

In an age of the 'global home,' literacy practices of the past are reduced in their power to determine the practices of the future.

(Mills)

Ways of thinking about literacy research arise in particular historical moments, and in relation to the social, economic, political and technological factors that set the stage and call for different ways of doing and theorising literacy. This book is an attempt to acknowledge the multiple and coexisting paradigms that are making a significant difference to the way we understand literacy in what I have called the 'digital turn' – the rapid digitalisation of literacy practices generated by human action, across a growing number of spheres of practice in the 21st century (Mills, 2010b: 246).

Globalisation

Children and youth today are growing up in a very different world than generations past: they can potentially use digital toys, tablets and mobile devices anywhere and anytime from much younger ages and earlier stages of language development than ever before. With the rise of the global home, a pun on McLuhan and Powers' (1989) book entitled *The Global Village*, the way young children are socialised in literacy practices is radically altered when compared with previous generations. For example, with the advent of touch-screen technologies, such as the iPad, babies and toddlers in many households can interact with an array of educational apps before they are able to correctly hold a pencil. At the same time, they are often surrounded at home and early childhood settings by an array of non-digital literacy materials, such as books, crayons, paper, craft, puzzles and alphabet blocks: the children switch between these and digital literacy practices with ease. The elementary school age child can potentially interact with a broadened selection of screen-based entertainment, from handheld to full sized video game consoles, tablets, personal computers and laptops for multiplayer online games. They can view user-generated content from peers on YouTube about the latest crazes, from tutorials about loom bands to Minecraft parodies. Teenagers and adolescents use the internet for both social and nonsocial purposes, including support of their offline friendships with peers (Gross, 2004). In the context of continuing urbanisation and more blatant commercialisation through globalised media, children and youth are often surrounded by digital displays from small to large, from the handheld devices in the home to the electronic billboards on buildings, buses and almost any commercial object that has a vertical surface.

A walk through Times Square in New York provides an extreme example of the pervasiveness of the digital image by global corporations and economies. The large-scale distribution of mass media and popular culture that saturates urban life through globalisation and technological progress brings with it both new opportunities and new risks (Jones Diaz *et al.*, 2007). Beck (1992: 22) foresees that, 'Along with the growing capacity of technical options grows the incalculability of their consequences'. These social and technological changes bring new security concerns for end-users, such as cyber bullying, identity theft, social engineering, piracy, malware and phishing, while events such as the 11 September attacks demonstrate the presence of an instant global audience for the transnational organisation of terrorist acts on a global scale (Giddens, 2002).

Literacy has become a process of commodification in which literate learning is entangled with commodities. It is similarly implicated by what Kinder (1991: 3) terms a 'transmedia intertextuality' – a conglomeration of interconnected texts across modes and media. In the context of capitalist accumulation, literacy learning throughout the life course involves interaction with multiple objects, video games, websites, toys, movies, books, figurines and licensed merchandise, as literacy is made and remade in networks of practice, and as material texts circulate and are adapted into diverse commodified forms. Within these discursive repertoires, which are often tied to global commercial corporations, children actively construct and reconstruct their sense of self and identity (Hughs & Macnaughton, 2001). This calls for a problematising of the ideological effects of the hybridised textual environment, and nuanced accounts of everyday and school-based literacy practices within the social conditions of globalisation (Makin & Whiteman, 2007).

The paradigms in this book are theorised in response to a series of social transformations known variously as the 'knowledge society' or the 'new economy' (Kalantzis & Cope, 2005: 16). For students to participate effectively in a globalised society they need new capabilities and knowledge assets that contribute value to organisations, communities, online networks and nations. One of the most significant and expanding areas in the new knowledge economy is what can be called technological knowledge – the technical content and process knowledge required for innovative digital media production. This includes knowledge of two areas: machines, such as handheld devices; and media applications, such as widgets, apps (applications) and other software. Elementary students enjoy using new technologies for digital media production, but we cannot assume that all students have the necessary skills for participation in the knowledge economy simply because they play video games for pleasure (Mills, 2010d).

The knowledge economy is heavily dependent on technologies that assist the flow of information – '...within enterprises, between enterprises and between enterprises and consumers' (Castells, 2000b: 16). Technological knowledge is a means of productivity gain and competitive advantage. Those who lack the newest technological knowledge may find themselves debilitated socially, economically and culturally, as others find information faster, work more efficiently and flexibly, and produce knowledge, media and commodities that have global influence. Castells (2000b: 17) observed more than a decade ago, 'Indeed, technology is now very much a relationship between tools and the knowledge of these tools in people's heads'. Clearly then, societal and technological changes require shifts in the way we think about knowledge in literacy practices (Mills, 2010d).

At the same time, there are risks associated with overproduction and over consumption of new technologies that may be incalculable or invisible into the future. We can liken this to Beck's (1992) discussion of the overproduction of food and the shift from the historical problem of hunger to the new problem of obesity in contemporary society. Texts and textual practices that are temporally and spatially dissimilar become drawn together in unanticipated ways in the lives of children and youths, and in homes, schools and other institutions, and require social responsibility.

When we consider the inclusion of responsible processes of digital media design in schools, students need textual knowledge, which includes both knowledge of the social and cultural context in which the text is produced and used, and the multimodal elements within the text. This includes the visual, audio, spatial, gestural and linguistic design elements that are combined in unique ways to synergistically represent meaning (Mills, 2009). By linguistic elements, I am referring to the phonological, lexical, grammatical

and generic structures of language that typically form the substantial content of English curricula (Mills, 2010d).

Multimedia information and new communications technologies are tied
to the hybridisation and expansion of new textual knowledge, which play
with conventional notions of genre, and which apply modified vocabularies
and new grammars. Digital technologies and the related convergence of the
industries of computing, broadcasting and publishing have contributed to
shifts in choices of modes, genres and linguistic structures (Cope & Kalantzis,
2000a). For example, instant messaging among English and Cantonese users
draws on common grammatical errors and shortenings, unconventional verb
forms and lexical choices, and creative orthographic representations (Lee,
2007). These patterns of spontaneous hybridisation of grammar, vocabulary
and orthography are causing linguists and literacy educators to reconsider the
shape of textual knowledge in a digital age (Mills, 2010b, 2010d).

In the process of digital media production learners also require content
knowledge of the subject or field. Content knowledge refers to funds of facts,
concepts and theories in the designer's head. Depending on the social purpose and audience of the multimedia text, this prior knowledge may include
sources such as personal experiences, experts, authoritative sources, and less
formally recognised knowledge texts. To engage in digital media production
involves knowing certain information about the subject represented, including the ability to use particular discourses and domain-specific vocabulary
for different communities of online users (Mills, 2010d).

Whether viewing or uploading podcasts, social networking, microblogging short posts of 140 characters or less, playing video games, instant messaging or engaging in any new hybrid textual and social practice, there is a
need to understand what students are coming to know. Students need critical literacy skills and discernment to judge the appropriateness, morality,
authenticity, truth, significance, relevance and substance of the texts they
encounter online, and to counter hegemonic discourses with their own critique and socially responsible text production (Makin & Whiteman, 2007).
The new knowledge assets for digital media production – technological, textual and content knowledge – describe in a coherent way the global supplies
of knowledge that learners combine synergistically to create or remix meaning in a digital age.

The World Wide Web (WWW) is a significant feature of contemporary
life, particularly for communication and social networking since the rise of
the social web or Web 2.0 (O'Reilly, 2005). When contrasted with the earlier
applications of the WWW, Web 2.0 has increased the ease and reduced the
cost of online collaboration, such as polls, blogs, podcasts, micro-blogs, social
networking sites, wikis and other more democratic forms of user-generated

content. Also referred to as the 'read-write web', Web 2.0 provides a means for free, rapid dialogue and instant feedback from significant international audiences (Wheeler & Wheeler, 2009). The third generation of web developments, combined with the proliferation of mobile devices with enhanced functionality and user-interfaces, is likely to bring new potentials for creating, cloud storing, collaborating and sharing digital media, and its associated user identities.

Mobile Lives

Outside of schools, students live in an expanding, mobile world of mobile lives and textual practices. This is not just about the use of mobile digital devices to communicate, but the portability of literacies and 'portable personhood' (Elliotte & Urry, 2010: 103). Identity and textual practices are essentially recast in terms of capacities for movement, and the expanded use of 'miniaturised mobilities' – handheld digital devices such as iPod, smartphones and tablets (Elliotte & Urry, 2010: 5). People are becoming more dependent on the ability to traverse national borders through air travel and other transport systems. During the 1800s, people travelled approximately 50 meters per day, mostly by foot or by horse and carriage; today they travel approximately 50 kilometres per day, using road, rail or air travel (Buchanan, 2002).

The new mobilities and their associated textual practices have transformed family life, the economy, security, work, citizenship, consumer behaviour and pleasure. Yet the flow of people, technologies and texts is not as open and fluid as it may seem, with tightly networked systems of regulation, surveillance and scheduling governing the organisation and control of mobilities. There are also those who are immobilised against the background of the movement and consumption of others, such as children who may travel less frequently than parents to attend the local school, or the economically marginalised workers who provide goods and services for the mobile professionals (e.g. mobile phone factory workers, hotel cleaners) (Elliotte & Urry, 2010).

Arguably, our increasingly mobile lives, the mobility of consumer goods and texts themselves, and the accessibility and affordances of mobile technologies, have wrought far-reaching changes to everyday literacy practices. Digitally encoded meanings now travel across great distances, whether in written, audio or visual form, such as e-books, e-journals, blogs, online chat, email, social media, global news, instant messaging, Voice-Over Internet Protocol, online purchases, digital movies, videos, video games, music and other forms of digital entertainment. Such changes necessitate the consolidation and generation of emerging paradigms for research, and new ways of thinking about digital media practices, literacy and social life – the aim of this book.

Digital Challenge for Education Policy

Educational policy makers should be explicitly concerned with the adoption of contemporary digital tools in the educational system (Merchant & Schamroth Abrams, 2013). Schools are confronted with the digital challenge – the challenge of embedding the new within the institution of schooling, which historically privileges linguistic or alphabetic modes of meaning.

Research in predominantly English-speaking countries has demonstrated that mandated testing of writing and literacy, such as the No Child Left Behind Act (2001) which authorised accountability testing in the United States, frequently positions digitally-mediated writing somewhat peripherally to English curriculum content (Applebee & Langer, 2009; Mills & Exley, 2014b). For example, here in Australia, school students have been required to participate in national testing since 2008 within the National Assessment Program: Literacy and Numeracy (NAPLAN). NAPLAN is a program of national tests that includes writing and language conventions (spelling, grammar and punctuation), to give schools and systems the ability to compare student achievement against national standards. Writing skills testing has become discursively constructed as a race in which states and territories, schooling systems and categories of students are positioned in opposition to one another by the media and the Australian government via the My School website (ACARA, 2012; Mills & Exley, 2014b).

The re-regulation of schooling – when central governments reclaim control of education – is also critically important for understanding the educational research context in the digital turn (Helgøy et al., 2007; Mills & Exley, 2014b). For example, in Australia, there has also been a recent shift from state English curricula to a centralised Australian English Curriculum that includes multimodal text creation using software (ACARA, 2014). This has been a positive development, arising from input into the curriculum by academics in the field. However, the reclaiming of federal control over educational outcomes, where multimodality and digital change is under-acknowledged, may limit the sustainable integration of new technologies in classrooms and the English curriculum. A search for the term 'multimodal' in the version of the Common Core State Standards (CCSS) in the United States at this present time, reveals no instances, providing an example of how the mandated literacy curriculum lags behind new literacy research (CCSSO & NGA, 2013). This sets up a potentially constraining context for teachers and researchers to embed new forms of digital textual practices (For an extended analysis of multimodality in the CCSS see Mills & Exley, 2014a).

Digital Challenge for Teachers of English – A Case Study

All social action involves a temporal and spatial dimension, and institutional ways of evaluating social performances, yet there are few studies of digital composition that simultaneously attend to these three dimensions. My classroom research with Beryl Exley demonstrated how multimodal and digital design involves changes to the delivery system of instruction, but more importantly, to the very nature of schooling (Mills & Exley, 2014b). We drew on Bernstein to theorise the symbolic and pedagogic struggles and resolutions observed as pedagogies for digital composition were introduced into an English curriculum in a low-socio-economic elementary school in Australia over several years. Specifically, the research examined changes to time, space and text in a digital composition program within three classrooms. Bernstein's theory of the pedagogic device explicitly addresses time, space and text to theorise social action in classrooms – a theory that has strong support in the discipline of sociology (see Bernstein, 2000).

The program taught students how to design multimodal and digitally written texts across a range of genres and text types. The students worked individually and collaboratively to produce web pages, sharing lengthy narratives and personal profiles, and inserted widgets such as maps and birthday countdowns. They handwrote scripts and recorded audio-visual podcasts in the school's purpose-built studio to record information reports. The teachers taught narrative writing activities through online comic creation. Students wrote scripts and created video documentaries containing interviews with characters from novels, and wrote web logs to recount everyday events and learning experiences, such as documenting their Lego robotics experiments in science (Mills & Exley, 2014b).

Many of these creative tasks were complex, involving new metalanguages to describe multimodal texts (e.g. shot types, cutaway shots, transitions), and technical proficiencies with a suite of software products. For example, the micro-documentary lessons included modelling and analysis of the features of micro-documentaries, responding to children's literature to imagine alternative plots, classifying shot types, learning digital camera skills, drawing storyboards, writing scripts, filming workshops, digitally editing movies, recording voice-overs and presenting movies to the school community.

Our research demonstrated that the selection, relation, sequence and pace for introducing specialist digital and multimodal design competencies into the writing curriculum was a function of embedding the instructional discourse into the regulative discourse through the pedagogic act (Bernstein, 2000; Mills & Exley, 2014b). The evaluative rule of the digital writing program often emphasised the performance of digital skills over the linguistic elements of the design tasks (e.g. punctuation, spelling, capitalisation, grammar, writing quantity). This is confirmed by other research in the United Kingdom and in the United States, where students are being taught to use digital applications, and tasks are sometimes restricted by the design of the user interface (Merchant & Schamroth Abrams, 2013).

We also observed a gradual shift from linguistic-based text criteria to one that included linguistic, visual, spatial, gestural and audio assemblages and their integrated modes. While a collaborative approach to pedagogical reform was upheld throughout the study, and brought about the transformation of writing practices in the curriculum, conflicts were created between the theoretical ideal and the system constraints.

The regulative discourse and its evaluative rules governed what aspects of multimodal and digital design did or did not constitute writing and literacies. For example, while the teachers and researchers worked together to develop a set of rubrics or criterion-referenced assessments to grade the students' web pages, digital stories, online comics, podcasts and other multimodal creations, only the most experienced teacher provided the students with time to edit and display their texts, and utilised this assessment information in formal school-based reporting. The other teachers nominated to leave the students' multimodal writing samples unfinished and unassessed in school reporting processes, because the digital compositing content and criteria were not aligned to the prescribed state curriculum at the time of the study (Mills & Exley, 2014b).

There was a tension between the evaluative rule of mandated testing of writing skills – the official recontextualising field created and dominated by the state – and the differing evaluative rules for assessing multimodal text creation. Writing in its various forms carries with it epistemologies and values that are deeply embedded in disciplinary and cultural practices (Ackerman, 1993). Without the wholesale transformation of the evaluative rules for writing throughout all levels of the system, the instructional and pedagogic discourse of schooling will continue to relegate the broadened range of semiotic codes and media production skills to the margins of the elementary English curriculum (Mills & Exley, 2014b).

Our original research in classrooms demonstrated that the pedagogic device or cultural relay of schooling regulated, to some extent, how digital and multimodal writing and communication practices were embedded in the English curriculum in a low socio-economic and culturally diverse elementary school. The changes created an ideological struggle as digital text production practices and multimodal grammars were adapted from broader societal fields to meet the instructional and regulative discourses of a conventional writing curriculum that prioritised written words in paperbound textual formats (Mills & Exley, 2014b).

The teaching teams and researchers embedded a broadened range of multimodal composition using different media practices within the English curriculum, and this recontexualised time, space and text to some degree. For example, we observed important differences to the regulative discourse used by teachers, and with the use of space, with certain digital practices, such as audio recording, involving different practical requirements, including access to quiet spaces or rooms away from other noise interference. Time was also specialised by the use of the digital tools and multimodal design. Reflecting a performance model, the writing curriculum prioritised the future tense as the temporal modality because the program was oriented towards moving students rapidly through an ambitious set of new technical skills and creating texts in new genres. Time for students to construct their own pedagogic agendas was limited (Mills & Exley, 2014b).

The significance of the regulated timing and pacing of the pedagogic discourses observed in these new writing lessons is that the act of pedagogising new writing knowledge and communication skills specialised meanings to time. The social grammar of schooling influenced the transformation of new literacy knowledge and practice as it moved from specialist media work in industry domains into pedagogic classroom communication. The new writing and text construction practices became recontextualised as official school knowledge, with all the institutional trapping of time and its regulation in schools through the pedagogic device (Mills & Exley, 2014b; Moss, 2000).

We observed that the teachers took hold of new digital and multimodal text production practices more readily when they were aligned to the requirements of writing in the national literacy test. During the final months of the project, we observed that despite some incremental changes to the three teachers' content and practices, the ordering of curriculum time, classroom space and the evaluative rule of the required texts, remained largely unchanged, due in part to the constraining nature of the existing cultural relay of schooling. We perceive that in respect to evaluative rules in English curriculum, the reproduction of existing pedagogies in classrooms is often tied to the historically established regulative discourse of schooling, maintained by government agencies through the inherent nature of pedagogic acts in contexts of institutional power (Mills & Exley, 2014b). We believe that this is a major reason why the institution of schooling is often slow to embrace the digital turn, and more visionary paperless schools.

Our findings from this study generated understandings of the dialectic relations of pedagogic time and space in classrooms to the product of the pedagogic device when teachers take up digital writing practices within the elementary school curriculum. When transforming modes of practice in the curriculum, the selection of curriculum content, and the ordering and expected speed of students' progression through the revised curriculum, can be theorised as a function of the instructional discourse becoming embedded by teachers within the regulative discourse. This occurred through pedagogic acts to produce texts that met both similar, yet different, evaluative rules to the sanctioned curriculum (Bernstein, 2000; Mills & Exley, 2014b).

Our research highlights the need for a reordering of time, space and text – the principles of the pedagogic discourse – to embed multimodal design into conventional literacy curricula. There were initial heavy investments of time in the acquisition of digital skills and multimodal textual knowledge, a reordering of the classroom space for certain media production practices, and the detailed development of new evaluative rules and criteria for assessing the quality of the students' digital text creations. We acknowledge that future teacher-researcher collaborations to embed digital writing practices within the elementary school curriculum may unfold in somewhat different ways, tied to changing historical, cultural, technological, political and economic factors that influence social action in schools (Mills & Exley, 2014b).

The pervasiveness, convergence and increased accessibility of digital technologies for multimodal writing call for an extension of the boundaries of what constitutes writing practices in schools. As Dalton and colleagues (2011) have observed, writing programs often include technology as an add-on to a print-based curriculum approach, with teachers feeling underprepared to teach digital writing effectively with technology. Perhaps more importantly, teachers need expanded knowledge of multimodal semiotics, including visual, audio, spatial, gestural and linguistic elements, to encompass the full range of design grammars involved in digital composition using various media (Mills & Exley, 2014b).

While some schooling authorities have begun to include multimodal and digital text production in standardised English assessments, this is currently the exception rather than the rule. It is timely for governing agencies to reconsider the changing nature of writing across all levels of schooling, and to reconsider the necessary shifts to curriculum time, classroom social space and development of evaluative criteria to accommodate new specialist forms of digital text creation. The systematic and continual inclusion of writing in digital formats needs to become a fundamental part of transformed evaluative criteria, particularly in contexts of externally imposed national and state-wide testing where what is not tested is not privileged (Mills & Exley, 2014b).

Digital Pedagogy: A Model for Practice

One of the central challenges of classroom practice involves exploring the pedagogical patterns that can enable teachers to navigate innovative digital text production in the literacy classroom. This can assist teachers to integrate any number of new technologies for text production at the level of curriculum planning. The pedagogy presented here, called iPed, was generated in the context of a longitudinal digital literacy intervention in a school that services low socio-economic and ethnically diverse students (see Mills & Levido, 2011).

The iPed model was beta tested with Year 4 teachers and their cohort of 75 students (aged 8.5–9.5 years). We introduced students to the features of new digital text types – blog pages, podcasts (video recordings in web pages), micro-documentaries (short factual videos with interview segments), web profiles, digital stories and online comics. Students were also introduced to new metalanguages to describe media texts, such as shot types for different purposes, and learned technical proficiencies with a suite of Apple media software.

Throughout the year, we observed pedagogical transformations in the writing classrooms, and the development of new technical competencies. The iPed model reconfigures theory about literacy pedagogy with four recurring features of the pedagogy cycle – link, co-create, challenge and share. iPed is timely in the contemporary context given the rise of the social web or Web 2.0 of user-generated web content (O'Reilly, 2005). The social web allows users to sustain an active presence on the web with an online identity or profile, while also allowing for customisation (Mills, 2013a). When contrasted with the earlier applications of the WWW, more recent affordances of the web have increased the ease and reduced the cost of online collaboration. Democratic forms of communication have taken centre stage, including polls, social networking sites, blogs and micro-blogs, where users are simultaneously authors and audience. Open access authoring space, such as podcasts and images, can be shared with ease. Also referred to as the read-write web, Web 2.0 provides a means for free, rapid dialogue and instant feedback from significant international audiences (Mills, 2010b; Wheeler & Wheeler, 2009).

In educational practice, these shifts in web-based social practices call for changes to print-based pedagogies for writing to include authentic digital forms of communication used in society today. The iPed model can guide learners to become creative and collaborative producers, rather than simply consumers, of digital media texts in schools.

Link

Link is the first principle of iPed, in which teachers assist students to make three kinds of connections between media texts: text to self, text to culture and text to world. Link centres on culturally inclusive practice. Students were most engaged in texts when the teachers selected multimedia (e.g. web pages, videos) and print-based texts (e.g. books) that addressed themes that were familiar in some way to the students' experiences. The students' world of everyday lived experience, which includes shared cultural assumptions, is referred to as their lifeworld (Cope & Kalantzis, 2000a: 206).

Some examples of Link that were observed in our study included a unit about the text structure and grammatical features of biographies, in which the teachers incorporated texts about Indigenous heroes to relate to the cultural background of our Aboriginal and Torres Strait Islander students. Another example of this pedagogy is when students wrote about their home life and community interests in an online blog (short for 'web log'). Similarly, when choosing pictures for their story writing (presented on web pages), the students were permitted to select their favourite cartoon images from the internet, applying ideas from popular texts of their out-of-school experiences of popular texts. The students created web profiles about themselves at the beginning of the year. They shared information about their likes and dislikes, making intertextual connections with popular texts such as Harry Potter and High School Musical. They shared their future ambitions, and insights into life at home and at school. The students' engagement with the task was not simply tied to the novelty of the technology, but to the activity structures that invited them to share the cultural experiences of their lifeworlds.

Link is an essential pedagogy in globally connected societies where local teaching contexts, like ours, are comprised of heterogeneous groups of learners from varied cultural backgrounds. By beginning with familiar texts from students' homes and communities, teachers can embrace the diversity of interests and experiences of the class, while leading them to new experiences of the world and unfamiliar textual practices. Link emphasises cultural inclusiveness, negotiating differences among learners, and creating bridges for those who have the greatest distance to travel to make links to new competencies. This pedagogy also draws on principles from cognitive learning theory, which concerns the assimilation of new knowledge to make links to the new (e.g. Piaget, 1952a).

Challenge

The second pedagogy of iPed is Challenge – a practice stemming from Street's ideological model, and extended more consciously by critical literacy. This is important because of the increasing accessibility of uncensored texts on the WWW by young children. Challenge acknowledges that texts and textual practices are ideological and social; that is, they are located in specific social and cultural fields, and are tied to power relations (Luke et al., 2003). This pedagogy specifically concerns new issues that have evolved in relation to the ease and accessibility of producing and consuming media-based texts on the WWW. Students need to know about online security, censorship, democracy and changing perceptions of ownership of intellectual property.

Students need skills to select texts from a much larger quantity of online information than ever before, requiring selectivity and discernment. Challenge involves teaching students how to judge the authenticity and authority of web sources. This requires identifying the intended consumers, and assumptions about gender, age, social class, ethnicity, belief systems, silences and whose interests are served by the text (Mills & Levido, 2011).

Co-create

Co-create is the third pedagogy of iPed. It specifically draws attention to co-producing media for real audiences within and beyond the school. This orientation is reflected in a Web 2.0 textual environment, where there is an emphasis on the collaborative design of knowledge and texts. A key feature of the pedagogy is that expertise and authority are distributed among the students, rather than located in a single individual. This pedagogy extends principles of situated cognition by key theorists Vygotsky (1962), Lave (1993) and Brown (1994) to the specific field of media text production in a digitally networked age.

Levido and I developed a pedagogical strategy to scaffold the print and digital dimensions of learning within the Co-create phase of instruction – Predict, Demonstrate and Do (Mills & Levido, 2011).

(1) Predict – Students are guided to anticipate the functions of the software to help students accommodate or assimilate new knowledge with existing knowledge.

(2) Demonstrate – Teacher or other experts show examples of how to create a digital text, focusing students' attention on important text features and an age-appropriate number of new digital functions in one lesson phase.

(3) Do – Students apply knowledge of how to construct a digital text in a supportive classroom environment with hand-on access to the technology.

This teaching cycle can occur once or even several times within a lesson. For example, in an elementary classroom unit on web page creation with Apple iWeb software, a teacher used her laptop and a data projector to show the whole class the iWeb interface. The students were seated in front of their own laptops, while able to view the teacher's screen. The teacher gave step-by-step instructions for creating a personal website, frequently asking students to predict where to locate some of the icons to achieve their intentions. To guide students' digital text creation, the teacher alternated very short periods of expert instruction with time for students to apply the instruction using the technologies. During the students' practice, they also received timely support and signposts by experts (peers, teachers, researchers) in the room to focus their attention on significant aspects of the design. This pedagogy emphasised guided social participation or joint construction of texts among co-creators, whose digital text production was scaffolded by peers, experts, technologies, screen displays, help sheets and other learning tools (Mills & Levido, 2011).

Through such demonstration or guided participation students were able to anticipate the process before immediately applying the new knowledge to their own textual production. Demonstration involved guided participation in learning, or scaffolding, within students' many zones of proximal development. The expert took the students to the outer limits of their potential social and cognitive attainment (Vygotsky, 1978).

During times when students needed the most guidance, the expert's instruction and students' practice occurred almost simultaneously. The demonstration process meant that students received sufficient instruction to take some risks as they were provided with information immediately prior to application, when it could most usefully organise and guide practice. My research has shown that in the absence of demonstration, learners can spend a significant proportion of the time pursuing unproductive learning paths (Mills, 2006c).

During Co-create, the responsibility for learning was gradually released to the students, as the pedagogy shifted from demonstration to application (Do), supported by peer collaboration. The need for gradual reduction in the degree of scaffolding should be recognised as students become proficient. For example, in our research, the students demonstrated greater speed and independence with digital text production. They moved from scaffolded text creation when new literacy practices were initially introduced, to later internalise new knowledge and apply digital procedures for new social purposes.

An essential feature of Co-create was that a variety of strategies was needed to make learning collaborative and distributed among the students and teacher. As coined in the important work, *Distributed Expertise in the Classroom*, sharing expertise was paramount to the social interactions and grouping of students (Brown *et al.*, 1993). Competent students scaffolded the learning of novice peers, who in turn trained others. When creating web pages, the classroom teacher had specifically allocated competent and struggling students to work together.

The teachers also established a practice called 'the 5 minute rule'. This involved an initial 5-minute period during 'Do' when the students were not permitted to ask the teacher for help. Instead, students could attempt to solve problems independently through trial-and-error, ask a peer or consult the 'help' sheet. The longer the students continued using a particular digital interface, the less they relied on the classroom teacher to solve technical problems. Later in the year, the number of students with their hands up to ask questions, greatly diminished. This reflected their growing confidence to solve their own technical problems, drawing from the distributed expertise among their peers (Mills & Levido, 2011).

Share

The final pedagogy in iPed is Share – presenting texts to local community and global audiences. While teachers made formal, comparative judgments about students' textual products, learning was also judged informally by participation in digital practices within local and global communities. This practice draws on Bourdieu's principle of cultural capital – a form of social power, such as educational qualifications, that is convertible under certain conditions to economic capital (Bourdieu, 1986b). In Bourdieu's understanding, there are specific profits that children from different social backgrounds can obtain from the academic market.

Share is about translating students' proficiencies with digital media design in exchange for cosmopolitan recognition and status. For example, in our research, students' multimedia products were formally presented to the Indigenous and non-Indigenous local community, including students, parents, the school principal and deputy, and visitors from the university. The teachers also accessed virtual classrooms within the state school intranet, where teachers and students could receive constructive and positive feedback from others, while gaining credibility for their work.

An aim of iPed is to give students sufficient access to design and share digital products with new confidence, taking on the situated identities of filmmakers, web designers and specialists who engage in text production for genuine social purposes.

It is important for students to have an online international audience. Many school districts have secure online spaces for teachers to upload students' media products for certain online communities. With the availability of Web 2.0 tools, receiving international recognition for user-generated content is a powerful way to give the learners' achievements greater visibility and status in a competitive global economy.

The iPed model for pedagogy offers teachers a way to engage students with print using new media technologies, scaffolding learning in a way that supports collaboration among peers. Incorporating Link, Challenge, Co-create and Share into classroom practice can equip students to become both creative producers and critical consumers of user-generated web content. It begins by validating students' existing cultural knowledge and skills, while moving them forward to mature forms of textual practice.

Note

(1) This chapter draws on portions of the following journal article by the author: Mills, K.A. & Levido, A. (2011) Iped: Pedagogy for digital text production. *The Reading Teacher* 65 (1), 85–91.

2   Socio-cultural Literacies

The view that literacy as a set of cognitive skills is an ideology that ignores racial, cultural, and other forms of social difference.
(Mills)

This chapter provides insights into recent changes within the socio-cultural paradigm of literacy research, which became known as the New Literacy Studies (Gee, 1999; Street, 1997b). Drawing on my review published in the *Review of Educational Research*, and extending it to recent developments, I define the socio-cultural literacy theory and interrogate its key themes (Mills, 2010b). I address some of the tensions in socio-cultural approaches, such as the boundaries or limits of literacy – a criticism that has also been raised in relation to multiliteracies approaches (see Cameron, 2000; Prain, 1997). I also consider the confines of regarding literacies as local practices, against the emerging features of digital practices more globally. I evaluate the extent to which critical approaches and other paradigms have shaped and continue to influence the New Literacy Studies. I trace some of the shared characteristics of literacy practices that have emerged in digital situations of use, and provide a vision of the future for teachers to integrate digital literacy practices into school curricula.

Key Concepts of Socio-cultural Literacies

Defined concisely by Street (2003: 79), literacy practices are '... particular ways of thinking about and doing reading and writing in cultural contexts'. Varieties of literacy practice are always constructed out of specific social conditions, including political and economic structures (Cook-Gumperz, 2006; Luke, 1994). What was unique and distinguished this view from the prevailing psychometric or autonomous paradigm is that knowledge and literacy practices were reconceived as constructions of particular social groups, rather than attributed to cognition alone (Street, 1984). This view opposed theorists such as Hildyard and Olsen (1978), who appealed to the scientific, intrinsic and seemingly culturally and racially benign nature of literacy as a purely individual cognitive skill.

A key difficulty with interpreting literacy practices within any community is the problem of limiting what constitutes a literacy practice, an issue that has been raised elsewhere (see Barton *et al.*, 2000; Mills, 2010b). Gee (2012) provides an interesting answer to this question, using the term Discourses (with a capital D) rather than literacy. He defines Discourses as socially recognised ways of using words or other semiotic codes (e.g. images, sounds) and '... ways of behaving, interacting, valuing, thinking, believing and speaking ... and often reading and writing ...' (Gee, 2012: 3). These are used to identify members of a socially meaningful group. To put it another way, Discourses are instantiations of identity.

As Gee (2005) explains, a major function of language is to act out different kinds of people for different sorts of roles and occasions. For example, in a job interview, one can attend not only to supplying the 'correct' verbal answers to questions, but to projecting a certain kind of ideal persona for the role. This includes how one enters and exits the room, where one sits, how one sits and even the direction one's foot is pointed. Discourses include facial expression, eye contact, gesticulations, length of responses, volume, pacing, tone and expression of voice, grammatical choices, hairstyle, clothing, footwear and so on.

There are traces here of Goffman's (1959: 136) well-cited theory outlined in his book, *The Presentation of Self in Everyday Life*. Goffman theorised that language is more than what is communicated through words or verbal symbols that have attached meanings familiar to those in the interaction. It is more than the expression that one 'gives'. Rather, language is as much about the message that one 'gives off' – the wide range of action that is symptomatic of one's identity, as one participates in social life.

A critical point is that groups often have different home and community-based Discourses that have differing degrees of alignment with the required language and Discourses in schools and institutions. This contributes a great deal to appreciating why groups in society have differing degrees of literacy 'achievement', as defined by schooling systems. While Gee acknowledges that there are also cognitive features of literacy learning, this is not his emphasis, given that the prevailing view of literacy, particularly in educational achievement psychometrics, reading research and school accountability discourses, has often been a cognitive one (Gee, 2012).

Explicitly drawing on Gee's definition of Discourses, Lankshear and Knobel (2008: 255) similarly define literacies as 'socially recognised' ways of communicating '... through the medium of encoded texts ... as members of discourses'. They include the words 'encoded text' to refer to transportable texts that are rendered in a form to be retrieved, modified, and made available independently of the physical presence of another person. Encoded language is captured in a semi-permanent or permanent form, as distinct from speech and gestures. Somewhat narrower than Gee's view of Discourses, this view of literacy specifically attends to texts that are less ephemeral than speech, but places no limitations on the particular format or site of display.

The role that digital technologies have played in socio-cultural understandings of literacy is significant, particularly in literature and research published in recent decades. The consensus of New Literacy Studies theorists is that literacy is inclusive of sign-making practices that use various technologies, from pen to printer to podcast (Mills, 2010b). A good example is when Scribner and Cole (1981: 236) defined literacies as '... socially organised practices [that] make use of a symbol system and a technology for producing and disseminating it'. This definition is quite forward thinking for its time, both in terms of the role of technologies in the dissemination of texts, and in terms of the unspecified reference to symbol systems, which might include image, music and other non-linguistic modes. In relation to the technologies of literacy, Kress and Bezemer (2008) similarly conceive that sign-makers create a match between their intentions for designing, and the available cultural, symbolic, and material tools available at hand.

Barton (2001: 95) championed for a broader interpretation of what constitutes literacy, and acknowledged that the New Literacy Studies has '... accepted more fuzzy borders ...' in order to include forms of meaning that in essence, function in similar ways to linguistic meaning. To illustrate, Barton (2001: 95) expressed: 'People read timetables, maps and music, as well as novels and academic articles ... There is a great deal in common in the practices associated with these diverse texts'. At a time when technologies and their texts are endlessly superseded by new affordances of communication media, literacy practices encompass an ever-broadening range of textual features and structures, and possible formats and sites of digital display, and these concerns extend to anyone who claims to be a teacher or researcher of language and literacies.

The New London Group (1996) issued parallel arguments for reconceptualising literacy as multiliteracies (see Chapter 4 of this volume). Multiliteracies accounts for the multiplicity of communications channels, media and modes, associated with the availability and convergence of new digital technologies. The conscious pluralising of the term 'literacy' encapsulates a response to increased cultural and linguistic diversity as a consequence of migration and globally networked economies. The fragmentation of English into differentiated Englishes, and economic and cultural globalisation, are '... mutually reinforcing relationships . . .' that influence local settings (Iyer *et al.*, 2014: 10; Tollefson, 2007). Pennycook (2007) has similarly pointed to the emergence of new linguascapes, which display unexpected diversity against the tide of a relentless homogenising process (Iyer *et al.*, 2014). Socio-cultural and multiliteracies theorists are conscious of the danger that ensues when singular, 'standardised' views of literacy of the dominant, colonising culture fail to recognise cultural, language and discoursal difference.

Origins of Socio-cultural Literacies

The socio-cultural perspective can be mapped to social theories of learning that burgeoned in the 1980s, also known as situated cognition (Brown *et al.*, 1989), cognition in practice (Lave, 1988), situated learning (Lave & Wenger, 1991), and communities of practice (Wenger, 1998). The socio-cultural paradigm was increasingly applied to literacy studies and other academic fields, corresponding with a revival of the work of Russian theorist Lev Vygotsky (1962). Vygotsky perceived language as influenced and constituted by social relations or socio-genesis, functioning as a tool for shaping, controlling and interacting with one's social and physical environment.

The socio-cultural approach to literacy was paralleled by other important works with a critical and social edge, in the late 1960s, such as Labov's (1966) *The Social Stratification of English in New York City* (1970) and *The Logic of Nonstandard English* (Labov, 1969). Both drew attention to the social nature of language acquisition. Halliday's (1978) *Language as Social Semiotic in the Tradition of Systemic Functional Linguistics*, also emphasised the three metafunctions of language and linguistics that function together in relation to social purpose and social context (Halliday, 1985; Halliday & Hasan, 1989). Halliday (Halliday, 2002: 6) personally professed '. . . to the extent that I favoured any one angle, it was the social: language as the creature and creator of human society'. This is important because socio-cultural literacy studies did not arise in isolation from these corresponding approaches to literacy theory.

One of the earliest studies located squarely in the socio-cultural literacy tradition was Street's (1975) ethnographic investigation of how commercial discourses were developed within an Iranian community. For several decades, Street (1995, 1999) consistently contended that literacies carry meaning primarily through their entanglement with cultural values and orientations in communities of practice. Street specifically demonstrated the application of a socio-cultural approach in schooled literacy practices (Street & Street, 1991) and in cross-cultural contexts (Street, 1993), while providing a case for the important role of ethnographic methods in literacy research in communities.

Street appealed to Graff's (1979: 292) ideal that literacy '... can be established neither arbitrarily nor uniformly for all members of the population'.

Socio-cultural approaches to literacy began to flourish, with ethnographies of communication detailing how literacy practices in diverse communities are situated in different ways. Gee (2009) explains that the flourishing field of the New Literacy Studies includes linguists, historians, anthropologists, rhetoricians, cultural psychologists and educational researchers (Cazden *et al.*, 1972; Gumperz & Hymes, 1972; Labov, 1972; Street, 1975). These theorists emphasised the social, cultural and ideological construction or nature of literacy practices that become taken for granted in daily communication, whether in homes, at school or social contexts (Barton & Hamilton, 1998).

The socio-cultural literacy tradition was supported by ethnographic research in many communities, such as Nukulaelae, Papua New Guinea, Zafimaniry, Sierra Leone, the Horn of Africa, Alaska and Philadelphia (Street, 1993). One of the most comprehensively documented socio-cultural ethnographies in the early 1980s was Heath's (1983) *Ways with Words: Language, Life and Work in Communities and Classrooms*, conducted in three diverse communities who lived only a few miles apart in the Piedmont, Carolinas. Heath compared the everyday literacy practices and speech communities of working class children in Roadville (white community) and Trackton (African-American community) and the mainstream, education-oriented townspeople. Heath documented children's language and culture at home that structured the meanings that served either to support or conflict with formal school literacies.

Since the turn of this century, scholars within the New Literacy Studies have applied social and cultural understandings of literacy across an array of everyday digital contexts of use and social settings (Mills, 2010b). Interpreting and representing ideas and information in social contexts, both inside and outside of schools, is increasingly digitalised as mobile phones and other media become accessible to the masses, though with stratified degrees of sophistication to different groups (Warschauer, 2004). The pervasiveness and ubiquity of technologies for text production has seen the continual expansion of textual forms that learners can create, requiring a reconceptualisation of the scope of literacy in teaching, research and policy. Whether of three-dimensional virtual worlds, personalised profiles, avatars or 'skins', podcasts, gamis (videos of avatars or online personas), mobile applications, online comics, fan-site wikis, Tweets, video calls, status updates or blogs, communication forms are constantly modified. The socio-cultural perspective of literacy practices is equally relevant to online or virtual communities of practice that are characterised by meetings and departures in a virtual game or chat room, or who subscribe to online communities on the basis of interest, friendship, culture, belief or ideology.

Original research that specifically draws on the New Literacy Studies framework includes ethnographies and other qualitative studies investigating a wide range of literacy practices across many regions and countries, including the United States (Knobel & Lankshear, 2007), Mexico (Lankshear & Knobel, 2008), Australia (Mills & Chandra, 2011), Canada and the United Kingdom (Pahl & Rowsell, 2006), Rwanda (Mukama & Andersson, 2008), South Africa (Janks & Comber, 2006) and Greece (Mitsikopoulou, 2007). The research sites include schools (Damico & Riddle, 2006; Morrell, 2002), out-of-school contexts (Ito et al., 2009; Yi, 2008) and afterschool settings (Barab et al., 2005; Brass, 2008; Hull & Nelson, 2005). Multisite studies also document the connections between literacy practices across home, school, community and commercial settings, such as shopping malls (Bulfin & North, 2007; Nichols et al., 2012; Pahl & Rowsell, 2005).

Literacy practices using digital media within the socio-cultural tradition have been enacted and researched in higher education (Jacobs, 2005; O'Dowd, 2005), such as within pre-service and in-service teacher university programs (Koskos et al., 2000; Rowsell et al., 2008), and across the full spectrum of schooling, from high school (Knobel et al., 2002; Leander, 2003), to elementary (Mills, 2011a) and early childhood settings (Flewitt et al., 2009; Marsh, 2011; Pahl, 2003).

Surveying the participant selection patterns in these studies, the digital literacy practices of a broad range of groups are included. Studies have examined the literacy practices of monolingual English users as well as bilingual (Ernst-Slavit, 1997) and multilingual students (van Sluys et al., 2008) and those for whom English is a second language (Lam, 2000). The research participants are of varied socio-economic backgrounds, including working class (Marsh, 2003), middle-class (Jacobs, 2004) and urban students (Damico & Riddle, 2006; Knoester, 2009; Morrell, 2002).

Textual practices described in these studies frequently involve multimodal texts — when words are used in combination with visual, audio, spatial and gestural modes. For example, studies have examined popular culture (Clancy & Lowrie, 2002; Ranker, 2007), writing multimedia stories (Rojas-Drummond et al., 2008) and reading talking books in Indigenous languages (Darcy & Auld, 2008).

Research of online literacy practices include instant messaging (Jacobs, 2004; Lee, 2007; Lewis & Fabos, 2000, 2005), designing Japanese anime fan sites (Chandler-Olcott & Mahar, 2003), using web quests, creating e-zines or electronic magazines (Courtland & Paddington, 2008) and writing online fan fictions (Black, 2009). An example of some of the Web 2.0 practices, web practices that involve uploading user generated web content, include relay writing using microblogging platforms (Yi, 2008), blogging (Davies & Merchant, 2007), threaded discussions (Grisham & Wolsey, 2006) and wikis (Wheeler & Wheeler, 2009).

A recent trend has seen research of digital media production, including movie making (Brass, 2008; Mills *et al.*, 2013; Ranker & Mills, 2014), interactive digital art creation (Peppler & Kafai, 2007), programming of video games (Sanford & Maddil, 2006), authoring and performing spoken word poetry (McGuinnis, 2007), social media use (Hull & Stornaiuolo, 2010) and literacy practices using various iPad applications (Gruszczynska *et al.*, 2013; Neumann & Neumann, 2014). A distinguishing feature of these accounts is that they describe the semiotic and new features of literacy practices using the encoded word in culturally and socially specific locales, using the affordances of different digital platforms.

Review of the empirical research in this tradition confirms that in virtually all cases, the participants engage with written words in the process or product of their textual engagements, while frequently drawing on other modes and conventions. For example, in the Indigenous Ways to Multimodal Literacy project, middle elementary students (aged 9–10 years) created Gamis using the Tellagami iPad application to give an Aboriginal and Torres Strait Islander perspective of so-called 'trespassing on white land' during the colonisation of Australia. The students learned about the structure and content of historical narrative poetry, and then handwrote their poems on paper. They used the Tellegami application to digitally photograph Indigenous artwork to create backgrounds, personalise the physical features of their avatar, and audio record their handwritten poems. Using the application, the children could select moods (e.g. happy, angry, sad) to influence the gestures of their personal avatar. The replay of the audio recording was accompanied by the visual display of the life-like avatar, which lip-synced and gestured to match the recording. In multimodal and digital texts such as these, the written word continues to play an important role in meaning making (Mills *et al.*, 2015).

Another example from upper elementary students in the Indigenous Ways to Multimodal Literacy project, students aged 11–12 years created a whole class digital story retelling of the Aboriginal dreaming narrative, Nanji and Nguandi, which originated in South-East Queensland where many of the students' ancestral tribes were located. The students created vivid Aboriginal paintings on sheets of transparent plastic to represent each scene of the narrative visually. They photographed the series of artworks using iPads, and combined the images with audio recordings of their retellings using an iMovie video editing application. In digital literacy practices of this kind, as with many others, the encoded word continues to carry a significant functional load, or proportion of the meaning (Jewitt, 2006).

Language is described by Kress (2000b: 186), a member of the New London Group, as a multimodal system of representation that is '...fuzzy round the edges'. However, Kress makes distinctions between modes, describing them as the fully semiotically articulated means of representation and communication (Kress, 2005). For example, Kress (2000a) distinguishes between written and spoken words, images, gestures and music as particular forms of representation. All modes are considered important in communication, and the logo-centrism of schooling and institutions attracts Kress' critique.

The increasing role of digital technologies for communication is one of the major reasons why theories of literacy and semiotics associated with the New Literacy Studies, and other theoretical traditions such as systemic functional linguistics, are taking into account meanings that exist in modes other than words on the page. Broadening conventional understandings of literacy beyond the written word does not create ambiguity. Rather, it resists a narrow literacy curriculum that excludes everyday literacy practices that are augmented and modified by multiple modes in digital formats. Lemke (1998) describes how meanings in multimedia are not just words plus images. Rather, word meanings are modified in the context of image-meanings, and vice versa, opening up a wider range of meaning potential. Furthermore, as Unsworth (2014) demonstrates through the analysis of texts, image meanings can sometimes deliberately subvert or contradict the accompanying word meanings, a feature of some innovative picture books.

There has been a global response among literacy researchers to reformulate grammars of multimodal design, which at times may be a response to the call of the New London Group to heed the seismic changes to the textual landscape (e.g. Jewitt, 2011b; Pahl & Burnett, 2013; Price *et al.*, 2013). Linguists and academics have continued to develop new grammars for describing the confluence of words, images, sounds, gestures and spatial elements across a range of text formats (e.g. Mills, 2011d; Painter *et al.*, 2013).

The New London Group invited linguists and scholars to develop new multimodal grammars to describe a broadened range of semiotic systems that figure so prominently in the new digital communications environment. A growing body of research in multimodal semiotics has articulated extended grammars to describe the visual, spatial and other elements of texts that enrich, augment and modify word meanings (e.g. Jewitt, 2011b; Miller & McVee, 2012; Painter *et al.*, 2013). The multiliteracies argument has moved the New Literacy Studies, and literacy studies more broadly, to acknowledge the multimodal nature of semiosis. There is a shared recognition that reading and writing practices using words-on-paper-based text formats are necessary, but not sufficient, for communicating across the multiple platforms of meaning making in society (Mills, 2010b).

Theorists of the New Literacy Studies, multiliteracies and multimodal semiotics have concluded that conventional views of reading and writing are no longer adequate to describe the combination of sign systems used in most literacy practices. Reducing the English curriculum to a narrow repertoire of conventional genres and writing skills ignores the reality of literacy practices in society today by excluding new forms of digital text. The ease with which users of the new technologies can transmit, produce and print documents for everyday purposes has made encoded language and literacies predominantly multimodal.

Tensions for Socio-cultural Literacies

Limits of the local

Many of the original studies cited here within the New Literacy Studies have demonstrated the plurality and context-specific nature of the new literacies, but have yet to account for common patterns of literacy practice that hold across diverse case studies (Mills, 2010). For example, Brandt and Clinton (2002: 337) critiqued the 'limits of the local' apparent in much of the New Literacy Studies. They contend that the New Literacy Studies should work towards identifying some of the supposed autonomous features of literacy practices, but without necessarily upholding a skills-based approach to universal literacy standards. They recommend that the New Literacy Studies acknowledge the extent to which local literacy practices and the emic or insider perspectives of participants are influenced by external social factors beyond the community.

The New Literacy Studies has worked against a universalist view of literacy; that is, the notion that literacy is an ideologically benign set of context-free skills that can be taught without regarding children's background experiences and prior cultural knowledge (Street, 1999). The theoretical endpoint of the New Literacy studies view is to resist any efforts to formalise or solidify the components of practice as universal standards. However, the empirical studies of the New Literacy Studies have, from the beginning, used comparative research designs to examine both shared and unique features of literacy practices across informal and formal social sites (e.g. Heath, 1983; Street, 1997a). Within the digital strand of the New Literacy Studies, a number of studies have adopted multi-site research designs to yield comparative data. For example, the Digital Youth Project was conducted for the explicit purpose of examining how new media practices across different populations are embedded in a broader social and cultural ecology within the United States (Ito *et al.*, 2008).

While comparative data is difficult to obtain within single-site case studies, the increasing body of ethnographies and other qualitative research within the New Literacy Studies is sufficiently large for patterns to be identified across communities and countries. Many of the New Literacy Studies draw attention to features of the local literacies that hold across varied sites. For example, in the studies cited in this chapter, more than 50 authors of journal articles or book chapters made reference to the multimodal nature of the new literacies. From a synthesis of the emerging patterns of literacy observed across multiple local sites, the following list of characteristics is evident across many practices, though rarely all occurring at once: digital, hybrid (modifying text forms), multimodal, intertextual (referencing other texts), often immediate (i.e. where synchronous), abbreviated (e.g. game chat, instant messaging), informal, multi-authored, productive, creative, interactive, hyperlinked and often involve participants that are socially and linguistically diverse.

Digital nature of the dominant culture

Criticism has been made of the alleged tendency of the New Literacy Studies, and recent literacy studies more broadly, to focus on the practices of young people in predominantly middle-class family backgrounds in well-resourced countries. For example, Walton (2007: 197), writing from South Africa, believes that digital literacies, such as online chat, blogs, wikis, digital media production, games and podcasting, are 'exotic practices' that are '. . . sustained by resources and leisure that are simply not available to most people'.

Similarly, Prinsloo and Synder (2008) contrast their study of young people's use of information and communication technologies in Uganda against existing work in middle-class locales around the globe. While researchers have shown that children's literacy activities involving digital devices outside of school are typically more frequent, sophisticated, and more meaningful than those they encounter in school, they note that this is not the case in their Ugandan context. Prinsloo and Synder acknowledge that digital learning opportunities in out-of-school contexts can be created with positive outcomes for students from less-advantaged neighbourhoods. However, they recognised that physical access to computers in the home settings of young people from minority cultures has not necessarily translated into success for these students in school contexts.

The generalisation that literacy research has focused on the new and exotic literacies of the dominant middle-class in Western cultures requires examination. The empirical research generated by the New Literacy Studies is largely comprised of many small-scale ethnographic case studies around the world. For instance, empirical studies have examined new literacies of marginalised communities, including teachers and students, from countries such as Brazil (Junquiera, 2008), South Africa (Jacobs, 2005; Walton, 2007), Greece (Mitsikopoulou, 2007), Hong Kong (Lee, 2007), Rwanda (Mukama & Andersson, 2008), Spain (O'Dowd, 2005) and Korea (Ajayi, 2009). The range of countries and social contexts of inquiry, and the varied patterns of participant selection in these case studies, demonstrates that the New Literacy Studies have, in fact, contributed more to understandings about social practices in marginalised communities than in dominant or mainstream cultural contexts.

There is no predominance of New Literacy Studies that examine the literacies of middle-class youth (e.g. Jacobs, 2004). Rather, a greater proportion of studies in the United States, Canada, the United Kingdom and Australia have examined the successful integration of digital practices among literacy programs for multilingual, bilingual and low-socio-economic communities. The cultures represented in these studies include the following: Latino, African American and multi-ethnic (Damico & Riddle, 2006; Ernst-Slavit, 1997; Hull, 2003; van Sluys et al., 2008); Cantonese (Siu et al., 2005); Indigenous Australian, Thai, Tongan, Maori and Sudanese (Mills, 2011c); Filipino and Taiwanese (Black, 2009); Chinese (Black, 2005; Lam, 2000); Mexican, Cambodian, Nicaraguan and South American (El Salvador) (Ajayi, 2009; McGuinnis, 2007); Indigenous Mexican groups (Lopez-Gopar, 2007); and the Hmong (Hawkins, 2004). These studies consistently show that broadening literacy curricula to include multimodal and digital forms of representation results in significant English language learning gains for multilingual students.

For example, Ajayi (2009) described the benefits of using multimodal textual practices to engage English as Second Language (ESL) students in critically analysing media advertisements in a bilingual classroom. In a similar vein, McGuinnis (2007) reported an inquiry-based, multimodal literacy project for adolescents in a summer migrant educational program. These ESL migrants had recently arrived in the United States from rural areas of China, Vietnam and Cambodia (Khmer). Both studies illustrated that encouraging ESL students to draw upon their interests, cultural experiences, first language and multiple modes (e.g. visual, spatial) can promote their academic success.

These studies have demonstrated how students from culturally and linguistically diverse backgrounds can engage productively in multimodal, digital, abbreviated and spontaneous literacy practices in both institutional and non-institutional spaces. They also serve to defend the New Literacy Studies against a bias in participant or site selection, since these studies extend beyond dominant cultural contexts.

There is similarly little evidence that the New Literacy Studies has given preference to the digital literacy practices of the middle class. While some studies do not comment on the socio-economic backgrounds of the research participants, other studies explicitly focus on the digital literacy practices of economically marginalised students. Schools with socio-economically marginalised clientele confront particular system constraints and routine practices that militate against the effective integration of digital media in literacy curriculum (Mills & Exley, 2014b).

For example, a comparative literacy and technology equity study conducted across eight high schools in California, five of them located in underserved communities (almost half Hispanic), was described by Knobel et al. (2002). The study investigated whether there was a digital divide that separated technology access and use in poor and wealthy school districts. The study showed that there was not a single digital divide, but rather, a complex set of divides along overlapping lines, such as gender, geographical location, socio-economic background and ethnicity.

Clichés such as the 'global village' have pervaded discourse in the wider literature about technology in education (e.g. McLuhan & Powers, 1989: 1). While online forms of communication are becoming globalised, the New Literacy Studies have demonstrated that there are qualitative differences in the kinds of online practices of users that are patterned by ethnicity, English language learning, socio-economic background, learning difficulties, geography and coexisting categories of marginalisation (e.g. urban poor). While giving acknowledgment to the significant advances in digital communication technologies, there is not a single global village; rather, there are groups with varied levels of participation in media practices, with varied degrees of sophistication, across local villages around the world.

Recent Developments in Socio-cultural Literacies

Networks of literacy practice

Given that the world is continually deterritorialised and reterritorialised in unexpected ways, it is no surprise that textual practices are also constantly remade through actor networks that involve symbols, people and materials. Empirical research of the New Literacy Studies has frequently documented authentic literacy practices that are situated in multiple contexts of informal learning beyond schools (Heath, 2013; Reyes & Estebann-Guitart, 2013). Since the digital turn, research in this theoretical tradition has demonstrated that innovative and productive forms of learning can occur with digital media in peer- and interest-driven networks that are oriented toward social communication and recreation (e.g. Beavis *et al.*, 2009; Coiro *et al.*, 2008; Kristien & Harmon, 2009). Many adolescents and adults are engaging in 'friendship-driven' practices, such as Facebook and Twitter, to maintain and extend the social networks of those they deem important in their offline lives (Ito *et al.*, 2008: 1). Adolescents are also engaging in 'interest-driven' networks in which they connect with peers and adults, often beyond their local community, who are united by specialised interests, from online gaming, to music and fan art (Ito *et al.*, 2008: 1)

The features of interest-driven, online practices have been in communities of practice that extend beyond academic settings. Steinkhuehler (2007) and Black (2009) have highlighted the voluntary participation of teens in multimodal, online forms of communication inspired by activity on fan sites, which play an important supporting role in the literacy practices of multiplayer online game participants. At other times, fan sites make intertextual connections with other online text forms, such as anime fan art (Japanese animations), games, discussions, media products and movies.

Microblogging – short posts of up to 140 characters, known as Tweets in Twitter or status updates in Facebook – can play an important role in supportive virtual communities, while promoting self-initiated literacy practices. For example, Yi (2008) and later Mills and Chandra (2011), examined adolescent and adult students' writing composition in online communities. These studies examined the social practice of relay writing, which is the online construction of a novel written in short sections and forwarded to multiple authors (Mills & Chandra, 2011). In the context of using Edmodo, an open access site suitable for use in higher education, we observed that students' relay writing blurred the distinction between readers and writers, as contributors became both readers and writers of a multi-authored text. Elements of the composition process became transformed, such as the immediacy of the posting, and the publication of partially constructed texts in progress. Others have investigated youth engagement in e-zine (electronic magazine) and journal communities (Guzzetti & Gamboa, 2005), language use in teenagers' online chat (Merchant, 2001), social networking via online chat (Lam, 2000), instant messaging (Jacobs, 2004; Lee, 2007; Lewis & Fabos, 2005), social media use (Hull & Stornaiuolo, 2010) and video game play in virtual worlds (Barab *et al.*, 2005; Merchant & Burnette, 2013).

While such research has provided important information about self-initiated digital practices of youth, New Literacy scholars have urged researchers to forge investigations of the new literacy practices in institutional settings. At the turn of this century, Hull (2003), Street (2003) and other New Literacy scholars cautioned that an emphasis on learning in non-institutional settings needed to be tempered with the acknowledgement that the informal literacies of youth are not always rich, dynamic and relevant to education. Recognition of children's out-of-school literacies needs to be coupled with knowledge of the textual encounters that students still need to traverse (Mills, 2010c).

A strength of the broader New Literacy Studies tradition is its stance against dismissing youth engagement with non-institutional learning as merely frivolous, remedial or inconsequential. However, there is conversely little evidence of any resistance to official literacies in the digital strand of this tradition. The majority of studies reviewed here were conducted in formal contexts of learning, with an emphasis on reporting pedagogical recommendations to an audience of literacy educators. Theory-driven research has been conducted in digitalised after-school programs in the effort to bridge digital literacies across informal and formal contexts that often link universities to local communities.

Rather than locating digital practices as an in- and out-of-school dichotomy, recent large-scale empirical research – the Digital Youth Project by the MacArthur Foundation – has framed the discontinuities between practices in various sites as age-related, a struggle of competing versions of literacy across generations (Ito et al., 2008; Lemke et al., 2015). The research investigated digital media and literacy practices across multiple populations, and geographical and online sites, including schools. Given that the New Literacy Studies has been criticised for relying on small-scale research (Street, 2003), it should be noted that research led by Ito drew upon over 5000 hours of ethnographic field notes and 659 semi-structured interviews. Online data included discussion thread transcripts, 400 videos, 10,000 online profiles from sites such as MySpace, Facebook and Neopets, and a questionnaire completed by over 400 participants (Ito et al., 2009; Ito et al., 2008).

The research examined the specific ways in which digital media are changing the way young people learn, play, socialise and participate in civic life across multiple social contexts (Ito et al., 2009). Across the United States, basic access to digital production tools and the internet was found to be a precondition for youth participation in popular networked publics. Social media play a vital role in sustaining peer culture, gradually replacing the role played by physical meeting sites, such as malls, homes or the street. In formal settings, the most powerful examples of digital literacy programs were based on learner- rather than teacher-interests. These programs afforded time for unstructured experimentation with new media, rather than emphasising direct instruction from authority figures. Continuing this trajectory of research funded by the MacArthur Foundation, Lemke and colleagues (2015) have very recently reported on the learning gains of youth in media-rich environments, developing a new model for assessment across a range at least ten learning domains.

Hybridisation of literacy practice

A salient feature of the new literacies is the 'hybridisation' of textual practices – the blending and modification of literate practices of a culture that results in the emergence of new text forms (Mills, 2011c). Hybridity in literacy studies originates from poststructuralist theory, sociology and cultural geography (Moje, 2013). In literacy studies, the hybridity of literacy practices across cultures has been described in the late 1990s by Gutierrez *et al.* (1995) with reference to literacy practices that are blended across home, school and recreational spaces (Moje, 2013). Also appearing in work by the New London Group (1996) and Street (2003), hybridisation has been used to describe the continually modified genres of online practices. An example of hybridisation is relay writing – online story writing created by multiple participants (Mills & Chandra, 2011). This has evolved as a variation of other forms of microblogging, such as posting status updates of daily minutiae.

The hybridisation of literacy practices using digital tools occurs organically, typically in voluntary spaces of participation, where users are not required to reproduce historically reified textual conventions. For example, Black (2009) showed how adolescent females who contributed to online fan fiction sites used text creatively. Rather than emulating pre-existing genres and concretised social patterns, they employed language and other symbolic resources to experiment with new genres and modified text forms. Chandler-Olcott and Mahar (2003) similarly showed how adolescents designed online fanfiction sites that utilised various internet functionalities, and blended features of multiple literary genres, including fantasy, science fiction, and romance in novel ways.

The hybridisation of literacy practices can also be illustrated in cross-language comparisons of instant messaging practices. Lee (2007) examined factors influencing script and language choice in computer-mediated communication among multilingual Cantonese users of online text, drawing from a 70,000-word collection of email and instant messaging texts from youth in Hong Kong. New textual practices included Cantonese based shortenings, common grammatical 'errors' such as inappropriate verb forms and lexical choice, and creative orthographic representations of Cantonese. These patterns of spontaneous hybridisation of grammar, vocabulary and orthography have similarly been identified among English users of online instant messaging or online chat.

These examples from the New Literacy Studies demonstrate that youth are involuntarily developing hybrid genres, textual features, vocabulary and practices that are tied to original purposes for engaging in new literacies using digital media. These studies have demonstrated that people in various cultures and subcultures reinvent and modify literacy practices with digital technologies for different social purposes and parameters in specific ways that are often unforeseen by their designers (Luke, 2008; Mills, 2010b).

Alliances of literacy practice

A key feature in the digital turn is the orientation of text users to social alliances of literacy practices. Gee (2007) refers to engagement in joint activity as affinity spaces – the sharing of knowledge and expertise based on voluntary affiliation around a common interest or goal. Gee observed that many online and offline resources support this synergism. The empirical studies reviewed here have examined the nuances of these practices that are aligned with others, in both institutional and non-institutional learning sites. Extending beyond the limits of the local (e.g. Collins & Blot, 2002), the New Literacy Studies have generated new knowledge about recent global shifts toward user-generated, collaborative, democratic and interactive forms of online participation.

Empirical research by the New Literacy Studies has drawn attention to the collaborative nature of digital practices – engagement in joint activity that is centred on shared interests or knowledge domains. This has been facilitated by the rise of the Web 2.0, also known as the 'social web' (Wheeler & Wheeler, 2009: 1). New online tools have facilitated the collaboratively generated, interactive production of content (e.g. blogs, wikis and social networking sites), over conventional Web 1.0 practice, which emphasised individual publishing and consumption (e.g. read-only web content).

New Literacy Studies scholars have conjectured that Web 2.0 tools also leverage 'distributed intelligence', including fewer 'expert-dominated' or 'author-centric' practices than conventional forms of writing (Knobel & Lankshear, 2007: 9). Wheeler and Wheeler (2009), for example, have demonstrated the benefits of engaging pre-service teachers in wikis, which are collaborative webspaces to which all users can contribute text, images and hyperlinks. Participation in the wiki resulted in an improved quality of academic writing, which was tied to the authors' awareness of having a wide, online audience.

Exposing the challenges of collaborative online writing in a university context, Goodfellow and Lea (2005) investigated new ways of assessing these new literacies in higher education. The shift from standardised assessments and conventional notions of individual authorship to collaborative assessment measures created conflicting expectations and complexities among students and instructors. Specific recommendations were made for supporting students, particularly culturally diverse groups, to engage in new genres and forms of online assessment in collaborative contexts of learning.

Other empirical research of the New Literacy Studies has examined the collaborative, social and productive nature of social media in both school and informal settings, through the production of e-zines (Courtland & Paddington, 2008), social networking (Horst, 2009; Pascoe, 2009), photo sharing (Martínez, 2009), digital media in dating and courtship (Boyd, 2009; Pascoe, 2009) and wikis in high schools (Grant, 2006). These studies demonstrate how joint participation in online community practices facilitates the co-construction of knowledge. Confirming socio-cultural research in offline contexts, students progress from observing and learning from others, to gradually assuming a more central role as actors and competent participants in communities of practice (Lave & Wenger, 1991; Mills, 2011c).

Epistemologies and literacy practice

There is undeniably a changed dynamic between youth and adult interpretations of authoritative knowledge. Experienced peers or co-conspirators, rather than traditional authority figures such as teachers, play an important role in establishing communal norms in the interest-driven media practices of youth. In these settings, youth have significant ownership of their self-presentation, learning and evaluation of others. While adults sometimes participate with teens in online communities, conventional markers of status, such as age, are frequently altered (Ito et al., 2008). At the same time, even elementary students can distinguish between the greater reliability of official game wiki knowledge, in comparison with the authenticity of YouTube videos about the games from peers. However, YouTube videos are seen as the knowledge with the greatest currency.

Other New Literacy Studies research highlights the destabilising of traditional loci of authoritative knowledge and expertise, and the centrality of peer collaboration, mentoring and voluntary support to members of online communities. For example, Chandler-Olcott and Mahar (2003) describe how an adolescent engaged in self-directed learning in the process of constructing web pages filled with fanfictions, applying and deepening her sophisticated technical knowledge of HTML. Rather than seek assistance from teachers,

Rhiannon received mentorship from two online peers. When she reached the limits of her technical knowledge, more experienced peers provided necessary HTML codes and links to websites.

Whether in the context of providing online gaming tips to newcomers in virtual worlds (Gee, 2007), constructing web pages (Chandler-Olcott & Mahar, 2003), remixing anime (Black, 2009), adding entries to Wikipedia (Knobel & Lankshear, 2007) or collaboratively writing a story (Yi, 2008), the New Literacy Studies has demonstrated a shift from traditional authority to an epistemology of shared knowledge and expertise. In online social sites, institutional authorities, such as parents and teachers, do not establish writing standards and protocols, nor are they positioned as instructional experts. Rather, norms and criteria for participation are located in peer- and interest-based communities to gain new forms of social status and recognition (Ito *et al.*, 2009; Mills, 2010b).

User-generated contributions to the WWW

A trending characteristic of online literacy practices in the socio-cultural tradition has been an increased emphasis on children and young people's user-generated contributions to the WWW. Some literacy commentators have described this as a cultural shift from consumption of new media to creative production (Buckingham, 2007). While the notion of consumption underplays the critical and interpretative uses of online literacy practices involving reading, the shift from using existing web content, to authoring web content for others is apparent in much of the New Literacy Studies research, paralleling the rise of the Web 2.0.

Creative production of new digital media is a focus of the Computer Clubhouse in South Central Los Angeles (Peppler & Kafai, 2007). During its first two years of operation, the Clubhouse attracted more than one thousand children and youth, with 98% coming from underserved communities. The inner-city youth became creators rather than consumers of digital products, using leading-edge software to create artwork, animations, simulations, multimedia presentations, virtual worlds, musical creations, websites and robotic constructions (Resnick *et al.*, 1998). Analysing samples of these textual products, Peppler and Kafai (2007) demonstrated that education can provide young people with more sophisticated and robust creative production technologies than the basic tools that would otherwise be available to them.

Examining the collaborative production of multimedia texts among fourth grade children (aged 9–10), Rojas-Drummond *et al.* (2008) provided detailed evidence of significant student learning. They applied micro-genetic analysis to interactions between the learners and the way in which the students took up digital designing. The students appropriated collaborative creativity, intertextuality (making cross-references between texts and modes) and inter-contextuality (making logical connections between events in a text) in the process of producing their multimedia stories. Combining oracy, writing, and images using digital technologies, the students successful engaged in the co-construction of knowledge through digital media production.

These are examples of an emergent emphasis in the New Literacy Studies on the role of youth as the next generation of creators of multimodal content, including the critical design of texts, software programs, media images, discussions and other media objects. The new literacies involve making and remaking media rather than being made by them.

Intersections between Socio-cultural and Critical Approaches

Socio-cultural literacy approaches have a distinctive focus on how literacy is practised in communities, and used in everyday spheres of activity. Yet Barton (2001: 97) contends in relation to critical literacy studies and the socio-cultural, 'Inevitably, there is no clear line between what work counts as being part of Literacy Studies and what represents a distinctive approach'. Barton's view suggests that the boundaries of socio-cultural literacy are somewhat contested, but does so to enable socio-cultural literacy theory to subsume other theories that fit within it. Barton (2001, 97) states: 'One strand [of Literacy Studies] is the work associated with Giroux and others which draws inspiration from Critical Theory'. He interprets that divergences among literacy theorists are largely based on different methods of approach, such as discourse analysis and ethnographic case studies. Barton reminds us that literacy scholars, such as Luke (1988), whose research straddles socio-cultural literacy studies, critical literacy and critical applied linguistics, and Street (1999) whose work is most central to New Literacy Studies, maintains that literacy practices are ideological, and must be interpreted in relation to larger social contexts and power relations. Yet others such as Auerbach (1997) clearly separate socio-cultural literacy studies from critical approaches.

Certainly now, critical literacy has emerged as a distinctive approach in its own right, which maintains an emphasis on the social, but with an overt epistemology grounded in critical theory, and with a rationale to analyse, interrogate, challenge and change forms of oppression and privileging of certain groups in society through critical pedagogies. However, it is useful to observe the number of socio-cultural literacy studies in digital contexts of use that analyse key themes of critical theory, such as power (e.g. Hawkins, 2004; Mukama & Andersson, 2008; Stein, 2006). Attending to power relations in literacy studies, within and across communities, has yielded significant evidence of patterns of marginalisation that are socially and historically constituted.

For example, observing the ideological nature of literacy practices and their distribution in an upper primary classroom from a critical and socio-cultural perspective, Mills (2008a) described in a book-length monograph a teacher's enactment of literacy pedagogies to enable the students to create stop-motion digital films. Students' uptake of multiliteracies in the classroom was unequal because of interactions between the teacher's pedagogies, coercive power and the official discourses of the classroom. Students from Anglo-Australian, middle-class backgrounds had greater access to multimodal and digital literacies than those who were culturally or economically marginalised. Irrespective of the relative merits of the teacher's pedagogy over conventional approaches, its ability to provide equitable access was tied to power relations in the school that constrained and enabled its implementation (Mills, 2011c).

Tracing patterns of power and access to new literacies, socio-cultural research has demonstrated that socio-economic marginalisation is tied to a reduced quality of access to digital practices in the home. Snyder *et al.* (2002) described a multisite study that investigated the digital practices of four families at home and school, who had varied social and economic resources. While all four families appropriated the technology into existing family literacy practices, the precise social purposes, nature and quality of these literacies differed significantly, affording varying levels of economic power to the participants.

For example, the most economically disadvantaged family had one shared computer, which became a source of entertainment, such as constant instant messaging, gaming and downloading music. In contrast, the members in wealthier families had exclusive use of their own computers or laptops, which they used for work, information gathering and organising social aspects of their lives. Differing cultural resources in the families' homes mediated the varying quality and nature of digital practices (Snyder *et al.*, 2002). Other research confirms that even when youth have access to digital production technology at home, they rarely apply digital tools to creative media production unless socialised into these practices (Buckingham, 2007).

Other socio-cultural researchers have sought to draw from critical theory, examining how the local digital practices of youth in their informal spaces are implicated in wider patterns of power and marginalisation. A case study of adolescent males' engagement in video games in non-institutional settings highlighted the way in which gaming provides space to resist institutional authority and feminised spaces, while reinforcing hegemonic depictions of masculinity (Sanford & Maddil, 2006). The study demonstrated that video games could be a powerful learning tool for the transfer of knowledge, intertextuality and text design. However, little evidence was found that the video game players were engaging in social or moral critique of the cultural stereotypes. They lacked older mentors to guide conscious and responsible resistance to dominant masculinities.

The New Literacy Studies has examined how students can be taught to question and challenge implicit and explicit social messages of the new media. For example, Beach and Myers (2001) examined the use of new media, and in particular the juxtaposition of images, text and audio, to teach students how to critique authors' assumptions about the world. This research positioned the out-of-school literacies of youth as an important focus of attention, demonstrating how youth construct their identities within the larger context of media worlds, as well as within their local subcultures (Beach, 2000).

Applying critical media research and socio-cultural literacy to early childhood educational contexts, Crafton et al. (2007) described how students in a Grade 1 class engaged in the critical reading of texts, and constructed multimodal texts using computers to publically voice concern about issues in the local community. Initially, the teacher used technologies and texts in the classroom that tended to reproduce existing pedagogies. Through engagement in a supportive professional community, the teacher made instructional decisions that drew upon new technologies and media for sophisticated forms of collaboration, social inquiry, problem solving and critical literacy.

Domico (2006) described a similar critical and socio-cultural media project for fifth grade students called Exploring Freedom. The students were guided toward analysing and evaluating multimedia sources (websites, books, magazines and newspapers), and the multimedia texts produced included research reports, news broadcasts, editorials, films, dances and poetry. It demonstrated how an inquiry-based, critical media approach could be taught to contest racial prejudice and other social issues involving unequal power relations.

Diffusing the power differential between researchers and the subjects of their research, the Parent Project involved multilingual eighth graders in serving as co-investigators (van Sluys et al., 2008). They recorded data about their parents' engagement in weekly focus groups about multilingualism, digital practices and critical literacy. The study highlighted the positive outcomes for a bilingual community when linguistic diversity, particularly the freedom to code switch between English and one's first language, became a resource for collaborative inquiry.

In sum, the influence of critical literacy themes within the New Literacy Studies has yielded important findings about power relations and new digital practices across all levels of education, from early childhood to adult education. Studies have demonstrated the constraining and enabling powers at work when new digital practices are integrated in normative (school-sanctioned) and informal contexts of literacy learning. Likewise, these studies have demonstrated the specific ways in which social patterns of marginalisation are reproduced and resisted in the appropriation of digital practices across institutional, private, civic and recreational sites.

Yet taken as a whole, socio-cultural literacy research has given less attention to developing the mental frameworks and pedagogies for critically interrogating and analysing texts than critical literacy approaches have forged, as will be demonstrated in Chapter 3. While literacy researchers may combine principles of socio-cultural theory with those of other paradigms, the distinguishing feature of a socio-cultural literacy approach is the emphasis on describing and validating the varieties of literacy practices that are shared within and between communities, including communities of practice in schools and other institutions.

Implications of Socio-cultural Literacies for Practice

With the increased need for students to navigate, interpret, critique and create polyvalent digital text forms, teachers have an important role in the difficult task of embedding relevant literacy practices that coalesce with, and extend the digital and multimodal practices with which children and youth now engage in many communities of practice beyond schools.

Recognising the connections between school, home and other community practices is valuable for teachers. It can enable us to appreciate that the hybrid array of digital discourses and literacy practices is never contained in one social site or another. Rather, they flow and are modified across and between communities, sites, spaces and time. There is also much for teachers to gain from the strand of New Literacy Studies that examines exactly how other teachers worldwide are engaging in the innovative, risky and often political work of integrating an expanding repertoire of literacy practices in the formal literacy curriculum. This work is political, because it often requires a paradigm shift in schooling and curriculum policies to acknowledge the value of digital text production beyond handwriting, of creativity beyond reproduction, of collaboration beyond individual tasks, of multimodality beyond monomodality (single mode), of textual critique beyond reading comprehension, of online navigation beyond reading the book and of virtual communities beyond the local school community. These are new directions for socio-cultural literacies.

The New Literacy Studies has investigated a broadened range of digital literacy practices across multiple technologies, media, modes, text formats and social contexts. This work has highlighted specific ways in which innovative digital practices are significantly more complex and varied than conventional literacy curricula and externally imposed standardised assessments currently permit. Large-scale tests generally do not measure students' ability to self-monitor comprehension in online reading, collaborate in online writing, produce digital media and critically evaluate media (Mills, 2008b).

The digitalisation of print is sometimes taken for granted by educators in their own lives, as they engage in routine practices such as sending text messages, making online financial transactions or using search engines. The digitalisation of literacy is no longer an argument that researchers must continually defend (see Mills, 2008a, 2009, 2010a, 2010c). Conventional literacy performance indicators such as print-based examinations cannot capture the unintended cognitive and social 'collateral achievements' of digital practices (Luke, 2008: 9). More importantly, such measures lack life validity, since they do not reflect the authentic digital literacy practices in social contexts beyond schools. There is scope for the New Literacy Studies to reform conventional measures of literacy by generating, implementing, refining and disseminating innovative models and modified rubrics for the assessment of digital and multimodal composition.

There is potential for the New Literacy Studies to identify factors that impinge on achieving specific pedagogical goals for digital literacy practices by applying qualitative, quantitative and mixed-methods research that extends beyond single- and multi-site ethnographies. Sustainable research interventions continue to be needed in institutional and non-institutional sites. These can investigate the changing out-of-school literacy practices of toddlers, children and youth, as well as the processes by which different types of material technologies become integrated with literacy curricula to develop approaches to curriculum and assessment. For example, design experiments and participatory methods are approaches to research that have directly informed policy and practice in authentic educational contexts (Clark, 2011; Cobb et al., 2003). Such approaches can account for how designs function, such as literacy interventions in educational sites, and design experiments have received the research funding support of governments.

The New Literacy Studies engenders new visions for educational research, practice, assessment and policy that take into account the transformed nature of the new literacies in the 21st century. Such research can continue to address the normative concerns of those who have a responsibility for guiding state and national accountability measures, using nomenclature that brings formerly polarised fields into a productive international dialogue[1].

Note

(1) This chapter is an expanded and updated version of the following journal article by the author: Mills, K.A. (2010) A review of the digital turn in the New Literacy Studies. *Review of Educational Research* 80 (2), 246–271.

3   Critical Literacies

We find contemporary society and culture wanting in many ways and believe that research should support efforts for change.
(Carspecken, 1996: 6–7)

Key Concepts of Critical Literacies

A critical orientation to literacy studies begins with a concern about social inequalities, social structures, power and human agency. Power relations mediate all thought and language, so that all language, textual practices and linguistic conventions are the product of relations of power and struggles for power. Poet and social activist Adrienne Rich once wrote:

> My daily life as a teacher confronts me with young men and women who had language and literature used against them, to keep them in their place, to mystify, to bully, to make them feel powerless. (Rich, 1979: 61)

Critical orientations to literacy, whether in relation to new media or old, derive from varied schools of thought, from the Frankfurt School Institute of Social Research to Paulo Freire's ideals. However, centrally, critical approaches to literacy aim to disrupt hegemonic discourses about what counts as literacy and for whom. Such approaches consider the power of discourses in terms of who has access to literacies and literacy practices, and how the inequitable distribution of literacy can be changed. As Dewey perceived:

> When language is used simply for the repetition of lessons, it is not surprising that one of the chief difficulties of schoolwork has come to be instruction in the mother tongue. Since the language taught is unnatural, not growing out of the real desire to communicate vital impressions and convictions, the freedom of children in its use gradually disappears. (Dewey, 1971: 55–56)

Critical approaches consider both power in languages and discourse, as well as the power behind language and discourses – the social structures and power relations that give rise to, maintain and reproduce language, and limit access to formal discourses for certain groups (Fairclough, 1989). Students need to be taught flexible and wide-ranging social competencies for educational, occupational and other social purposes, coupled with the ability to challenge ideologies of texts, textual practices and one's own place at any given point in time within the social structure (Luke, 1994). And regardless of what grammatical forms, bilingual approaches, modes or technologies are taught within the literacy curriculum, literacy pedagogy isn't inherently democratic or critical in nature. Critical approaches to literacy directly address the ideologies in books and media, and work towards the development of a critical consciousness (Shor, 1999).

Literacy events in schools are rule-governed social contexts that have embedded values, identities and symbols of the social world. The social roles and images circulated in school texts are not natural or inevitable, but can be interrogated. Critical approaches reposition teachers and students to deconstruct dominant selective traditions in schools and society, particularly in the complex textual and multimedia environments of navigating and remixing digitally mediated texts.

Domination and privilege

From a critical orientation, any serious analysis of literacy studies requires an attendant understanding of the way in which literacy pedagogies function in the process of social struggle, whether tied to race, class, gender, belief or other identities, and how literacy pedagogies may also legitimate or alternatively critically challenge the continued privileging of dominant groups (Apple, 1982). Literacy practices in schools need to be reinterpreted and repositioned with an attendant awareness of the changing demands of the historical, cultural and political context in which they are used (Luke & Freebody, 1997). As Luke (1997: 2) concluded, 'There is compelling historical and contemporary evidence that, the best intents and efforts of teachers notwithstanding, many school systems are not providing equitable access to powerful literacies'.

Providing new evidence for these patterns of literacy marginalisation in Australia, ethnographic data from students' home and school lives demonstrates that students' ability to take hold of multimodal design in the classroom is partially bounded by the consequences of social action more widely distributed (see Mills, 2011c). For example, in an Australian classroom, multilingual and Indigenous students who were not of the dominant, white culture – Paweni, Daria, Ted, Wooraba and Meliame – possessed differing language resources, including speaking different dialects of spoken English at home. The unintended consequences of these differences in students' home experiences were conditions for the social reproduction of differing access to digital literacy practices at school. Many hundreds of instances over a 10-week period were video recorded and coded in which students from minority cultural backgrounds demonstrated unfamiliarity with the classroom discourse.

Paweni, who was Thai, could speak few words of English, so would become silent when asked to give an account of her contribution to the collaborative movie-making tasks. Paweni often became silent when asked questions by the teacher in both whole class discussions and small groups, and was reprimanded for unsatisfactory attempts at audio recording, and for not making a significant contribution to the group planning (Mills, 2011c). Ted, who was Indigenous, often received negative sanctions for incorrect uniform (e.g. hat indoors), for excessive movement around the classroom room, inattentive posture and incorrect verbal grammar. He was relegated to the repetitive aspects of designing, such as keeping a tally of the photos taken by others, and adding myriads of similar sized pieces of plasticine grass for the props (Mills, 2006a). In contrast, there were many observed instances in which white students were able to verbalise convincingly that they were working hard (Mills, 2008a). They dominated the roles of photographers and lead designers in the group movie making, because they were familiar with the expectations for designing, the discourses for negotiating roles and the tacit requirements for schooling success. They were voted by peers as producing the best movies (Mills, 2007). The students had widely varied structures of action to draw upon, and accordingly, had wholly unequal access in the classroom. Familiarity with the dominant culture in many parts of the world (e.g. Maori education: Bishop, 2003; South Africa: Janks, 2010b) continues to play a role in either enabling or constraining students' possibilities for action in the literacy classroom.

Ideology

Elucidating what is meant by 'ideologies' in social practices is also important to critical approaches. Ideology is meaning making that supports forms of domination (Kincheloe, 2007). All thoughts, acts, uses of language and social relations are inherently political (McLaren, 1994). This view of ideology can be traced back at least as far as Engels' 'false consciousness' where ideology is seen as '...a process accomplished by the so-called thinker, consciously...but with a false consciousness' (Marx & Engels, 1968: 700). Marx and Engels theorised that one's underlying intentionality or motive remains unknown even to oneself '... otherwise it simply would not be an ideological process' (Marx & Engels, 1968: 700). In other words, those who hold ideologies are often unaware of the origins of their falsehood, do not honestly examine their motives for propagating them, nor examine the reasons for their perpetuation. Ideologies often have an historical origin, so that over time, they become invisible or naturalised by groups and individuals, rather than challenged. An oft-cited example is the political and social situation that ensued in Latin America in the 1960s and 1970s, which required cultural action in order to break the 'culture of silence' (Freire, 1970a: 72).

In the context of schooling the literacy curriculum is seen as a selective tradition, and pedagogies seen as disingenuous practices. These are sometimes ideologically coded in the same way as goods and services, in the sense that they are subject to the logic and processes of commodification and capital accumulation (McLaren, 1995; Mills, 2013b). Literacy is ideological because people master the codes and conventions of their communities, which have differing degrees of alignment with the literacy practices valued by the dominant, white culture (Luke & Freebody, 1997). Literacy is socially constructed, as a form of historically solidified ideology, and an assemblage of socially approved communicative practices for different social contexts (Cook-Gumperz, 2006).

Literacy is often complicit with an ideology of politics and exclusion (Riggins, 1997), a form of cultural capital that is distributed in selective and uneven ways to different groups. Literacy is also ideological with respect to the stratification of literacy achievement socially and demographically. For example, differences in achievement are often strongly correlated with socioeconomic status, race, first language background and geography (e.g. urban, rural, remote), rather than accounted for by individual cognition alone. Furthermore, reading in the Freirian sense involves 'reading the word and the world' (Freire & Macedo, 1987: 35). It is not just about learning the rudimentary aspects of textual competence, but about critically evaluating how literacies are used and valued, and how they are exchanged for status in different fields or linguistic markets (Luke & Freebody, 1997).

Oppression

From the position of critical pedagogy, oppression is also worthy of attention, and has many forms. There is a need for educators to identify and understand how oppression works in educational systems and society, and within the professional and informal communities that inhabit how we live and work (McLaren, 1994). The meaning of oppression has shifted in critical theory, with an original focus on colonial domination and conquest extended to interrogate the many forms and sites of oppression. For example, since the 1990s, critical theories have addressed the social relations of capitalist production, globalisation, institutional hierarchies, the reproduction of inequity and false beliefs that impinge on everyday practices (Young, 1992).

Oppression is experienced in many parts of the world in the form of inadequate educational provision for certain groups, such as those in poverty, racial and migrant groups, those with disabilities, rural communities, females and children. Few would challenge the view that increased access to literacy practices, including those mediated by digital technologies, often leads to better economic outcomes than for those who are illiterate. However, literacy alone provides no insurance against unemployment, particularly in volatile economic markets, and when ideologies about societal, occupational and domestic roles limit individuals from participating equally in the public sphere. Patterns of inequity will continue to persist in capitalist societies as literacy requirements increase, including the need for skilled use of information-based technologies, self-promotion via texts, and creative text production. In addition, higher levels of post-secondary education have become a necessary prerequisite for accessing and maintaining entry to many professions in an information and Web 2.0 digital ecology. Oppression can begin to be addressed in literacy practices when we teach children to see that '...meanings change according to the social positions of those who hold and make them' (West, 1992: 85).

Agency

The notion of agency or emancipation is a third concept discussed here, central to critical pedagogy. It refers to the ability to shape and control one's life, free from the power or hold of oppression (Kincheloe, 2007). In Freire's view, humans are unlike animals in the respect that we are active agents who can critically reflect on our action in the world. Human action can lead to humanisation or dehumanisation, to the growth of people, or to our diminution (Freire, 1970a).

In classrooms teachers and students are as seen as possessing agency, able to critically and consciously transform the world, though always within the constraints and enabling structures and politics of schooling and society. More specifically, according to Freire, humans have the capacity for 'conscientisation' – the processes through which agents gain a '...deepening awareness of the socio-cultural reality that shapes their lives and of their capacity to transform that reality' (Freire, 1970a: 65).

Applied to literacy, agency is seen as central to all acts of communication, but becoming literate does not guarantee access to social power. Educating the masses through basic literacy has historically functioned as a form of citizen regulation and control, relayed through a hidden curriculum of bodily control and discipline (Luke, 1992). Agency through literacy may begin to unfold when children are taught literacy practices that provide the foundation for participation in work, community and family life, and are encouraged to challenge and critique the assumptions and hidden curriculum in textual practices. Critical theorists consider that while no one is ever completely free from the social struggles within one's socio-political context, a certain degree of social emancipation can begin when we expose the forces that prevent individuals and groups from shaping the decisions that crucially affect their own lives, and the lives of other members within an oppressed community (Kincheloe, 2008).

Origins of Critical Approaches

Prior to its influence on literacy education, and in educational theory more broadly, critical theory has a long history in the academy. The Frankfurt School was central to the development of critical theory, an approach to cultural criticism and social philosophy associated with the theoretical contributions of Horkheimer, Adorno, Marcuse and Benjamin. These theorists engaged with earlier philosophies and the social thought of Marx, Kant, Hegel and Weber. The Frankfurt School grew out of the Institute of Social Research, founded in 1923 by Felix Weil, and directed by Carl Grunberg from 1923–1929. Horkheimer, who wrote while in exile in the United States, directed the Institute of Social Research from 1930–1958. This school drew on Marxist theories that addressed, among other social themes, the rise and contradictions of capitalism and class exploitation, against the prevailing Liberalism and Enlightenment rationality of modernity that celebrated scientific progress and capitalist accumulation (Robertson & Dale, 2009). Against the backdrop of post-World War I Germany, and moving beyond Marxist orthodoxy, Frankfurt School critical theorists were united in the view that injustice and domination shape the world. After escaping to California during World War II, the Jewish membership of the Frankfurt school returned to Germany in 1953 to re-establish the Institute of Social Research (Kincheloe, 2008).

At the same time, critical theory diverged from Marxism in clearly defined ways, including a move away from the base-superstructure model of society – in essence, the economic organisation of society to meet basic, material needs of life as 'the base', and everything else of culture in society as the 'superstructure'. The base includes the social relations and technological means of production of material goods (Carspecken, 1996).

Paralleling developments in social theory more broadly, critical theory began to attend less explicitly to the material and economic relations that constitute the reproductive function of institutions, to acknowledge the possibilities for social change and transformation. A key feature of neo-Marxist critical theory was a focus on the superstructure, in particular the ideologies that shape social action through media, art and other cultural domains. It also emphasised the role of dialogue and reason in social life, while providing a reconstructed critique of some of the limitations of societies that are driven by technical efficiency and instrumental or means-ends rationality, such as the loss of moral values and the depersonalisation of social life. Similarly, greater reflection on the system of constraints that are humanly produced, and the dialectical critique of political economy, essentially diverged from Marxism (Robertson & Dale, 2009). These developments occurred in the context of other movements around the world, such as the beginnings of the Civil Rights Movement in the United States, and the emergence of the New Left, influenced by the anti-colonial liberation movements in Latin American, Africa and Asia.

One of the most well-cited extensions of critical theory to education was Paulo Freire's (1970b) *Pedagogy of the Oppressed*, which became available in English in 1970, based on the original 1967 version. It amalgamated traces of liberation theology with German Frankfurt School critical theory. These ideas were elucidated in the context of his work against poverty in northeastern Brazil (Kincheloe, 2007). In this and other key works, Freire's central thesis was that schooled forms of reproduced knowledge could not transform life for those who are oppressed in society. Rather, liberatory educational practice requires a dialectic between the conversion of transformative action into knowledge, and conversely, the conversion of knowledge into transformative action (McLaren, 1993). Friere's pedagogical project was about action both in and on the world.

Seventeen years later, Freire and Macedo's (1987) volume, *Literacy: Reading the Word and the World*, became an international success. It sought to apply transformative principles to literacy practice. The Freirian model of pedagogy involves the presentation of a problem situation, which can be generated by the students, which is then analysed and coded critically by the students, and a plan of action developed (Au, 2009). It involves three phases. The first uses codes to enable learners to see themselves as makers of culture, whether through stories, collages, songs, performances, drawings or other representations. Through these codes learners are encouraged to challenge discourses and norms that serve to marginalise individual and groups within the social order.

In the second phase, students are taught generative vocabulary, both discussing situations associated with key terms—*favela* (slum), *comida* (food), *terreno* (land) and *salario* (salary) – and envisaging spaces through which they can challenge and transform the social forces and circumstances associated with these problematic themes. During the third phrase, various symbol systems, such as drawing and writing, are employed in combination with the generative themes (Lankshear & Knobel, 2005).

Two essential approaches are used to develop this praxis – problem posing and dialogue. Problem posing involves students and teachers generating critical questions of the world in which they live, including of the material relations of daily experiences, and determining what actions can be taken to change one's material conditions. Dialogue is also integral to these processes, which stems from Freirian dialectical philosophy. From this viewpoint, ideas are seen to be a reflection of the material world, and events are interpreted as processes that are constantly in motion, a chain of interdependent relationships that must be understood in relation to each other (Au, 2009). Essentially, Freire's contribution to knowledge was the establishment of a critical relationship between pedagogy and politics, that is, critically addressing the implicit and explicit ideologies or myths of the dominant powers that shackle oppressed groups (Freire, 1998).

Freirian critical pedagogy first enables students to develop a critically conscious knowledge of the world and become conscious of their relationship to the world. Second, in developing consciousness, it envisages that the teacher and students will become 'an instrument of choice' (Freire, 1982: 56). Education that allows for critical agency is both liberating and authentic (Freire, 1982). Students and teachers learn to critically reflect on reality, and take transformative action to change their reality.

Critical literacy is a process of literacy learning that enables the learner to become conscious of one's historical location in ideological power relations with view to democratising education (Shor, 1999). Critical literacy involves using and analysing language with an awareness of the social construction of identity, power and social implications. The key issue is that no literacy pedagogy is value neutral, and that literacy is always taught for some political purpose, whether recognised or not. Critical literacy is an approach to literacy learning that makes transparent the ideologies and power relations at work in texts, in literacy learning, and in the production and use of the texts that circulate in society. In short, language forms are taught through pedagogy that aims for democratic development.

With respect to the teaching techniques of critical literacy, there have been many useful approaches developed toward an agenda for positive social and democratic change. For example, bi-dialectical approaches have been promoted by Shor (1999) and Freire and Macedo (1987) in ways that equip students with powerful uses of dominant forms of English, while honouring students' community language as a resource. Bilingualism, bidialectalism and translated versions of students' community texts are all valuable tools for language learning, while at the same time needing to go beyond the teaching of functional language skills.

Language learning has failed if it teaches students only the minimal skills of the language of the colonisers to simply reproduce the rhetorical forms, standard usage and academic discourses. Critical literacy provides students with the conceptual tools necessary to critique the omissions in texts, the silences and the social and cultural bias of text producers – whether in relation to race, gender, beliefs, values, age, social class, geography or other social dimensions. Students also gain the analytic tools and textual production knowledge to create a vision for a more socially just future, to challenge the status quo, and to address intellectually and pragmatically the social, cultural and political problems that influence marginalised communities, with a view to individually and collectively transforming society.

Critical literacy can take many forms, from critically analysing an array of real texts used in schools and society – books, news articles, websites and billboards – to publishing counter-narratives, arguments, research papers, online media and public forums and events, and involving students in advocacy or social change projects with local councils, organisations and governments. Freire and Macedo (1987) advanced the view that reading and writing is about actively reading both the word (or image, or other mode) and the world, acting on the world rather than being passively unreflective of the place of texts and people in the world, and of the social configurations of power that shape how texts and people are used to benefit certain groups.

Tensions for Critical Literacy Approaches

The entire area of critical research, within and beyond its application to literacy studies, has been the subject of intense debate (Carspecken, 1996). One of the main tensions concerns debates about the role of schools in the structural reproduction of hegemony, a view that overlooks the opportunity for schools and teachers to generate real possibilities for individual or collective human agency. Hegemony is seen here as the '... spontaneous consent given by the masses of the population to the general direction imposed on social life by the dominant group' (Gramsci, 1971: 12). Any teacher, researcher, student or other individual who dares to lead self or others in disrupting the status quo, of uncovering hegemony, of challenging the cultural, gendered or racist scripts that dictate who one should become, is likely to contend with opposition. And any theory that challenges the dominant social groups, that seeks to elevate subjugated knowledge or beliefs, or that promotes counter-hegemonic social structures, is by its very nature political.

In waging a 'war of words', critical theorists can expect a social skirmish (Shor, 1999: 3). Critical pedagogies cannot make the poor rich, reverse the wrongs in society, punish the unjust or free all marginalised groups in society from the weight of oppression. What critical pedagogies can do is guide self and others in '…the process of becoming conscious of one's experience as historically constructed within specific power relations' (Anderson & Irvine, 1993: 82). In this process, accounts of critical literacy have demonstrated that teachers can strive to work towards more just social outcomes in at least their corner of the world, and in relation to textual practices (see Comber et al., 2001).

Applications of critical theory to literacy pedagogies can be fraught with potential problems. Shor (1999: 8), who has co-authored with Freire and is a keen proponent of critical literacy forewarns: 'Coming to critical literacy is a rather unpredictable and even contentious process filled with surprises, resistances, breakthroughs and reversals'.

In relation to the theoretical tensions and arguments raised against critical pedagogy, some concern the accommodation of poststructuralist viewpoints, particularly refinements in understanding the relationship between knowledge and power (Foucault, 1980). These have included issues such as the impossibility of having one grand meta-narrative under which relations of domination are subsumed. Critical education has sometimes been seen to overemphasise oppression in relation to race, gender and class, at the expense of multiple, overlapping and changeable identities. Consequently, postmodern views and other 'post' theories have been grafted into critical educational studies, which as Au and Apple (2009: 91) concede '…has been important, though not totally unproblematic to say the least'. They maintain that the '… "newer" postmodern and poststructuralist analyses were not replacements for those understandings that were grounded in the more structural and materialist positions'.

Addressing some of the difficulties of critical literacy practices more specifically, Comber (1997: 272) asks: 'How does one immersed in and constructed by a particular culture, manage to stand out of it and examine some its integral and implicit tenets?' This is a criticism that has been raised of critical pedagogies more broadly, akin to the problem of uncovering a false consciousness, which is by very definition invisible to the knower. West also contends provocatively:

> It is when we come to the claims for critical literacy that the real difficulties begin…The history of literacy is littered with broken promises…

Literacy…is no guarantee of either freedom for the individual or economic prosperity for the nation… Are the claims that could be made for
critical literacy any different? (West, 1992: 90)

Many critical literacy theorists actually do not hold the view that literacy
guarantees economic freedom, particularly when there is no reflexive understanding of the social circumstances and historical traditions that influence
how literacy is taught. They ask questions such as: For what purposes are
literacies powerful? In which institutional sites is literacy powerful? Whose
literacies are being privileged in the social system? (Luke, 1994)

Key works by critical literacy theorists, such as *The Social Construction of
Literacy: Studies in Interactional Socio-linguistics* by Cook-Gumperz, and *The
Social Construction of Reading in the Primary School* by Luke, devote significant
attention to the social reproduction of literacy inequality in schools. Cook-
Gumperz (1986) reviews social conceptions of literacy since the advent of
compulsory schooling, providing evidence that differentiation through
schooling achievement became a marked feature of 20th century life. Luke
(1994) theorises that different educational institutions – technical colleges,
universities – and different 'streams' within schools dispense and require
differing kinds of practice and capital that don't have the same currency or
exchange rate. What is taught in schools does not necessarily lead to transfer-
able competence and knowledge in life beyond schooling. Critical literacy
advocates have indeed challenged the premise that literacy means future
employment.

Others believe that the claims of critical literacy are often embedded in
pejorative language that militates against its advancement. For example, the
'oppressor' is defined, not on the basis of one's intention or wish to oppress,
but upon one's location in an oppressive structure. More specifically, the
oppressor is usually defined as a middle class, white male holding a senior
position in a hierarchical institution. In discourses with powerful political
figures, such as in efforts to reform institutional structures and educational
policies, the pejorative nature of the term 'oppressor' renders it difficult to
employ, particularly when those who have the capacity for political and systemic change are still often white males (West, 1992).

Critical literacy advocates have conceded the need to acknowledge, articu-
late and critique their own underlying values and socio-political agendas
(Knobel & Healy, 1998). Critical pedagogy is historically grounded in neo
Marxist foundations, left-wing politics and anti-capitalist persuasions,
though it is has also been taken up by the political right. Teachers need to
reflect continuously on how they construct a particular version of critical
literacy in their classroom, ensuring that they are not engaging in a form of

political manipulation and the possible suppression of students' different points of view. For example, teachers have traditionally had a propensity to claim the high moral ground based on the negative critique of children's popular culture (Faraclas, 1997). At other times, students' belief systems and those of their religious, spiritual or cultural communities may conflict with the secular foundations of critical literacy, which is not consistent with their own systems of textual hermeneutics, worldviews, historical texts and authority structures (Skerrett, 2014). Kenway and Bullen critique critical literacy:

> They offer their teaching as a non-oppressive, enlightened, and empowering alternative to popular pedagogy and the corporate curriculum. This is not necessarily the way it is understood by students who may experience it as authoritarian. (Kenway & Bullen, 2001: 155)

It is possible that through critical literacy practices, teachers may offer students the implicit message that certain popular and pleasurable discourses are not condoned by adults (Kenway & Bullen, 2001). Taking a critical literacy stance will not neutralise classroom literacy practice, since it is driven by its own political agenda for social change.

Nevertheless, schools play a strong normative role in society and any actions that pose a serious threat to social institutions may involve negative ramifications. It is important to take a critical position with regard to both texts and textual practice in schools, subjecting the critical literacy classroom itself to analysis and critique. Despite its many merits and contributions to education, critical literacy alone is not the panacea to cure the uneven distribution of knowledge and inequalities of power in contemporary society. However, a strength of critical literacy continues to be its attention to the social and cultural nature of literacy, in which materially and symbolically unequal relationships of power are often implicated and constructed (Green, 1997).

Recent Developments in Critical Approaches

While critical pedagogy is not new, it is certainly no less relevant in literacy studies in the current times, when attention and interest is given to digital forms of communication. Critical theorists have contributed insightful critiques of the global circulation of texts on the internet, the ease of creative media production and consequent increased democratisation of knowledge, the unequal distribution of powerful digital practices and the social implications of heightened accessibility to the internet and popular culture through mobile technologies. The discourses of technological change are critiqued as potentially problematic, particularly when there are hints of technological determinism, valorising of technological advancement, and overly optimistic views of the benefits of media production for education.

Critical theorists see that ideals such as participatory culture (Jenkins *et al.*, 2009), democratisation of knowledge, and their associated transformed epistemologies through the web (Knobel & Lankshear, 2007) need to be tempered with critical analysis of texts and textual practices. Digital textual practices are caught up in the same capitalist agendas, power relations, domination, marginalisation and historical and political struggles as face-to-face interactions. The colonising of online spaces by the most powerful is experienced just as viscerally, such as through advertising or cyber-bullying, as in offline worlds. Where terms such as 'agency', 'voice', 'freedom', 'flexibility', 'collaboration', 'community' and 'production' abound in communication and media studies, the online world is still dominated by corporate media and market conglomerates in ways that require critical pedagogies like never before. When we 'Google it', do we really get knowledge, or do we get a list of corporate sponsors? How does one ever get to the six hundred millionth (marginalised) result from a typical search?

Critical theory uncovers the myths associated with heightened internet interconnectivity, arguing that the new post-Fordist subject is a '…cultural citizen of mobile privatisation' (McCarthy *et al.*, 2009: 40). While online from anywhere, anytime, users require less face-to-face contact with fellow citizens and become less meaningfully related to their immediate locales and environments. Social technologies can often breed social isolation. Similarly, virtualisation in education, '…the rise and intensification of virtual interactions' within institutional sites, tied to the desire for speed and efficiency, is often exploited by organisations, not to free the oppressed, but to have greater surveillance, information and image control and dominance over those at the bottom of educational hierarchies (McCarthy *et al.*, 2009: 42). Critical theory is wary of technological determinism that is tied to discourses of scientific progress and societal advancement, with important commentaries appearing on critical theory and technology calling for democratic participation in technological decision-making (Feenberg, 1991).

Critical pedagogy also critiques the neoliberal operations of universities and schools, such as quality control processes and audits. Colonised by processes such as electronically delivered student experience surveys, the teaching and learning relationship becomes one of product-consumer, with surveys functioning as consumer complaint hotlines, and feedback loops for venting the emotions of students who are under the stress of continual evaluation, competition and meritocracy. Apple (1996: 11) has critiqued the global commodification of the educational enterprise: 'Education is seen as another product, evaluated for its economic utility and as a commodity to be bought and sold like anything else in the "free market"'.

Without the voice of critical education, institutions such as schools, colleges and universities may become uncritically implicated by the capitalist agendas, power relations and hegemonic relations that dictate education markets, distorting educational and research values, and diminishing equity and social justice for those who have been historically marginalised by structural inequality that over time has become naturalised. The literacy practices that occur in universities, their logo-centrism and the integration of digital technologies for delivery of knowledge, can be viewed as institutionalised processes to mass markets that often centre on transmission, due to their economy and efficiency. Technologies are often offered to students as different ways of achieving the same reproductive ends, consistent with the selective traditions that have historically dominated institutions.

Intersections between Critical Literacy and Multimodal Literacy Paradigms

The connections between socio-cultural and critical literacy paradigms were synthesised in Chapter 2, tracing a strand of critical work within the New Literacy Studies, while maintaining the distinctions between these theories. The interrelationship between critical literacy and multimodal paradigms are also deserving of some attention, because key themes of critical approaches, such as power, ideology, knowledge and language have parallel lines of thought within the historical development of multimodal approaches.

Kress and van Leeuwen (2006: 2) acknowledge the direct influence of Critical Linguistics of the East Anglia School in the 1970s, '...with whom one of us was connected' (i.e. Kress). Key volumes exploring the relations between ideology and textual analysis include Hodge and Kress' (1979) monograph, *Language as Ideology*, which was published around the same time as their co-authored book with Fowler (1979), *Language and Control*. Grounded in Halliday's systemic functional linguistics, both volumes aimed to demonstrate the subordination of language use within institutions, drawing attention to both paralinguistic and non-linguistic features of language, and the use of language as an instrument of domination.

Closely associated with multimodal theorists is the work of Fairclough (1989) who published the later, but yet significant work, *Language and Power*. Like theorists of critical approaches, Fairclough emphasised the need to develop a '...critical consciousness of domination through language and its modalities, rather than just experiencing them' (Fairclough, 1989: 3). This account of power in language was not deterministic or hopeless. Rather, through the critical raising of consciousness of the exploitative functions of language, it demonstrated how discourses operate, and how language can be used to disrupt power relations and lead to emancipation, breaking down dominant discourses in the ideological struggle against dominant social groups. Fairclough aimed for children of oppressed social groups to be equipped with critical language awareness to be collective producers and interpreters of new discourses that would disrupt the *status quo*. Fairclough is included here because of his membership with the New London Group, and his contributions alongside multimodal theorists, such as Kress, in the volume edited by Cope and Kalantzis (2000a). Fairclough (1989) saw the visual mode as carrying some of the richest elements of meaning within language.

Multiliteracies is important in traversing the intersection of critical and multimodal approaches (Cope & Kalantzis, 2000a). This dynamic movement brought together key theoretical developments, such as Kress' (2000b) concept of multimodality, dominance of the visual, ideology, and the semiotics of consumption, with Faircough's concepts – power in language, marketisation, commodification and intertextuality. At the most fundamental level, the multiliteracies arguments forged the idea that meaning is made in ways that are multimodal, with increased multiplicity of meaning making through electronic hypermedia, mass media and the WWW. Multiliteracies also addressed the realities of local cultural and linguistic diversity and global connectedness, including the rapid domination of English around the globe.

Fairclough's (1989) earlier work is also significant in relation to the intersection of critical and multimodal approaches, because he sought to demonstrate how socio-linguistic conventions have a dual relation to power, both arising from and giving rise to power relations. He enumerated persuasively that ideological assumptions are embedded in language conventions, as a means of legitimising certain social and differential power relations.

At the outset of their later volume, *Reading Images: The Grammar of Visual Design*, Kress and van Leeuwen similarly emphasise the importance of ideological positions in the different interpretations of experience and their representation, whether pertaining to linguistic cultural resources, or visual, spatial and audio modes. The multimodal literacy paradigm begins with an acknowledgement that the production of language and knowledge are issues of power with normative sanctions – the dominance of semiotic modes in public communication, the constraining of rules in language and the inscribing of grammatical rules in education are clear evidence for this point. The intersection of language and power is realised in the specialisation of language by elites, the explicit and implicit shared grammars of members of certain groups and cultures, and the very organisation of genres, such as the rules of scientific diagrams that are maintained by scientific communities. As Kress and van Leeuwen (2006: 3) make evident, any multimodal textual analysis begins with the questions: 'What is the group? What are its practices?' Only then can one outline the grammatical rules and elements of texts established by members of those groups.

The consciousness of linguistic imperialism among theorists of multimodal semiotics is an example of a backgrounded understanding of how ideology operates in the construction of grammars and meaning (Mitchell, 1999b). Linguistic imperialism is when linguists blindly impose modes and methods of discourse onto new areas of study without a sensitivity to difference, seeing what one expects to see, thereby concealing the nature and ways in which other modes function. Linguistic imperialism is a demonstration of power, and can be seen as a type of ideology that conceals grammatical differences that perpetuates the dominant modes of language. Kress (2000) sees that the dominance of words in schools and institutions operates in this way, often leaving visual and other modes outside a general theory of communication.

Forms of visual communication are also similarly perpetuated through discourses of power, with the dominant visual language controlled by globalising forces of the mass media, and the reproducibility of memes and images in computing, creating a homogenising influence on the worldwide distribution of image banks. Evident in the work of multimodal theorists is the explication of broad historical, social and cultural relations that recursively influence and are influenced by the grammar of visual design (see Kress & van Leeuwen, 2006).

The analytic themes of power and ideology are woven through Jewitt's (2006) multimodal approach outlined in her volume *Technology, Literacy, Learning: A Multimodal Approach*. One of her purposes for '... analysing the structure of an interface...' is to '... bring the ideology, hidden agenda or curriculum of an application into the open' (Jewitt, 2006: 12). When applying multimodal analysis to classrooms and technology use in schools, Jewitt foregrounds pedagogy as design, and teacher agency as maintained and constrained within socially regulated institutions that interact within a complex social web or activity system that is layered with policies, regulations and legislation. In other words, differences in teachers' pedagogical styles and choices are less about individuals and more about the power and knowledge relations within which teachers must operate. Thus, critical themes have maintained an influence on key theorists of multimodality from its early development, and its precursors in critical language awareness.

Implications of Critical Approaches for Literacy Practice

The application of a critical orientation to education is no simple feat, since educational systems and institutions are primarily establishments of cultural reproduction. Cook-Gumperz' (1986) edited book, *The Social Construction of Literacy*, republished 20 years later as a second edition (Cook-Gumperz, 2006), recounts how the introduction of compulsory schooling was aimed to bring literacy to the masses. Yet throughout history, the pedagogies of schooling have tended to separate literacy from its local cultural foundations, differentiating the school population by achieved levels of literacy. Effectively, there was a differentiation of the distribution of knowledge that contributed to maintaining the social stratification of the literate in society.

Public education provided the organisational conditions for the development of such ranking of individuals. This was supported by psychometric testing of 'universal' developmental processes and the refinement of measurement instruments, providing opportunities for the social mobility of some groups, while selecting and separating others to lower streams, and ultimately, life pathways and occupations with reduced economic opportunities (Cook-Gumperz, 2006). Such processes were supported by the pedagogies of schooling, which Durkheim describes as the knowledge that is embodied in the way the content is transmitted and evaluated. The end result of twentieth century schooling was that literacy '... served as a mobilising force ... in which the cultural patterns of small and localised groups were supplanted by allegiance to the wider and more uniform cultural and social base in which all classes appeared to contribute, only in a differentiated form' (Cook-Gumperz, 2006: 41).

Social interactions everywhere are entangled with power, and include a function to educate others, whether through media, popular culture, advertising, universities, family life and workplaces. Educational discourses and texts have a homology of structure with other societal institutions and processes. Discourses are systematically-organised modes of talking, and these determine what one can say or not say, when one can speak, and when one must be silent (Kress, 1985). In this way, critical views of discourses in institutions constitute a vital part of current understandings of language modes and pedagogies in schools, and have done so for several decades.

Applying a critical orientation to literacy learning itself, literacy is not just about learning graphophonic, syntactic and semantic knowledge; it is about cultural knowledge and symbolic codes that are occur in specific social situations where relations of power are constructed, maintained and waged (Luke, 1994). Critical literacy is an extension of critical pedagogy applied specifically to texts and textual practices. It builds on a recognition that reading is an ideological practice, and that teaching literacy includes helping students to interrogate '...how, why and in whose interests particular texts might work' (Luke & Freebody, 1997: 218). It includes understanding how texts situate readers, and how reading practices situate and construct the 'model reader'. Texts can be juxtaposed against each other, and against one's own reading. Students can learn to see through texts, rather than simply comprehend them. They can deconstruct texts, and situate them within the historical, cultural and political context in which they are written, and in which they are used and taken up.

As Green (1997: 231) acknowledges, '...texts are always already implicated in history, including the history of their own regimes and practices of production and reception'. Texts do not exist independently of the wider system and circulation of discourses, but typically follow rules and symbols of the speech communities to which they belong. Literacies become powerful when we critique other literacies, examining the extent to which they attempt to constitute us as persons and situate us socially (Gee, 2012).

To give an example of such critique, I refer here to Reese's (2008) caution to seek alternative perspectives on given facts in history textbooks. Many children's books report that Columbus discovered America. The term 'discover' in this usage refers to being the first person to find something, preventing readers from perceiving Columbus as an invader of a land already occupied and owned by native peoples. Literacy practices should be more than an uncritical reading of texts and the reproduction of meaning. Another clear example in a Grade 1 classroom was collected by Jennifer Hammond, and first published by Luke (1994). The teacher is guiding the shared writing of a fairy-tale about a princess:

Teacher: A long time ago there lived a princess [reading story modelled on paper for students]. I think I can make it a bit better than that...What do you think she'd look like?
Student: Ah...
Teacher: With long hair? What colour?
Students: Yellow, black [chorus laughter]
Teacher: What about long, long golden hair?

As Luke perceives, here, there is more than a lesson about how to make story writing more descriptive. It is an example of how literacy practices are constructed as narrative writing, in the selective tradition of the white

European fairy-tale, with implicit assumptions about race, gender and power. One of the Torres Strait Islander students had suggested that a princess might have black hair. Luke (1994) contends that a pedagogy that is inclusive of race may require a critical reconceptualising of the fairy-tale genre.

A positive example of literacy occurred in my research when a media teacher introduced web profile pages (Mills & Levido, 2011). Several examples of websites were used to help students understand some of the features and purposes of websites. The students were guided to answer a series of critical questions, listed below, that were tailored to match the specific content of example web pages:

(1) What is this website about?
(2) What is the purpose of this website?
(3) Who created this website?
(4) Who will benefit from the website?
(5) What are the features of the website?
(6) What does the website suggest about people of different ages, and what are some opposite views about age and social roles?
(7) What does the website assume about the tastes of boys or girls, men or women, and do you agree with these?
(8) What does the website suggest about people from different races, cultures or community, and whose viewpoint is left out?
(9) Can you trust the information in this website? Why or Why not?
(10) Whose viewpoint or perspective is left out, and could have been included?
(11) What are some counter-arguments to the views presented here?

Learners can present their critique in a variety of formats, such as discussions, matrices, debates, interviews, and written textual products. Throughout the process of textual design, students interpret, select and evaluate knowledge sources for different audiences and social purposes.

Critical literacy also involves reflecting critically on the cultural and social assumptions represented through the students' own digital compositions. For example, teachers in our research guided students to think about issues of audience, purpose, interests and internet safety as they created blogs (web logs) in a secure and monitored intranet administrated by the local state department of education. The students had to plan and think about:

(1) Why am I creating this blog?
(2) What text features (e.g. words, images, audio) will best suit my purpose?
(3) Who is my intended audience?
(4) Who else potentially has access to my blog?

(5) What information about myself should I share or hide?
(6) How does my blog build on the contributions of my peers in the discussion thread?
(7) How do my blog entries show respect for my teacher and others in my class? (e.g. manners and language use)
(8) What do my blog entries say about people of different ages, occupations and cultures?
(9) Whose views have I included or left out? Why?
(10) Who benefits from my blog? Why?

These questions are important, because students' user-generated web content will not automatically work towards democratic participation and voice if students merely reproduce or circulate the pervasive hegemonic and oppressive messages, images and viewpoints in contemporary media environments. Web texts are best seen as key sites where cultural discourses, political ideologies and economic interests should be contested, rather than unquestioningly transmitted. Teachers' selection of written composition tasks in schools is also ideologically value laden, and typically influenced by educational policies. The criteria for judging the quality of students' written compositions are shifting in the context of society and culture.

Critical literacy can include classroom discussions about social issues that are perhaps only indirectly connected to the written texts that circulate in society, but are of direct relevance to the spoken modes of discourse that shape the way children think about the world. Critical pedagogies in literacy have not been limited to the reading of texts, but have also been applied to writing and text production. For example, podcasting students' audio-recorded auto ethnographies can be used by students to describe themselves in ways that engage with representations others have made of them, but which turn ideologies on their head. Students can be taught rhetorical techniques of parody, comparison and critique, applied to digital or conventional literary forms, so as to strengthen students' abilities to deflect, transform and speak back to the digital and other textual products of the dominant culture.

Giving students the linguistic resources and knowledge of multimodal grammars, coupled with technical proficiencies, can enable them to digitally create texts and counter-cultural messages on wikis, websites, blogs and YouTube. Transculturation – an artistic technique for selecting and inventing from the materials transmitted by the dominant culture – can be used by marginal groups to remix, use or oppose, rather than simply absorb, the dominant cultural messages into their own culture or subculture (Shor, 1999).

To use an example from my own research, Allan Luke, colleagues, teachers, and I conducted a critical literacy unit of work that involved digital video design with Year 5 students (students aged 9.5–10.5 years) who attended a school in one of Brisbane's most socially and economically disadvantaged areas (Mills *et al.*, 2012). We wanted the students to have a voice in their local community, so we arranged for them to present their movies at the national Building Child Friendly Communities Conference held in Logan, Queensland. The conference drew a national audience of community activists, health workers, city council workers and chief executive officers as part of Australia's response to the Unicef International Child-Friendly Cities Initiative. The documentaries involved envisaging their social roles as community leaders, including evaluating their local area.

At the conference, the voiceover of a documentary created by two of the Year 5 boys filled the room: 'If I were a community leader, I would put more trees in, and put more bins and more skate parks'. A second movie by two girls continued: 'If we were community leaders, we would make more parking spaces around the school for children's safety'. After the movie screening, the children sat at a long table on the stage forming a panel to respond to questions from the audience – as active agents for change in their local community. Knowing, for these children, was not about grasping objective facts that were separated from their lives. In order to know the world, children have to make the world their own (Hegel & di Geovanni, 2010).

The movies were the culmination of a series of learning events over several weeks that aimed to teach students that places where we live, work, play and learn directly influence our sense of happiness and well-being (Sunderland *et al.*, 2012). The students applied multimodal literacy skills to shape and share their new knowledge – combining written and spoken words with moving images, music, spatial layouts and gestures (Mills, 2011a). They observed local places with the researchers and filmed interviews with community members in the local shopping centre and recreational spaces. They created micro-documentaries for both national and international audiences. The project also engaged the students in understanding Indigenous ways of experiencing the natural world, with Indigenous students represented in the class. Symbols like the 'message stick' were used as examples of the richness of Indigenous culture on the country (Davis, 2012). We were open with the students about our roles in society and our connections with education. After spending time with us, some students shared their aspirations to attend university, and become future teachers and filmmakers.

A capstone moment occurred during the student panel at the national conference, when a member of the local city council asked: 'How does it make you feel to tell us your story?' One of the students replied: 'I feel very good because I see happy faces in the crowd'. Another responded: 'I feel good because everyone liked our movies'. Finally, another student announced loudly and clearly:

'I feel proud that I did this!'. The students had appropriated the world for themselves. They had taken a step toward transforming their world, and in doing so, were transformed themselves. It reminds us that true learning and change is possible only by continuous action in community, and not by sheer contemplation, or passive and objective receptivity (Mills *et al.*, 2012).

New Directions for Critical Approaches

Critical pedagogy has been described as a radical theory of education that is interminably committed to the oppressed (McLaren, 1989). Critical educators share the view that the cultural politics of schools and other education systems historically perpetuate a meritocratic ideology that tends to reproduce inequality, racism, gender inequality and other unequal power relations. Too often, education works against equity through influences of competitiveness, hierarchy and control, white dominance, androcentric ideologies, logo-centrism and market-driven agendas (McLaren, 1995). In relation to literacy more specifically, Brandt and Clinton (2002: 1) discern the complexity of literacy and its relation to social and economic ends: 'Literacy in use more often than not serves multiple interests, incorporating individual agents and their locales into larger enterprises that play out...'. It is for this reason teachers need to know how to critique texts, and their associated historical, cultural and political formations, rather than teaching reading as decoding and comprehension alone. The texts that are selected in literacy curriculum function as mediating technologies in the institutional shaping of discourses and social practices (Stevens & Bean, 2007).

Critical pedagogy can be a paradigm shift to counter ideological views of literacy achievement and schooling. Narrow measures of literacy standards in schools that are aligned to the colonising white middle class have become the benchmark for the literacy practices of culturally and linguistically diverse communities. It has awakened school administrators and teachers to the some of the problems of tracking or streaming students, oversized schools and classrooms and the inequitable distribution of funding and human resources. It has alerted teachers to the problems of reproductive pedagogies and the unreflective selection of texts and classroom discourses that unwittingly marginalise students often by race or socio-economic background (Cook-Gumperz, 1986; Luke, 1998; Mills, 2011c).

Much research still remains to be done in understanding the social struggles of specific groups at specific historical times, including those related to literacy and race, indigeneity, culture, gender, religion, ability, age, appearance, health, poverty, mobility, rurality and other subjectivities, and the fight against oppression. This is because capitalism, the media and other social forces are dynamic and constantly changing. While it is important to broaden research beyond historical forms of oppression (e.g. race, class, gender) to acknowledge multiple relations of power (Au & Apple, 2009), this needs to be done cautiously so that subjectivities of real oppression do not become meaninglessly extended to encompass almost everyone in the world, nor oppression normalised as the ways things should be.

More importantly, there must always be the goal to conscious social action and transformation, both of individuals and the social structures that constrain particular groups, rather than simply the resignification, retheorisation, interrogation and deconstruction of oppression. Critical pedagogy has, at times, become a theoretical project that emphasises material and economic relations, class formation, capital accumulation, and political and economic privilege, over immaterial forms of agency, such as spiritual, emotional and value-centred forms of freedom and emancipation. This is perhaps a by-product of its theoretical and philosophical roots in historical materialism and Marxism, which accounts for the mode of production of material life – its relations of production, that is thought to condition social, political and intellectual life (Marx, 1970).

A future line of critical literacy research pertains to studies that account for rapid cultural globalisation, diasporic communities, cultural communities and hybridised critical literacy practices as tied to the movement and flow of communities experiencing migration and transmigration. For example, we need to ask: How are critical literacy practices and pedagogies emerging in these communities? How do these practices travel or flow across time and space? What new concerns, practical and policy implications, and internet reading practices extend and support the repertoires of critical literacy capacities of students and teachers (Gutierrez, 2013)?

The internet is also central to critical literacy practices in a digital era, opening up new possibilities for researching how children and young people apply critical literacy practices to navigate, construct, evaluate, select and interpret online texts across different social contexts of use, whether in open-ended or institutionally-defined internet practices (Cho, 2013). We need to gain new understandings of students' critical encoding and decoding of new media forms that are powerfully motivating, such as self-initiated interactions in social networking sites (e.g. Instagram, Facebook, Twitter), virtual worlds (e.g. Second Life, Club Penguin, Moshi Monsters, Minecraft), and photo-, video- and music sharing sites (e.g. Flickr, YouTube, SoundCloud), video calls (e.g. FaceTime), blogs and wikis.

Possibilities remain to examine the extent to which users co-create, simulate, play, experience and interact in online spaces in ways that serve to reproduce, resist, accommodate, escape from, blur, transform or do otherwise, in relation to the contemporary and historical forms of oppression that circulate in institutional and textual sites, and their pedagogic practices, in the changing textual landscape. This is particularly important when the ubiquity and mobility of electronic media is transforming the way children see the world, and the ways in which these semiotic domains might be designed to encourage active and critical textual practices (Gee, 2007).

While it was envisaged that the WWW would offer greater opportunities for democratic forms of societal participation (see for example Hague & Loader, 1999), there continue to be stratified constraints on access for certain groups to prestigious forms of online discourse, such as paid access to peer reviewed journal articles, online memberships, reliable internet connections or to hardware and software. Visible and invisible constraints for online membership and struggles to have one's voice heard amidst the online 'noise', are examples of the concerns of critical education. Such issues of restricted access are not necessarily overcome by online spaces, which are potentially influenced by the social constraints of formality that marginalise groups from discourses (Fairclough, 1989). Access to participation in online spaces is unequally distributed along with economic capital, is still subjected to material and ideological constraints, and has enabled new issues of virtual forms of marginalisation, such as children's encounters with cyberbullying, an old problem in a new guise (see Campbell, 2005). Users may experience constrained access to powerful subject positions, to sophisticated and advanced material apparatus, and to skills that require formal training in text production (e.g. graphic design, information retrieval, html programming and advanced animation). Undemocratic online participation is associated with other societal structures and barriers that parcel out differing forms of participation to different groups in new media practices.

Language is the mode of exchange through which education is conducted, and it is never value neutral (Bruner, 1986). Texts are manifestations of discourses, and the social positions and histories of individuals influence their access to the sets of discourses in society (Kress, 1985). Even when teachers are uncritical or unreflective about their discourses, or about the stance implicit in texts and textual practices used in classrooms, values are 'caught' by students, rather than necessarily 'taught' by teachers. Critical literacy serves to make educators cognisant of ideologies that often constrain students who would otherwise choose differently. In short, through critical pedagogy, teachers can show students '...that they are much freer than they feel' (Foucault, 1988: 10).

4　Multimodal Literacies

A multimodal approach to technology-mediated learning offers a way of thinking about the relationship between semiotic resources and people's meaning making

(Jewitt, 2006: 16)

Key Concepts of Multimodal Literacies

Multimodal approaches to literacy are currently prolific in educational research, indicated by the steady increase in the number of research studies of digitally mediated literacy practices (Mills, 2009). The popular terms 'multimodal' and 'literacy' now appear together in over 30,000 scholarly texts accessible to Google Scholar, though definitions of multimodality are not always alike. The dominant theory of multimodality addressed in this chapter is positioned within the theoretical framework of social semiotics (Kress & van Leeuwen, 2006). Social semiotics explicitly attends to meaning-making of diverse kinds, whether of words, actions, images, somatic meanings or other modes (Thibault, 1993). Therefore, by definition, social semiotics acknowledges the role of non-linguistic modes in human social meaning.

Multimodality is defined as '...the use of several semiotic modes in the design of a semiotic product or event' (Kress *et al.*, 2001: 20). Reading and writing have always been multimodal, since these literate practices involve the decoding and encoding of words, while similarly attending to spatial layout of the text, images and other modes of representation (e.g. gestural meanings of represented characters, material features of the book). Yet undeniably, people-driven technological developments of communication have given rise to a much more diverse range of texts and textual practices. There is more rapid dissemination of a greater number of multimodal texts than ever before, and more prolific flows of textual practices across cultures, sub-cultures and national borders via the internet (New London Group, 2000), particularly given the ease of uploading user-generated content using Web 2.0 technologies (Mills & Chandra, 2011).

Humans have always learned to communicate through multiple sign-systems or modes, each of which offers a distinctive way of making meaning (Kress & Bezemer, 2008). However, many theorists see that there is cause for heightened interest given the affordances of digital technologies to capture, create, modify, combine and disseminate images on a much broader scale than in the past. The multimodal ways in which we remember our lived experiences, and preserve our heritages through the visual, are similarly more fluid and configured differently, coupled by greater immediacy and increased portability to share these representations (Giaccardi, 2012).

There are changing social roles and identities associated with multimodal assemblages of audio, visual, gestural, spatial, tactile and other modes that are combined and disseminated with greater ease by everyday users via mobile devices, and disseminated via social media sites, such as Twitter and Facebook (Mills, 2009) and image or video sharing sites (e.g. YouTube, Instagram, Pinterest, SoundCloud). While theorists see that conventional offline literacy practices and new online communication practices are epistemologically different (Knobel & Lankshear, 2007), culturally more participatory (Jenkins et al., 2009) and defined by new online social orders (Snyder, 2001), it is fundamentally the transformation of modes to which multimodal approaches attend.

Modes as sign-systems

Definitions of the multiple resources that humans use to communicate have been multiple and varied, including definitions of 'modes'. For example, the New London Group (2000) uses the term 'modes' in conjunction with 'design'. They identify six major areas or modes of meaning: linguistic, visual, audio, gestural, spatial and multimodal. Multimodal design is considered the most significant, since it concerns the interrelationship of different modes of meaning and the patterns of interconnection among modes.

While Kress (2000b) has several chapters located within Cope and Kalantzis' volume by the New London Group, his interpretation of modes in his sole authored chapters differs slightly to the New London Group. For example, Kress includes music as an example of a mode, as opposed to the broader classification used by the New London Group – audio design. In the New London Group's account, music is listed as a sub-category of audio design, which can be grouped with other examples of audio, such as sound effects, recorded speech and silence (New London Group, 2000). Kress' usage of the term 'modes' is similar to Suhor's (1984) use of the term 'sign-systems', because music, unlike the audio mode more broadly, includes a specific set of formalised conventions that are recognisable to others within a culture. Ten years prior to the New London Group, Suhor (1984: 250) had preferred to discuss 'sign-system' rather than 'modes' to describe categories of meaning and their systems of conventions, such as written words, drawing, dance steps and music notation. Each sign system or mode has unique organisational principles involving elements and conventions that do not have precisely equivalent meanings (Semali & Fueyo, 2001). The terms 'modes' and 'sign-systems' are used interchangeably here to describe socially and culturally shaped resources or semiotic structures for making meaning. They are organised, regular, socially specific means of representation, such as writing, drawing, dance, image, music and mathematics (Suhor, 1984). Specific examples of modes include still image, moving image, writing, music notation, speech and gesture.

Translating meanings across multiple modes: Transmediation

So why does multimodality matter to literacy practices? Theorists of social semiotics have attempted to address this question from various angles. For example, in Jewitt's (2006) volume, *Technology, Literacy and Learning: A Multimodal Approach*, Jewitt envisages that new technologies have the potential to reshape knowledge as curriculum. An illustration of this is seen in her research involving children learning about characters in narratives. The students' reading or viewing of a novel via CD-ROM introduced new practices for designing, navigating and deciphering the character of the narrative. Jewitt also demonstrated how the use of new technologies in the classroom can reshape teachers' pedagogies for learning.

I maintain that transmediation is a central principle that distinguishes multimodal literacy practices from literacy practices involving written or spoken words alone. Suhor (1984: 247), in a significant article called 'Towards a Semiotic-based Curriculum', coined the important term 'transmediation' to describe the meaning-making process of translating content from one sign-system to another. This involves searching for connections between sign-systems to make meaning. This concept was then extended by Semali (2002), Semali and Fueyo (2001), Siegel (1995, 2006) and Short (2000). In my studies of young children translating content from book to image, storyboard to film and from drawing to online comics, I developed three key principles of transmediation that are fundamental in understanding children's multimodal and digital meaning-making (Mills, 2011a).

The first principle is that transmediation is more than the simple reproduction of knowledge, and involves a process of knowledge transformation by degrees. This means that even if a literacy task, at face value, seems to involve the mere reproduction of knowledge (e.g. story retelling through drawings), the act of translating semiotic content via a different expression plane necessitates the transformation of meanings. For example, if the child's drawing translates the meanings of words in an author's book, or a child's drawing plan of movie frames (storyboard) is used as the basis to create a digital film, there is never mere reproduction. Rather, the cross-channel of communication involves inventing connections and weaving between two or more very different symbolic forms. In such communication practices, children must choose from multimodal semiotic resources that do not have direct equivalence, thus inviting creativity and transformation.

The second principle is that transmediation involves a process of continual adaptation of intentions for representing knowledge in response to the possibilities and limitations of sign-making systems, including the affordances of digital systems (Mills, 2011a). When transmediating semiotic content—from words and drawings in the storyboard, to moving images on the screen—users must adapt the affordances and constraints of the filmic medium. For example, when students translated their script into speech and drama, they modified the original script. They often changed the sentence mood and vocabulary and added accents that were not indicated in the script as they took on the role of different characters in meaningful ways. Certain scenes they had imagined and depicted in their storyboards needed adaptation to better suit the limited range of material props and background scenes in the school grounds.

Similarly, when students translated their comic drawings to become digital comics using comic creator software, the constraints and possibilities of the pre-formed images in the digital platform necessitated selection of different semiotic resources than those used in their drawings. Students substituted their intended images with those that were available in the comic menu, which also generated new ways of representing their ideas. In the absence of one-to-one correspondence between sign-making conventions, transmediation across modes establishes an anomaly for the learner. This tension invites learners to invent a way to cross this gap by engaging in both evaluative and generative thinking (Mills, 2011a). This is another reason why we should give attention to multimodal literacy practices in schooling and research.

The final principle is that transmediation across modes is central to digital text production because it involves translating semiotic content via the discrete sign-making systems inherent in software interfaces (Mills, 2011a). In the context of observing students engaged in digital media production, I demonstrated that each digital interface is more than a simple tool for sign making, akin to a pencil or paintbrush. Theorists of semiotics have conceptualised digital technologies as mediating tools. Yet what had not previously been acknowledged in literacy research is that each digital interface requires users to understand a discrete sign-making system of the tool itself (e.g. icons, navigational tools, drop-down menus) with an inherent logic that must be understood in order to mediate meaning. In the context of children's online comic creation, I demonstrated that transmediation involves a process of continual adaptation of the children's intentions for representing knowledge in response to the possibilities and limitations of the sign-making system, including those embedded in digital software. Children engage in a continual process of problem solving as they seek ways to work within the constraints and possibilities of the digital conventions to communicate meaning. Therefore, the use of digital platforms in literacy practices adds another layer to meaning making, requiring new technological knowledge of the sign-systems that are associated with the technology.

Origins of Multimodal Literacies

While the concept of multimodality within a social semiotic framework has greatly influenced literacy research in educational settings through the work of Kress, van Leeuwen (2006) and colleagues in the 1990s, semiotics has attended to non-linguistic modes of communication since as early as the 1930s. Kress and van Leeuwen (2006) acknowledge the first wave of Prague School semiotics from the 1930s to 1970s. The foundational theories of Birdwhistell (1952), Hall (1959), Goffman (1959) and Pike (1954) in the *Natural History of the Interview* were seminal in conceptualising language and nonverbal communication in the 1950s (see Scollon & Scollon, 2009). Semiotics addressed the meanings inherent in non-linguistic forms such as art (Mukarovsky, 1976), costume (Bogatyrev, 1976) and theatre (Honzl, 1976).

These theorists paved the way for a burgeoning interest in how language works in collaboration with other modes in communication studies, linguistics, poetry, film and other disciplines (Kress & van Leeuwen, 2006; Scollon & Scollon, 2009). A notable contribution to this development was Pike's (1954) *Language in Relation to a Unified Theory of the Structure of Human Behaviour.* In this work, Pike articulated the semiotic basis of linguistics to unify the study of human behaviour, so as not to separate the written word from nonverbal modes of language. At the same time, Ruesh and Kees (1954) published an important volume, *Nonverbal Communication: Notes on the Visual Perception of Human Relations,* in which they used pragmatics to demonstrate the relations between the verbal and the non-verbal (Scollon & Scollon, 2009).

According to Kress and van Leeuwen (2006), a second wave of social semiotics became popular in the 1960s and 1970s, through theorists of the Paris School, based on Saussurian semiotics, who applied linguistic structures to the analysis of photography and fashion (Barthes, 1967, 1984), film language (Metz, 1974) and music (Kress *et al.*, 2001; Nattiez, 1976). The philosophies and linguistic theories of Charles Sanders Peirce (e.g. signifier and the signified) are considered a part of this movement. These formalist ideas of autonomous or independent language structures of Peirce contrast the Hallidayan school, where the functional and instrumental nature of language was studied in relation to social contexts of use (Davidse, 1987).

Clearly, social semiotics has since Goffman, Pike (1954), Barthes (1967), Hall and others earlier last century, been much broader than alphabetic inscription (Scollon & Scollon, 2009). For example, Pike's (1954) unified theory is grounded in the view that a theory sufficient for the analysis of language must be applicable to all of human behaviour, such as the larger cultural structures, which like language, are the products of human behaviour (Hoijer, 1956). Goffman's (1959) acclaimed work, *The Presentation of Self in Everyday Life*, draws attention to how two radically different sign-activities are involved in impression management: the expressions that one gives through verbal symbols or their substitutes that are recognisable to others, and more importantly, the expressions that one gives off – a wider range of action – the nonverbal, the contextual and theatrical kind, sometimes purposeful and sometimes unintentional. Similarly, the field of language and non-verbal communication has existed for at least five decades, perhaps strengthened by the need for covert and subtle forms of communication in times of war or political instability (Scollon & Scollon, 2009). As Ruesh and Kees wrote mid last century:

The trend of a number of approaches has been toward an essential concern with nonverbal forms of communication and with the verbal form largely in its pragmatic aspects... Although books can be burned, the use of certain words legally outlawed, and even the act of listening to particular broadcasts or speeches marked as a criminal offence, communication through silent action is more difficult to suppress. (Ruesh & Kees, 1954: 3)

According to Ruesch and Kees (1954), the move toward analysing nonverbal modes of communication was in part a move toward safer and more subtle codes of communication in the aftermath of two world wars, but can also be seen in part, as a reaction against the over-evaluation of the spoken and printed word, and against commercialism, radio propaganda and other circulating forms of media (Scollon & Scollon, 2009). Ruesh and Kees (1954) made this case long before the current social critiques of capitalism and uses of language for profit.

The point is that the growing intellectual interest in language and non-verbal communication, and later, the study of gestures, expressions and posture in paralinguistics, has a longer tradition than multimodal theory, dating back to the mid-1950s, prior to the rapid circulation of images in the digitally-mediated and networked textual practices of the world as we know it today.

What was missing in these earlier models of nonverbal communication was the concept that not all modes were structurally analogous to written language and its grammars. For example, one's interpretation of meanings in a built environment is not linear, as is the grammatical structure of a written sentence, but simultaneously draws on multiple visual, aural, tactile, olfactory and other embodied sensory information that is perceived through the moving body, and which includes an awareness of one's orientation toward other static and moving human and non-human elements sharing the space. Understood in this way, Scollon and Scollon appreciate the complexity of meaning-making:

In a world of logos, flashing light boxes, and texting, even linguistics is hard put to use conventional theories of language to account for the forms of pragmatic language use, much less provide the foundation for studies of meaning across all modes. (Scollon & Scollon, 2009)

Thus, while non-verbal communication studies have burgeoned since the 1950s across a range of fields of communication, earlier structural and linear models of non-verbal language have been subjected to critique. Multimodal theorists acknowledge that human language is done in placed, material contexts of use, and performed and interpreted across many different, often non-linear, timescales that differ to those of speech and written words (Lemke, 2002). There is also a clearer recognition that modes of meaning do not operate in a monomodal way, but involve complex relationships among multiple modes.

Technology, modes and literacy studies

A paradigm shift acknowledging the role of technology transformation and its influence on the plurality of communication modes and media practices began to emerge in literacy studies during the 1980s. For example, Graff (1987: 39) envisaged: 'What is needed is a broader view of reading and writing that integrates and emphasises the many human abilities in a context of a changing world that requires their development and use'.

Sensenbaugh (1990), coordinator of the ERIC Clearinghouse on Reading and Communication Skills, wrote a short document entitled Multiplicities of Literacies in the 1990s. Sensenbaugh summarised the changing organisation and categorisations of literacy research in the ERIC database. He already foresaw that, 'Clearly, literacy has broadened beyond skills used in reading and writing to include terms in other disciplines' (Sensenbaugh, 1990, ¶5). Again, preparing the way for the idea of multiliteracies, Graff perceived that there are:

> ...many literacies in addition to, or beyond, traditional alphabet literacy, from those of science and numeracy, to the spatial literacy that some geographers term 'graphicacy' to... 'cultural literacy', 'historical literacy', and 'moral literacy'... teleliteracy and other media literacies. (Graff, 1995: 321)

A new paradigm of the pluralised nature of literacies was unequivocally recognised.

Writing from Australia, prior to the formation of the New London Group, Green (1993: 209–210) observed that the shift to an electronic order '... opened up the possibility of asking about those forms of human semiosis which are currently slighted, if not suppressed, in the official discourse on curriculum and schooling'. Green (1993: 210) advanced that it is 'inappropriate' to employ the term literacy, except in a metaphorical sense, since the notion of literacy, 'strictly speaking', is specific to the written word. Green (1993) cites theorists, such as Spencer (1986) in relation to emergent literacies, and Ulmer's (1989) *Teletheory: Grammatology in the Age of Video*, to argue that the '...development of new information and communication technologies, including but not limited to the computer, will have particular and decisive impact on pedagogy and literacy' (Green, 1993: 210).

An explicit focus on understanding the semiotic potentials of modes and multimodal texts began to appear in academic titles throughout the late 1990s, such as by Kress and colleagues in the United Kingdom, Martinec (1996) on rhythm in multimodal texts, and among genre theorists in Australia (New London Group, 1996). Sometimes multimodality was discussed as multisemiotic – two or more semiotic resources (see for example O'Halloran, 1999, 2009). It is generally agreed that multimodality – the concept that all modes of communication are important to meaning making – is theoretically framed by Halliday's (1978) social semiotic theory. This theory begins with the important recognition that language is social, and that semiotic resources are not entirely fixed, but are socially and culturally shaped conventions of a community; that is, they arise within situational and cultural contexts of use (Halliday, 1978; Jewitt, 2006; O'Halloran, 2009). Hallidayan systemic functional linguistics flourished in Australia, where the acknowledgement of spoken language and other modes gradually became grafted onto Halliday's social semiotic theory, organised by the three meta-functions of language. Halliday associates his own functional grammar with that of the Prague school (Dirven & Fried, 1987).

Paving the way for multimodal approaches and the New London Group's multiliteracies approach, a surge of educators and theorists saw the need to integrate digital environments in literacy pedagogy, and to gather evidence examining the specific elements of reading and writing processes that were unique to the digital sphere of literacy use. For example, in the late 1980s, Foster *et al.* (1989) studied computer access for English classes. In the early 1990s, Landow and Delany (1991) identified the role of hypermedia in literacy studies, and Selfe (1992) saw the need to prepare teachers for the virtual age. Shortly after, Reinking and Pickle (1993) addressed how computers affect reading and writing. Bigum and Green (1993) began to envision the technologising of literacy, and Green (1995) published numerous articles on literacy and technology issues, including digitalised writing composition. Leu (1996) examined the social aspects of literacy learning on the internet, while Burbules and Callister (1996) also researched hypertext learning environments. Pre-dating or coinciding with the formation of the New London Group, these theorists were united in the view that computer-based technologies were decisively changing existing understandings of literacy, curriculum and research. It was not simply that the tools of literacy had changed, but the very nature of texts, language and literacy were seen to experience some noteworthy alterations.

Well-cited contributions further challenging conventional notions of literacy, but not particularly oriented to the term 'multimodal,' included Lankshear, Gee, Knobel and Searle's (1997) edited volume, *Changing Literacies,* and Snyder's (1997) monograph *Page to Screen: Taking Literacy into the Electronic Era.* Shortly after, Reinking *et al.* (1998) published the well-cited *Handbook on Literacy and Technology.* Theorists such as Snyder (1999) published numerous books and articles in Australia about information technologies in literacy education, and Strassman (1997) on information systems and literacy.

In 1996 the New London Group coined the term 'multiliteracies' in the title of their article to propose that the changing textual and technology landscape, including multimodal forms of communication, called for a new pedagogy for literacy (New London Group, 1996). The theory of multiliteracies was further elaborated in Cope and Kalantzis' (2000b) edited volume with the New London Group, *Multiliteracies: Literacy Learning and the Design of Social Futures*.

Shortly after, Kress, a member of the New London Group, and van Leeuwen, published *Multimodal Discourse: The Modes and Media of Contemporary Communication* (Kress & van Leeuwen, 2001). Kress's co-author, Jewitt, published her (2006) monograph *Technology, Literacy, Learning: A Multimodal Approach* to look more specifically at multimodal pedagogy and curriculum. In Australia, working from a Hallidayan approach to semiotics, Unsworth brought together children's literature studies with technology in his volumes *Children's Literature and Computer Based Teaching* (Unsworth, 2005), and *E-Literature for Children: Enhancing Digital Literacy Learning* (Unsworth, 2006).

Tensions for Multimodal Literacies

While multimodal approaches to literacy and research have been widely accepted and cited by international scholars, they have not been exempt from criticism, particularly when the concept of multimodality first took hold in the late 1990s (Cameron, 2000; Pennycook, 1996; Prain, 1997; Trimbur, 2001). Multimodal theories have been met with resistance in the English curriculum, in contexts where teachers and pre-service teachers often have a responsibility to uphold a politically charged back-to-basics curriculum with a linguistic emphasis, and where the traditional disciplinary boundaries of English are created and dominated by the state and its agencies (Bernstein, 2000). For instance, Hamston (2006: 39) reported in Australia that '...some student teachers continue to define literacy in terms of foundational skills alone because they have not witnessed the use of multimodal texts for instructional purposes during school practicum placements'.

The difficulty of shifting literacy practices in schools to incorporate digitally mediated textual practices has been covered elsewhere in research (Mills, 2011b), and contributing factors include the failure of government policies, inadequate technology infrastructure in schools, insufficient professional development for teachers, ideologies about the superiority of print, lack of time and funding, short-term quick-fixes, fear of change and pedagogical reproduction (Warschauer & Matuchniak, 2010). Hamston (2006: 39) surmised that resistance from certain teachers to take hold of multimodal design and digitally-mediated reading practices in their literacy pedagogies is often associated with limited personal use of certain text forms, and the persistence of problematic conceptual binaries between conventional and new platforms for reading.

A criticism of multimodal theory arises from the claim that semiotic grammars are dynamic or changing in response to social context. For example, Prain (1997) criticises the New London Group for their claim that static rules do not govern meaning making, yet in practice, the New London Group provides elaborate codes and checklists of multimodal and linguistic elements, that are essentially static categories of meaning. This endeavour, Prain (1997) suggests, contradicts their appeal to the multifarious, hybrid texts that are proliferating and ever changing.

It can be observed that similar criticisms were made of Kress and van Leeuwen's (1997) work in the first edition of their volume, Reading Visual Images. In a critical review of this major contribution to visual grammar, Forceville (1999) observed that there is an underlying problem of categorisation. While acknowledging that categories need to be able to show what is included and excluded in a group, categories of visual grammar are not definitive, and are often better represented as a continuum.

Kress and van Leeuwen explicitly address this tension, arguing that their categorisation of visual meanings should be seen as tools for analysis, rather than as unalterable rules:

Our discussion above has, we hope, made it clear that we see these distinctions as tools with which to describe visual structures rather than that specific, concrete visuals can necessarily always be described exhaustively and uniquely in terms of any one of our categories. (Kress & van Leeuwen, 2006: 86)

However, Forceville sees that this clarification stands in contradiction to the way in which Kress and van Leeuwen present their classifications, which are typically presented as tree diagrams, often with a hierarchical structure, and thus, obscuring the malleability of these grammars. Forceville (1999: 169) suggests that such diagrams imply exhaustiveness and hint at '... stable, authoritative hierarchies'. Using his own approach to visual interpretation, Forceville (1999: 172) elaborates: 'My own work on pictorial metaphor, while fully acknowledging that metaphors have a strong ideological dimension, primarily tries to outline what forms pictorial metaphors can take, and suggests how word and image texts guide, but cannot enforce, interpretations'. He then continues:

In short, Kress and van Leeuwen often too easily assume (a) that their examples are representative and (b) that their personal interpretations have intersubjective validity. One of the tasks of the project of developing a more refined and sophisticated visual grammar is to be more specific about the differences between shared and non-shared interpretations of (elements of) pictures. (Forceville, 1999)

Such criticisms of their 1996 work have not been levelled against the second edition published in 2006. These tensions also need to be contextualised with an understanding of the history of multimodality, which is sometimes explicitly grounded in a Hallidayan social semiotic theory of communication (Halliday, 1978, 1985). For example, Kress and van Leeuwen's (2006) multimodal theory is mapped to Halliday's three meta-functions: the ideational, interpersonal, and the textual. The ideational function involves representing the objective and subjective world, the interpersonal function concerns the enactment of social interactions as social relations, and the textual function presents a coherent world of the text or composition.

From a Hallidayan perspective, all meaning making is social, and therefore, the selection of semiotic resources both shapes and is shaped by social and cultural practice so that there is always some resemiotising of the signifier material for meaning making in use (Iedema, 2001). In the introduction to Kress and van Leeuwen's second edition in 2006, published 10 years after the first, they (2006) devote several pages to the issue of what constitutes a 'grammar'. The maintain that grammars are merely described by linguists, and that others then interpret and apply these normatively in rule-governed social sites, such as schools and workplaces. However, they also envisage that, over time those who are not visually literate may have social disadvantages, while visual literacy is becoming a matter of survival in the workplaces (Kress & van Leeuwen, 2006). The marketisation of educational discourse in recent decades has already seen an emphasis on creating a strong corporate image through visual signs, such as logos, uniforms, websites and advertising materials, and visually pleasing built environments and learning spaces (Mills, 2013b).

A related tension is the pragmatic issue that ensues whenever literacy becomes pluralised – the need for delimiters on the categories of literacies. This is the same criticism that has been levelled against socio-cultural views of literacy practice, such as the scope of literacy having 'fuzzy borders' (see Barton, 2001: 95; Mills, 2010b). For instance, Prain maintains that the reformulation of linguistic grammars by Kress and others in the New London Group to include the five modes of design has opened up an unmanageable number of text types to be addressed in literacy education, requiring semiotic tools of analysis that the New London Group has not provided (Mills, 2009).

Being mindful that over a decade of multimodal research and practice in schools and other social sites has been published since Prain's (1997) early critique, Prain considered that the theoretical and practical boundaries of multimodal design were inadequately developed for formulating curricula, and at that time, were unsuitable for classroom implementation

(Mills, 2009). Prain was not alone in raising these objections, which were reported among pre-service teachers, and among teachers in research projects (Hammond, 2001). Similarly raising this issue of the scope of literacy practices in multimodal approaches, literacy theorist Cameron contends:

> The point is well taken that text often co-exists with talk...and new technology tends to make traditional boundaries between modes or media redundant. Nevertheless, I sometimes find myself wondering where literacies stop? Why not count, say, arable farming as a literacy practice on the grounds that it marks the landscape? (Cameron, 2000: 206)

This *reductio ad absurdum* is a search for the limits of what constitutes meaning making and representation within the framework of literacy curriculum. While semiotic theory can acknowledge that all forms of representation, visual, gestural, spatial and so on, have meaning, there are pragmatic implications when recontextualising multimodal approaches from their location in social semiotic theory, to their application in the school curriculum. There are ideological and value-laden issues of selectivity within the school English curriculum that are different to the concerns of the semiotician debating what constitutes meaning making.

Decisions about what literacy practices to include and exclude inevitably involves political struggle within schooling systems that typically reproduce a national consciousness (Bernstein, 2000), and which increasingly reflect the ideologies of education markets. Within the English curriculum, learning sequences can be designed that simultaneously attend to genres of written text, but which are also supported by visual, spatial, gestural or audio modes. There is no agenda among multimodal approaches to supplant or replace linguistics with grammars of visual or other modes. Opposition to the rise of the visual as a full means of representation is often not in opposition to the visual mode as such, but of the possibility that the dominance of linguistics – of words – might be threatened among elite groups (Kress & van Leeuwen, 2006).

In the second decade of the 21st century, it no longer holds that multimodal grammars are immature in their development for real curriculum use (Prain, 1997). There has been an international effort from social semiotics to develop and systematise comprehensive volumes outlining detailed visual (Kress & van Leeuwen, 2006; Painter et al., 2013; Unsworth, 2001), audio (van Leeuwen, 1999), moving images (Burn & Parker, 2003; Mills, 2011a) and gestural grammars (Kalantzis & Cope, 2012; McNeil, 1992), demonstrating the integration of a range of media in literacy practices in institutional sites. Recent work by Kalantzis and Cope (2012) has given attention to further elaborating tactile, gestural and spatial modes of design in their substantial volume, Literacies, as well as additional previous monographs similarly attending to the pedagogical dimensions of multimodal design (Kalantzis & Cope, 2008; Kalantzis & Cope, 2005).

One good example is a knowledge-sharing website and wiki called New Learning devised by Cope and Kalantzis. The site showcases curriculum units and accounts of teachers who have applied the multiliteracies pedagogy, including multimodal grammars, in educational sites around the world (Cope & Kalantzis, 2014). Teachers and researchers have demonstrated that multimodal and digital design can be productively integrated within the English curriculum, from early childhood to primary and secondary levels of schooling, and to higher education (Mills, 2010c, 2011a, 2011d; Mills & Chandra, 2011a; Mills & Levido, 2011).

Another criticism of multimodal approaches, and one that could be levelled against the social sciences more broadly is that of ocularcentrism – the emphasis on what can be seen with the eyes over what is perceived through other senses. While multimodal approaches emphasise the need to attend to multiple modes of meaning, in practice, there has been much greater emphasis on elaborating the metalanguage of images and words over olfactory, tactile, gestural, kinaesthetic, spatial or audio meanings. Any perceived focus on the visual mode in current theories of multimodality is partly a consequence of the disciplinary lens of communication studies, visual culture and linguistics.

When comparing a multimodal approach to approaches of phenomenological anthropology, a key criticism has been levelled by Pink (2009) against Kress and van Leeuwen's (2001) view that vision gives access to the world differently than touch, smell and taste. Writing from the point of view of distinguishing multimodal approaches to her own sensory ethnography, Pink contrasts the multimodal view to Ingold's (2000: 268) suggestion that eyes and ears are not 'separate keyboards' for the 'registration of sensation', but function within the body as a whole. In other words, Kress and van Leeuwen's work analyses the discernible patterns of visual meanings, thereby creating a distinction between the modes, rather than interpreting them holistically. Pink (2009: 102) sees this as a fundamental distinction between multimodal approaches and those of phenomenological anthropology, seeing this as 'One of the limitations of the multimodality approach'. The distinction is perhaps less sharp when we take into account other clarifying statements by Kress (2000b: 181) such as: '... none of the senses ever operates in isolation from the others'.

An issue here is that while one perceives the world using multiple senses simultaneously, their meanings can be separated for the purpose of analysis.

Further, even though anthropologists, such as Ingold, claim that the eyes and ears should not be understood as separate keyboards for registering sensation, in practice, Ingold attends to theorising the significance of one sense at a time. We see this, for example, in his article, 'Culture on the Ground: The World Perceived through the Feet', where locomotion is salient (2004).

However, another concern is that literacy research is becoming saturated with journal articles that include the search term 'multimodal', while the multiple dimensions of textual practices are equally being transformed by new media. This is not a critique of the original theory of multimodality, but with the way in which literacy theories tend to have a bandwagon effect (Mills, 2005). For example, the aggregate of semiotic choices are always recontextualised and resemioticised (Iedema, 2001) resulting in discernible patterns of text structures that are also able to be modified, called genres (O'Halloran, 2009). Genre is a key element that received attention by Hallidayan systemic functional linguists in Australia, particularly during the 1990s, led by leading theorists Martin and Rothery (1980, 1981, 1986), Kress (1993), Christie and Martin (1997) and Cope and Kalantzis (1993) with *The Powers of Literacy: A Genre approach to Teaching Writing*.

Many genre theorists became the first advocates of multimodality, while attention to the term 'genre' gradually receded in academic titles. Literacy education in Australia, particularly writing, has been greatly strengthened by curriculum policies that followed from genre research, with the explicit teaching of the purposes and discernible features of discourses and genres, such as literary recounts, literary responses, poetry, historical narratives, analytic expositions and so on (Richardson, 1991; Unsworth, 2002). Despite the rigid adherence and codification or static descriptions of genres in text books and resource materials for teachers (Mills, 2005), the discernible patterns of textual features in genres do provide a guide for young learners, who once familiar with the structure and grammatical features, can learn to adapt it creatively and generatively.

In addition to changes in mode, there are new configurations of text structure, syntactic structures, vocabulary usage and hybrid orthography. For example, limits of 140 characters in tweets and text messages require users to search for abbreviations, and these new vocabularies are used with some regularity within the online communities. Changing cultures of participation in online media are less restricted by schedules of face-to-face interaction, affording almost anywhere-anytime textual practices across time zones and geographies, but within the constraints of divergent timezones across hemispheres for synchronous communication (e.g. real time).

Blurred boundaries between private and public have emerged, such the display of personal videos on YouTube, and similarly, between consumers and producers of texts, as text users read and write simultaneously (Leadbeater, 2010). Modified forms of heritage collection, representation and communication have taken centre stage in communities, and new publics are forming around key historical events, interests and affinities (Giaccardi, 2012). There are cultural, social, economic, political and epistemological shifts in textual practices that cannot be explained in relation to a theory of multimodality alone.

Recent Developments in Multimodal Literacies

With such a long and ideological history of non-linguistic forms of meaning making, and a long history of research bringing together technology and literacy, what's so new about multimodality? Scollon and Scollon posit this question in their detailed chapter outlining the history of multimodality and language:

> …What happened to the body of work, which extended across so many disciplines, and in which so many figures who are now considered the founders of several fields participated? Why is multimodality now having to be reinvented? (Scollon & Scollon, 2009: 174)

Scollon and Scollon maintain that the dissipation of the growing interest in the relationship between verbal and nonverbal form of communication was tied to an erosion of the structural-grammatical model of analysis by post-structuralist, generative analysts, and a growing view that other modes of communication did not function like spoken and written language. Scollon and Scollon conclude of the structural-grammatical model:

> In a few words, the project failed because of the fatal assumption that all modes of communication were structurally analogous to language, and would be patterned with analogous grammars. (Scollon & Scollon, 2009: 175)

Yet while structural models of linguistics from the 1950s were met with criticism for applying linguistic structures directly to nonverbal communication and other modes, theorists of multimodality have a distinctively different approach. Theorists such as Kress, van Leeuwen, Jewitt, and others have not simply imported the theories and methodologies of linguistics directly into visual and multimodal analysis. Unlike Pike (1954) and the theorists of the monumental study, *The Natural History of the Interview* (Leeds-Hurwitz, 2005), this third wave of social semiotics does not look for the analogues of sentences, clauses, nouns, verbs and so on in images, music or gesture. This is an important departure from structural and linguistic approaches. As Kress and van Leeuwen (2006) uphold, there is considerable congruence between the language of words and the language of images, since they belong to and are structured by culture, but each form has its own possibilities and limitations for meaning making.

Multimodal approaches demonstrate that there are discernible patterns of coding orientation in visual communication (Kress & van Leeuwen, 2006; Painter et al., 2013; Unsworth, 2006b); music and sound (van Leeuwen, 1999) and many other modes. With the growing number of digital texts that combine words, images, audio and other modes to communicate meaning, we can no longer ignore the non-linguistic elements of textual design in literacy practices, but interpret words in relation to the complex set of modal meanings that function in concert and in hybridised forms across a range of media.

Multimodal approaches comprise an important strand of research within the recent digital turn in literacy studies since the beginning of the 21st century. My research has examined the multimodality of the classroom – itself, a multimodal text. I developed a taxonomy of the social spaces of the classroom — dialogic, bodily, embodied, architectonic and screen spaces. In my observations of children filming clay animation movies in the classroom filming studio, I theorised how students' multimodal learning was tied to important transformations of space (Mills, 2010a). This work is an example of a cluster of studies of multimodality in classrooms in which social action, rather than the classroom texts alone, are analysed multimodally, such as Norris' (2004) study of the multimodality of classroom interactions (e.g. gaze, gesture, posture) and Moss's (2003) research of boys' reading practices, such as the interactions associations with their reading of non-fiction multimodal texts.

There is a large and growing type of research conducted in schools that analyses the multimodal features of different text types, extending the kinds of semiotic interpretations of still images demonstrated by Kress and van Leeuwen (Kress & van Leeuwen, 2006). For example, my research in schools has included multimodal analyses of clay animation movies as kineikonic texts (Mills, 2011d), and of emotion or affect expressed through images in children's video productions (Mills et al., 2014). Unsworth (2001, 2006a, 2006c), and also with Painter et al. (2013) have elaborated a book-length, detailed metalanguage or visual grammar, to extend social semiotics in relation to appraisal – affect, judgement and appreciation – in multimodal texts. Other original studies of multimodal texts include Ormerod and Ivanic's (2000: 199) research of the home and school connections evident in young children's multimodal text samples in the United Kingdom, and the multi-modal meanings in manga comic books (Schwartz & Rubinstein-Ávila, 2006), and within science texts (Wilson, 2008).

In relation to studies of multimodal design with different populations, there are studies of the multimodality of young children's text making at home (Pahl, 2003), and children's drawings (Mavers, 2009). There are studies of multimodal design among adolescents in contexts of poverty (Hull & Nelson, 2005; Mills, 2010c; Vasudevan, 2007; Warner, 2013), of second language learners (McGuinnis, 2007), multilingual learners of Indigenous groups (Menezes de Souza, 2004), pre-service teachers (Hamston, 2006), early childhood education contexts (Flewitt et al., 2009) and in higher education discourses, including the persistence of monomodality to accentuate the dominance and authority of institutions (Mills, 2013b).

The transformative potentials of multimodal communication for pedagogies, learning, curriculum, and assessment in the English or Language Arts curriculum has been another important trajectory of research among educators. As Jewitt (2006) has demonstrated, while pedagogies can remain unchanged in classrooms, such as multimodal texts used with direct instruction, or computer games with 'fill-in-the-blank' exercises, there is great potential to reconfigure the agency and subjectivity of teachers' and students' multimodal learning environments, to which our attention turns now in this chapter.

Intersections between Multimodal and Socio-cultural Approaches

Multimodal literacy is by no means a solidified and consistently unified theory, but rather has many historical influences, trajectories, and junctures with other literacy approaches. Not to be seen as simply a strand of socio-cultural theory, multimodal semiotics contains at least three strands of its own – social semiotic multimodal analysis (e.g. Hodge & Kress, 1988), the systemic functional approach (e.g. Halliday, 1978), including multimodal discourse analysis (e.g. O'Halloran, 2004), and multimodal interactional analysis (see Jewitt, 2011b). Multimodal semiotics has enriched the theoretical tradition of the New Literacy Studies, which from the beginning has emphasised the need to validate the variety of modes and materials of communication, such as music composition, cartography, filming, interpreting timetables, and reading academic articles and books (Barton, 2001).

The aims of the two approaches are contrastive: multimodal theory describes modes and their relationships in texts and textual practices, while socio-cultural theory describes literacy practices as they belong to communities or cultures. It is vital to establish from the outset that socio-cultural theory did not begin with the aims or intention to develop detailed multimodal metalanguages or grammars to describe and analyse the variety of visual literacies and other modes of text forms that circulate in textual environments. For example, Street's fieldwork in Iranian villages in the 1970s primarily demonstrated how literate identities located in Qur'anic or *maktah* literacy practices differed to literacy in school contexts, and the *lingua franca* or vehicular trade language of buying and selling.

Conversely, multimodal semiotics did not begin with the aim to observe and document how literacy practices, including written and spoken language, are situated in specific domains of social practices within different communities, such as in villages, schools, markets and religious centres. For example, Kress and van Leeuwen's (2001: 20) work on multimodality focuses on describing semiotic modes in the design of a semiotic product, including images, writing, gesture, gaze, speech, spatial arrangements and posture. How these features of multimodal design are realised in texts is more central to multimodal analysis than a description of the text-making culture of the community of designers.

At the same time, multimodal and socio-cultural theory both function to honour the diversity of funds of semiotic knowledge available to groups in society for different social purposes. As Street (2012: 27) states, the socio-cultural perspective '...entails a recognition of "multiple literacies"', while Jewitt (2011b: 2) states that multimodality examines a wide range of modes in '...a variety of contexts, including workplaces, the home, the museum exhibition and online environments...'. The theories are united in the view that there is not one monomodal, Standard English literacy, and both theories attempt to account for the variability of forms of meaning making, rather than interpreting literacy as a set of grammatical rules. Both theories are underpinned by an awareness of the social, cultural and historical contexts of communication.

However, the extent to which there is congruence of texts and textual practices across cultures is a point of difference for multimodal and socio-cultural theorists. Many systems of multimodal grammar, such as the visual grammar of Kress and van Leeuwen (2006: 3), were forged as '...a quite general grammar of contemporary visual design in "Western" cultures'. In other words, multimodal theorists have often articulated the structures of grammatical patterns that are found to be somewhat consistent across textual practices. In contrast, theorists at the turn of the century raised the concern that the New Literacy Studies was focused primarily on localist literacy practices, rather than attempting to highlight the similarities of literacy practices across cultures and the globalised communication environments (Collins & Blot, 2002).

Multimodality and socio-cultural theory both take into account times-cales in relation to literacy practices. In multimodal accounts, there is a focus on how images or other modes have changed over time – such as how the configuration of modes in texts become modified by technologies. In volumes such as Kress and van Leeuwen's (2006) *Reading Images: The Grammar of Visual Design*, and *The Routledge Handbook of Multimodal Analysis*, edited by Jewitt (2011), there is from the outset a stated emphasis by these theorists to account for historical changes to textual practices. Specifically in the case of kineikonic (moving image) texts, timescales of the action are central to the analysis of the text (Mills, 2011d).

Socio-cultural theory focuses on literacy events or moments in time, and literacy practices, which are repeatedly observed in communities over time, and then conceptualised (Street *et al.*, 2009). Collectively, original studies within socio-cultural theory have also mapped literacy practices over time, with a significant body of New Literacy Studies conducted around the world mapping literacy practices in changed digital contexts of use (Knobel & Lankshear, 2007; Lankshear *et al.*, 1997; Mills, 2010b).

While both traditions share the understanding that meaning-making resources are shaped by cultural and social context, the two traditions also remain distinctive in their methodological beginnings. Socio-cultural theory began as a tradition that drew on anthropological methods of inquiry, predominantly ethnography, with an emphasis on observation and participant observation of literacy events and literacy practices. Consistent with the use of ethnography is a concern to gain *emic* or insider participant perspectives, to be self-reflexive, and to focus on eliciting theoretical insights about a set of particular circumstances, rather than an emphasis on generalisation from a sample to a larger population (Street, 2012).

The methodologies of multimodal approaches emphasise the collection and analysis of multimodal textual data, such as video observations, billboards, online textual environments, picture books, animations and other material instantiations of meaning. Intersemiotic and intermodal relations between resources are often transcribed multimodally, such as by creating a series of still image frames from a moving image text, matched to the accompanying dialogue and descriptions or visuals of participant action (see for example Flewitt *et al.*, 2011). The focus of multimodal analysis is often on intersemiotic relations – 'the specific work of each mode' and how each mode interacts with other modes (Jewitt, 2011a: 25). Multimodal analysis can involve specialised terms, such as functional load (see Jewitt, 2006), transmediation (see Mills, 2011a), modal density and modal configurations (see Norris, 2011) and parametric systems (see van Leeuwen, 2011).

Socio-cultural theorists share some common ground with multimodal literacy theorists, and often theorists draw on both traditions throughout their research trajectories. For example, Pahl (2014, 2006) has published on New Literacy Studies and at other times attended specifically to modes in children's writing (Pahl, 2003). Hull (2003) has published on New Literacies and digital media in youth culture and digital media, while also analysing the multimodal semiotic features of students' digital stories (Hull & Nelson, 2005). Mills and Exley (2014b) recently drew on New Literacy Studies arguments to introduce new theorisations of time, space and text in original research of digital and multimodal composition classrooms. Jewitt (2011b: 38) supports the notion of bringing multimodal and New Literacy Studies concepts together, in order '. . . to fill out a larger more nuanced picture of social positioning and group practices, texts, contexts, space and time'.

Street *et al.* (2009) have devoted a chapter to the tracing of studies that draw on both traditions, while attempting to bridge New Literacy Studies and multimodality. They believe that bringing together the local nature of socio-cultural literacy studies with the theories of multimodality allows texts to become more salient within their research contexts. Similarly, Rowsell and Chen (2014) have specifically attempted to bring these traditions together as a new approach. Any merging of literacy approaches can be beneficial when overlaying multiple theoretical lenses sharpens rather than blurs the focus on new and relevant themes of literacy inquiry. Multimodality and socio-cultural traditions have had substantial take up by researchers in the 21st century, firmly grounded in the socially-situated nature of meaning-making and accounting for transformed digital and culturally-diverse contexts of literacy.

Implications of Multimodal Literacies for Practice

The implications of multimodal approaches to literacy learning are far reaching, but it is within schools that the weight of a logo-centric culture is felt and experienced by teachers and students most viscerally. This is what Green (1993: 196) referred to as the 'Insistence of the letter', and in many classrooms, this continues to hold true 20 years later:

This is a view of teaching and learning that is organised around particular versions of alphabetic literacy, and already the seeds are sown for the discursive construction of a distinctive school subjectivity. (Green, 1993)

The distinctive school subjectivity entails the learning of letters, words, and the grammatical rules, as well as the regulation of the disciplined body of the learner through routines. There is a persistence of pedagogies and the ideological dominance of written words in literacy curriculum and assessment. I have observed many schools in Australia in which the elementary school day is divided into periods for spelling drills, and direct instruction in copying letters in handwriting books (Mills, 2011b). The literacy curriculum in colonial New England in the United States began with the teaching of the smallest components of written words – letters – and then moved to sentences. There was an emphasis on penmanship, as Monaghan and Saul (1987: 96–99) describe: 'Mastery of the pen was to be achieved by constant repetition – namely, copying'. Often, under such a curriculum, what matters is what can be measured, and technocratic discourses of prescription were governed by assessment of basic writing skills that were seen as aligned with the goals of industrial models of education (Green, 1993).

The point is that writing tasks in schools are important, but need to be expanded further to incorporate a widened range of digital text types with their associated generic structures that play on the boundaries of conventional genres. Genres and features of texts have arisen that are exclusive to the digital landscape, such as blogs and micro-blogs, podcasts, digital stories, memes, tweets, e-books and the related convergence of linguistic and visual codes has prompted textual theorists to examine these shifts in meaning making (Mills, 2010b; Mitchell, 1999a). Conceptions of literacy include the visual arts and representational literacies in digital formats that make possible a fluid relationship between word, sound, image, gestures, movement and other modes. The profusion of networked digital platforms has created opportunities for users to communicate for different social and personal purposes, and generic features of reconfigured, screen-based genres.

With regard to reading, multimodal texts should be incorporated into the literacy program because online environments challenge conventional notions of reading (see Burbules & Callister, 1996; Green & Bigum, 2003; Landow & Delany, 1991; Luke, 2000; McKenna et al., 1999; Snyder, 1998). The physical non-linearity of electronic texts involves increasingly sophisticated navigational skills and search capabilities. Author-controlled textual environments, characterised by the arrangement of words in top-down, left-to-right, beginning-to-end tangibility, have changed. Virtual communication uses flexible, reader-controlled, dialogical environments that are open to manipulation (Leu, 2009).

The reading and comprehension of online texts recruits text mapping skills that differ to those used to read lengthy, linear strings of page-bound print. While the non-linear reading of text appeared long before the internet was accessible, such when readers look at a contents page to skip to a section, the internet makes non-linear intertextual pathways and connections between texts, resources, and terms more explicit and more extensive. Navigating hypertext – electronically networked text – diversifies the direction of significant connections to a potentially indefinite degree, and reading comprehension processes are distinctively different to other forms of reading (Burbules & Callister, 1996; Leu *et al.*, 2007). For example, readers must actively process online texts in a way that tends to involve an open-ended cycle of linkages. One must reluctantly pull away from an internet search, knowing that there is no definitive end point of possible resources, in order to make meaning.

There are reshaped social practices and conceptions of multimodal textuality and communication. For example, electronic environments allow readers and writers who are physically remote to occupy cyberspace in a transformed interactivity (Burbules & Callister, 1996). Two-way communication occurs through electronic networks, with hypertext blurring the distinction between reader and author as both become readers of hypertext pathways (Mills & Chandra, 2011). This occurs, for instance, in Facebook status updates, where multiple participants continue a flow of comments about another's post. Digital texts of all kinds tend not to be static, discrete units, like a printed book, but are often dynamic and malleable, open to re-authoring multiple times (e.g. word processing). At other times, words are published and unchangeable too soon, such as in the case of instant messaging, where once sent, it cannot be retracted from the thread. There is often an abandonment of the single-minded, authorial voice for scholarly texts, which has been augmented by multi-vocal metadiscourse, that is, writing in discussion threads and micro-blogs, which reflects upon itself (Mills & Chandra, 2011). Web 2.0 technologies allow users to comment about what is posted, encouraging increased dialogue between author and reader, with a responsibility to acknowledge and engage with others who hold opposing views (Mills, 2013a).

Educators cannot simply assume that students are competent in productive and mature literacy practices in digital contexts of use because they upload photos and videos to YouTube and Instagram to access from their mobile phones. There is a need for multimodal research in educational settings to investigate the multimodal resources, actions, texts and social practices that are associated with the digital communication environments that are required for meaningful participation in a changing society.

New Directions for Multimodal Literacies

While the schooling of literacy has often been tightly confined to writing and speech, there are many accounts of teachers' multimodal textual practices or use of multimedia learning resources in the English curriculum

(Mills, 2013a; Ranker & Mills, 2014; Unsworth *et al.*, 2005). The hegemonic bounds of print-based or alphabetic only literacy practices in schools are gradually crumbling, to become supported by a much greater multiplicity of hybrid forms of communication, including audio, visual, gestural, spatial and linguistic modes (Mills, 2006b; New London Group, 1996).

The emerging communications technologies generate new forms of text that existing English literacy curriculum and assessment in schools cannot ignore forever. Communication is increasingly multimodal as multimedia technologies, screen-based interfaces and electronic networks proliferate.

Students today will engage in Massive Open Online Courses, external and internal modes of university study, and take up roles in globalised corporate markets. Students are already interacting with peers in online learning environments at times and places that extend beyond physical proximity to a desk and computer, and beyond the constraints of institutional timetables, often via multiple mobile devices. Some of the existing and emerging social practices in which students must engage range from reading a traditional textbook, to reading an e-book, and from interrogating TV advertisements to ignoring consumer links to sponsors that dominate the top internet search engine results. Students use digital machines to scan multimodal documents, record voice, locate businesses online, conduct internet transactions, make video calls, use online maps and plan their public transport journey online from a mobile device. Toddlers who have not yet begun school use touch screen devices, such as tablets and smartphones to play apps, often synchronised to their toys (e.g. Furby Boom). People continue to handwrite very little – memos, phone messages, forms, diaries and greeting cards – but the main modes of communication are multimodal and digitally-mediated (Mills, 2006b).

Multimodal approaches to understanding how we live and communicate in different social, political, and cultural contexts will open the door to more relevant practices of schooled literacies. Challenging monomodal interpretations of literacy practice (Mills, 2013b), multimodal approaches acknowledge that the sites of display are being transformed by the design of new and ubiquitous technologies, learning spaces, and architectural and cultural spaces (Jewitt, 2006). It is now imperative rather than optional for educators and students, from early childhood to adult, to become knowledgeable experts in sophisticated, hybrid, and typically hypertextual (electronically linked) systems of multimodal meaning, and their affordances for teaching and learning (Mills, 2006b; Mills & Levido, 2011). The way we communicate in society combines face-to-face interactions with digital interactions that often coalesce, and at other times, create tensions and struggle between competing societal roles and between offline and online interactions. The changes are not always positive ones, but the realities of change cannot be denied.

Throughout the first two decades of the 21st century, there have been some early forays into the relations between multimodal literacy practices and different cultural groups, reflecting the cultural diversity in schools and society (Menezes de Souza, 2004; Mills, 2008a; Stein & Slonimsky, 2006). There remains much work to be done in understanding how multimodal communication is becoming part of different ethnic, cultural and sub-cultural identities, heritages, epistemologies and community practices. Multimodal literacy practices have been taken up in different forms, dialects, and registers, including subcultural groups with every conceivable interest, style and sense of affiliation (Cope & Kalantzis, 1999).

The clientele of schools globally are often drawn from diverse ethnic, community, and social class cultures, with a wide range of texts, interests, and group identities. Written English is becoming a world language, yet all languages are influenced by the confluence of still and moving images, music, sounds, graphics, spatial, gestural and other modes, supported by multimedia devices that are marketed globally. Yet multimodal literacy practices differ conspicuously in ways that are related to membership in different groups – recreational, interest or friendship driven, cultural, political, religious and professional.

Rarely are lecture theatres, classrooms and webinars comprised mostly of Anglo-Saxon, monolingual users of English who are being prepared for a predominantly monocultural workplace. Participation in community life now requires that we interact effectively using multiple modes and communication patterns using transnational discourses (Lam, 2009). Those who are most successful in life are those who are competent to negotiate real differences, code switching between multiple semiotic systems, and hybrid, cross-cultural discourses for varied communication purposes (Mills, 2006b; New London Group, 2000). Cross-cultural communication and the negotiation of difference is now a basis for worker creativity and teamwork, and multimodal forms of communication are inextricably linked to these processes.

Pathways to success in vocations, higher degrees, and workplaces are also changing, with workers across every sector needing to accumulate academic credentials and technical skills at a much faster rate and over more years to keep pace with technological shifts, or to maintain their institutional roles. The rate of technological change in contemporary society means that multimodal and digital literacy practices are critical in a growing number of skilled and professional workplaces. Online technologies are being extended by means of elaborate communication interfaces, including iconographic, text and screen-based modes of interacting. An important role of schools is to prepare students for multimodal communication in the world of work.

On a cautionary note, the values and practices of the dominant culture are reflected in multimodal literacy practices, while those of minority groups may still become silenced (Mills, 2006a, 2007, 2008a). Since authority is vested in those who are members of the dominant white, elite culture, the privileged versions of multimodal cultures will tend to become dominant. Inexcusably, what is included, excluded, valued and denigrated is seldom an arbitrary, random or natural expression of quality of taste, as critical theorists have long understood (see Bourdieu, 1989; Kincheloe & McLaren, 1994; Luke, 1994), but flows from the power and status of particular groups and their associated multimodal representations of culture. Multimodal approaches to research can be strengthened by critically interrogating the intersection of power, race, whiteness and society that shapes texts and textual practices.

There is scope for research of multimodality and how it intersects with subjectivity, and how a sense of self is formed out of certain social practices, assisted by novel technologies that have become a resource for users' self-production (Green, 1993a; Green & Bigum, 1993; Green et al., 1994). This is even more evident in the Web 2.0 world of user-generated content. For example, I have observed children as young as seven producing Minecraft skins for avatars, and creating and posting YouTube videos to showcase Minecraft gameplay. Online identities are currently projected through gaming avatars, Facebook profiles, accumulated followers or through continually updated displays of tagged, digitally edited images and posts about self. Collectively, these online projections symbolise and fortify membership in groups. Learners need the ability to proficiently negotiate the divergent digital life worlds and identities each of them inhabits.

To summarise, multimodal research of the confluence of visual, audio, spatial, gestural and linguistic grammars applied using varied digital technologies needs continual expansion and refinement, just as the elaboration of semantically based verbal grammars were informed by linguistic investigations of many different registers and genres (Painter et al., 2013).

5 Socio-spatial Literacies

> ... *[S]paces ... are socially constructed ... This recognition alone opens up*
> *new ways of looking at literacy and learning.*
> (Soja, 2004: x)

Socio-spatial literacy research is transforming the way we think about the social and geographical distribution of literacy practices across regions. It has enriched our thinking most fundamentally about how literacy spaces are socially produced, and about how the social spaces of literacy are influenced by power (Mills & Comber, 2013). Literacy research is a field in which we have, for some time, acknowledged the interactions between globalisation and the circulation of literacy practices across transnational borders (New London Group, 1996).

There is a growing recognition that the spatial dimension of literacy, including the flows, networks and connections between literacy practices that circulate in society, are worthy of more serious attention in literacy research, including at the local level. For example, recent literacy studies have examined the connections between literacy practices in, within, and across specific social spaces of school and home (Bulfin & North, 2007; Nespor, 1997, 2008; Pahl, 2001), and within public spaces such as libraries (Nixon, 2003) and the mall (Moja, 2004). Others have examined literacies within institutional sites, such as prisons (Wilson, 2004), and in virtual environments (Valk, 2008). Fenwick and colleagues (2011: 130), who trace the spatial in educational research rather than literacy studies per se quip: 'Space is too important to be left to social geographers'.

These approaches that give priority to spatial themes in social and cultural geography have led to new theorisations of space as it pertains to literacy studies. For example, literacy theorists have borrowed Soja's term Thirdspace to take on a new meaning for literacy studies (Gutierrez, 2008; Lynch, 2008; Moje et al., 2004). New phrases to encapsulate this strand of literacy research include spatial theories (Gulson & Symes, 2007), spatialised literacy (Leander & Sheehy, 2004) and geosemiotic approaches to language and discourse that '...study the social meaning of the material placement of signs...discourses and...actions in the material world' (Scollon & Scollon, 2003: 2). These spatial theories are sometimes coupled with the view that systems of signs are always located in the material or spatial world – as a necessary condition of their existence – and that literacy is more than a mental construct, detached from the space-time dimensions in which it is practiced.

The recognition of space in literacy studies can be called the spatial turn (Mills & Comber, 2013), which has concord with other literacy research paradigms, from a critical turn (e.g. Comber & Simpson, 2001; Luke, 1998), to the social turn (e.g. Gee, 1992; Street, 1995) and within what I have called the broader 'digital turn' (Mills, 2010b: 246). The spatial turn in literacy studies is not unique to our work, but has occurred throughout the past decade, with edited works, such as Leander and Sheehy's (2004) book, *Spatializing Literacy Research*, which brings researchers together to reconceptualise literacy in ways that address spatial aspects of literacy practices. There is also an increasing number of literacy studies that demonstrate the significance of space in literacy practices, whether within single social sites or across social sites, at a micro-level (e.g. classroom interactions) or macro-level (e.g. globalisation) of social analysis (see Mills & Comber, 2013).

This chapter moves beyond general notions of space or à la mode spatial metaphors, to conceptualise a principled theory of spatial literacy. Soja perceives that spatial theory is sometimes at risk of becoming a '...now-fashionable attachment...to geographical facts and spatial metaphors' (Soja, 2004: ix). To avoid the conflation of spatial metaphors with a systematic theory of space and literacy, it is important to begin by articulating the central principles of social-spatial literacy research, which we have outlined elsewhere (Mills & Comber, 2015).

Key Concepts of Socio-spatial Literacies

In socio-spatial literacy studies, there is first the recognition that language practices are distributed socio-geographically in patterned ways, appearing in distinct forms in certain social sites, while having similarities to literacy practices in other social spaces (Mills & Comber, 2015). Spatiality in literacy studies includes the socio-material relations of space-time that are central to literacy practices, conceiving of spaces as more than storehouses of social action. The spatiality of communication includes the temporal dimension of flows and connections between literacy practices across social sites and geographies, and the spatial dimensions of texts themselves and their associated practices. It includes the spatial locations of literacy practices and texts, and spatial networks of textual practices, social actors and materials (Mills & Comber, 2015).

Second, spatial literacy research acknowledges that space and literacy practices, and the organisation and meaning of those literacy spaces, are socially constructed. This is a logical result of combining the principles that space is socially produced (Lefebvre, 1991), and that literacy is a social practice (Street, 1999). This conception of space extends spatial ideas to understanding literacy practices, while remaining consistent with the key assumptions of a number of social theorists, including Soja (1996), Foucault (1986), Lefebvre (1991), Harvey (1996) and Massey (2005). A key example of the social production of space is Lefebvre's (1968) much-cited work on urbanism and the contestation of entitlement to the city, in which cities are conceived as '...the pre-eminent site of social interaction and exchange...social centrality' (Shields, 2011: 280). Social spaces incorporate individual and collective social action, which occurs at definitive times and places (Lefebvre, 1991). The implication for socio-spatial research is that the multiple literacy spaces that we inhabit, both in private and public life, offline or online, are seen as fundamentally socially constructed. They are spatial geographies that shape our literate lives in multifarious ways.

Third, spatial literacy research acknowledges that the working of power influences all literacy spaces. Literacy scholars have demonstrated convincingly that literacy practices are ideological, and must be interpreted in relation to larger social contexts and power relations (Luke & Freebody, 1997; Street, 1999). For example, critical theorists of literacy have drawn attention to the 'exclusionary forces of the dominant discourse', while providing the marginalised with access to dominant literacies in ways that consciously reinstate the diversity of literacy practices, and the potential power of human agency to transform the stratification of literacy practices (Janks, 2010a: 26). Questions are asked such as: Who gets access to literacies and who is excluded? And more importantly: How can we challenge these inequities? Socio-spatial theory builds on these understandings of critical sociology to examine how power and space interact with literacy practices.

Educational researchers have examined the spatial dimension of literacy practices and its relation to power (Gulson & Symes, 2007). Acknowledging the working of power in the research of literacy practices both within and across social geographies has provided evidence that patterns of marginalisation are undeniably socially and geographically constituted (Soja, 1996). Spatial approaches to literacy have mapped the social and geographic stratification of literacy practices and power in order to understand the topographies of literacy disadvantage. As Dixon (2011: 7) writing from South Africa argued, the particular geographical locations of schools is not neutral. Rather, '...these locations are shaped and coloured by histories of class, race and culture'.

There is now a growing body of research that demonstrates the socio-spatiality of marginalisation in studies of classroom practices (Hawkins, 2004; Janks, 2000; Mills, 2011d; Stein, 2007). Such approaches have addressed equity issues, such as the uneven distribution of literacy practices, and spatial patterns of marginalisation and domination in relation to literacy practices and societal structures. For example, recent transnational theorisations of rurality and literacy demonstrate how literacy practices are connected to place in ways that are different to those of the metropolis, but which are equally valid (Green & Letts, 2007). Lipman (2007) has examined the spatial dimensions of urban inequality, while others have traced the patterns of power in institutions, such as schools, which provide homogenising contexts for certain literacy practices, permitting some practices and excluding others (e.g. Gutierrez & Larson, 2007). As Foucault (1980: 39) contends, power constitutes a 'capillary form of existence' that extends into the 'very grain of individuals'. We must acknowledge that power is inscribed in our very bodies, actions, attitudes and thought processes, and indeed, in the spatial configurations of human actors and their time-space pathways.

Origins of Socio-spatial Literacies

Social theorists have contributed significantly to understanding social space and power in the past century, which have been usefully extended to educational research and literacy studies. Here, I present three historically significant spatial shifts arising from social geography that have important implications for literacy research and practice in the early 21st century: new mobilities, deterritorialisation and social mediafication.

New mobilities

The spatial concept of new mobilities is about contemporary society, a 'society on the move' (Lash & Urry, 1994: 252). Movements of both people and things create orbits that comprise complex 'material transformations' that are 'remaking the social' (Urry, 2000: 2). The currents of this theory have implications for understanding changes to literacy practices in recent decades that arise in particular from the increased mobility of technologies for communication (e.g. smartphones, iPads, tablets), the more rapid circulation of information, education, texts and images across national borders, and also as a by-product of the movement of people through work and leisure-related mobility as travel.

The New London Group's (2000) theory of multiliteracies could be seen as a partial extension of Urry's new mobilities paradigm applied to literacy practices, without explicitly drawing attention to mobilities and spatial theory. Tied to a new mobilities paradigm is the politics of mobilities, such as economic and social barriers to accessing the benefits of the new mobility, including the production and consumption of international mobilities of literacy practices, technologies, texts, information, images and social interactions (Adey, 2011).

New mobilities of literacy practices are also important in the sense that mobile technologies have continued to play a more central role in literacy practices, with the multi-functionality of mobile devices becoming accessible in an increasing number of countries, including many developing nations. However, the technologies to access ubiquitous media, games, and literacy practice anywhere, and at any time, are only one dimension of the new spatiality of literacy practices. The increased accessibility of wireless communication is for some a means to overcome the constraints of a less mobile body, such as when care giving, recovering from illness, or when encumbered by transport delays or costs of travel (Bissell, 2009). As the frequency of travel to other spatial locations for work, study and personal communication is reduced by digital communication services in some sectors, there is a resultant sense of time-space compression (Fenwick *et al.*, 2011). This arises in part because most dominant functions in our societies, such as financial markers, transactional production networks and media systems, are organised around the space of flows – flows which are quickened by the speed and ease of digital technologies (Castells, 2000a). The idea of the new mobility is essentially tied to the economic processes and political relations of production (Adey, 2011), giving rise to new expectations for the faster effusions of money, news media, books, knowledge, products and personal communication. Literacy practices cannot remain unchanged in these changing spatial processes of the new mobility.

Deterritorialisation

A change related to new mobilities is the complex process of deterritorialisation – the seeming blurring of boundaries and geographical and political territories, such as the nation-state. The complex spatial changes of globalisation have weakened the borders and frontiers of literacy as skills that are required of citizens of the state. While literacy policies continue to determine the literacy practices that are taught and assessed in schools, there is an unavoidable sense that the literacy practices of children and youth are becoming realigned to forms of communication and media production that have global currency. These cosmopolitan shifts have been enabled by the growth of digital technological advances, and the accessibility of the internet; in particular, Web 2.0 technologies of production rather than mere consumption (Mills & Chandra, 2011). This does not mean that the literacies of the digital turn are not still materially, socially and politically constrained in definite ways (e.g. technological infrastructure, English core standards, copyright laws), but that literacy and literacy policies are part of the ongoing flux that involves 'tensions, struggle and conflict' (Urry, 2007: 25). Youth are increasingly connected electronically for periods that extend well beyond their hours of geographical proximity to educational institutions, involving different kinds of networked literacy practices that constantly traverse state, national and other geographical and political borders.

Deterritorialisation occurs when lines of flight of the rhizomes interact with the structuring of institutions, including disciplines of knowledge (Deleuze & Guattari, 1987). The concept of deterritorialisation is a useful heuristic to explain the gradual blurring of boundaries around what counts as literacy practices in the digital age within the discipline of education, to embrace more than linguistic forms of representation in page-bound contexts of use (Mills & Comber, 2015). As Morley and Robins maintain:

> New technologies are implicated in a complex interplay of deterritorialisation and reterritorialisation... Things are no longer defined and distinguished in the ways that they once were, by their boundaries, borders and frontiers... We can say that the very idea of boundary... has been rendered problematical. (Morley & Robins, 1995: 75)

While it would be a mistake to ignore the existing limits of technology, the fragility of material digital devices and infrastructure, and regulations that govern documents in cyberspace, the rhizomatic structure of communication networks nevertheless facilitate new flows of financial transactions, leisure, images, information, interactions and commodities across national boundaries. Similarly, reterritorialisation usefully describes the reclaiming of decentred literacy practices of marginalised cultures, or youth subcultures, as no less purposeful and valid than the literacy practices of the dominant white, middle class that have been most closely aligned to the discourses of Western schooling (Mills, 2011c; Mills & Comber, 2015). These processes are part and parcel of globalisation, which implicates time-space compression and an increased sense of connectedness across expansive geographical regions (Fenwick et al., 2011).

Processes of deterritorialisation have reshaped both the distribution of technologies and the distribution of ideas (Waters, 1995). Most relevant to literacy researchers is what I call 'literacyscapes', or the realignment of literacy practices to shifting spatial realities in the context of globalisation. These global processes have transformed the conventional ambit of literacy practice and research, and this integration does not supplant diversity, but reorders it (Fenwick *et al.*, 2011). Aspatial accounts of literacy research can often be substantially disrupted by bringing the spatial into focus with the temporal, such as by acknowledging how social practices, including literacies observed in places, are '... constructed out of a constellation of social relations, meeting and weaving together at a particular locus' (Massey, 1991: 28).

Social mediafication

Socio-spatial literacy research builds on the knowledge that literacy practices are increasingly hybridised and affiliated with digital technologies and social media platforms. I call this the 'social mediafication' of personal relationships and their associated literacy practices. This is not to be confused with a deterministic account of technologies, since autonomous human beings, who decide either to take up or ignore social media, drive this shift. Social mediafication has arisen with the rise of the Web 2.0 or social web, which is characterised by its facilitation of user generated content, deemed potentially more democratic, inclusive and participatory than the pre-Web 2.0 internet (Mills & Chandra, 2011). Jenkins described participatory culture as a media culture in which not everyone will contribute, but permits users to feel free to contribute, with the hope that others will value what they give (Jenkins *et al.*, 2006).

Despite the reality that much of what is posted on the web is regarded as 'noise', the now all-familiar platforms, such as Facebook, Twitter, Pinterest and Instagram, are used by millions of young people and adults for the individual sharing of profiles, status updates, hash tags, images, blogs, podcasts and bookmarks. Twitter membership of 145 million users in 2011 together produced, on average, 90 million tweets per day (Kietzmann *et al.*, 2011). Game-based fan sites (e.g. Minecraft wiki), question-answer websites (Quora) and web sharing of digital videos, music and photos (e.g. YouTube, SoundCloud and Flickr), have given rise to a heightened level of interactivity within the literacy practices of online communities. These participatory cultures include crowd sourcing (e.g. MTurk), professional networks (e.g. LinkedIn) and wikis for the collaborative and public disclosure of corruption (e.g. WikiLeaks) (Giaccardi, 2012).

Social mediafication of social relationships intensifies as users employ digital platforms to augment and map their offline connections in their education, work, business or recreational life. One of the spatial realisations of current times is that such online systems afford users an ever-present sense of connectedness to the world, uniting people from around the globe with shared interests, irrespective of spatial distance. Urban residents can co-ordinate their face-to-face interactions with residents next door using social media, rather than knock on the front door and catch an unannounced glimpse of the realities of private life. Globalisation of social media has not made localisation obsolete (Fenwick *et al.*, 2011). Rather, local connectedness continues alongside heightened opportunities for global networking, with social media sometimes enhancing or alternatively detracting from face-to-face interactions with co-present strangers. For example, travellers can use digital devices on the subway to maintain social distance from other passengers. Social mediafication of literacy practices has made important contributions to the spatial order of communication, enacted every day to constantly reconfigure the spatial networks of people, ideas, texts and images across geographies. This social phenomenon has modified the spatially confined relationships and flows of interactions that were formerly unassisted by networked hypermedia. As Castells (2000a: 14) maintains: 'The space of flows refers to the technological and organisational possibility of the...simultaneity of social practices without geographical contiguity'. Social media influences the clustering of literacy activities based on the shared interests of users, rather than literacy practices only influenced by actors within geographical proximity.

The implications of these global social and media shifts have presented new directions of inquiry for socio-spatial literacy research to understand precisely how literacy practices that we observe are simultaneously influenced by both global and local ecologies, and the flows and connections between them and across geographies. The social mediafication of literacy practices is reshaping the territorial parameters of social networks of the pre-Web 2.0 era, as youth and adults become entangled in a network of social relations containing multiple points of connection to the texts that circulate. The social and spatial dimensions of life need to be conceptualised together. This is more than the perfunctory superimposing of space as a motivating or explanatory factor: 'It is not spatial form in itself (nor distance, nor movement) that has effects, but the spatial form of particular and specified social processes and social relationships' (Massey & Allen, 1984: 5). Literacy practices, whether online or offline, are caught up in the entanglement of space, heterogeneously composed with expanded and open-ended networks of textual linkages, and having multiple pathways (Callard, 2011). Social mediafication of relationships and literacy has given rise to a range of social practices with augmented and transformed spatial dimensions. For example, children play face-to-face with friends at school, and then continue these relationships after school from their respective suburbs by logging on to multiplayer online game servers such as Club Penguin or Minecraft.

There are many positive accounts of the use of social media, such as the use of social media by communities, groups or clubs to facilitate a collective or heritage process of 'remembering together' through social media (Simon, 2012: 89). There is an important epistemic shift from the one-way directionality of 'information delivery' to networked 'sociability' (Wakkary et al., 2012: 217). Yet there are similarly cautionary examples of the use of social media, include the archiving of potentially risky digital images (Coyne, 2012), and the collection of millions of digital images that once uploaded to web can become commodities for mass consumption.

In sum, I have identified three key socio-spatial developments – new mobilities, deterritorialisation and social mediafication – that are a significant part of the human revolutionising of the spatiality of literacy practice in recent times. These changes to the socio-spatiality of literacy practices are tied to juxtapositions and transformations of 'aggregate' meanings of literate practices (Scollon & Scollon, 2003: 23). Literacy practices are progressively less dependent upon communities in geographical closeness. Socio-spatial research is a call to recognise the reterritorialised 'spatial grids' of social relations (Leander & Sheehy, 2004: 364). These extend beyond the observable routine movements of people from one physical space to another, and which come together to define 'articulated moments' that become placed literacy practices (Massey, 1994: 154).

Tensions for Socio-spatial Literacies

Socio-spatial literacy studies have not been directly resisted in the literature, perhaps owing to its recent incipience. However, a key challenge for socio-spatial literacy research will be to consistently demonstrate its robustness as a theory of literacy that can lead, not only to new spatial ways of analysing literacy, but to provide new solutions for literacy learning in the socio-spatial order. For example, in Australia, it is recognised that literacy practices are distributed unevenly throughout society, with a concentration of literacy practices that 'count', located in the urban sites of the middle class. This stands over against the marginalised and diverse forms of literacy practices in rural and remote sites, that are currently less recognised as official literacy skills (see for example Green & Corbett, 2013; Pegg & Panizzon,

2007). The distribution of literacies is inherently entangled with power relations, and the distance between social actors and groups in cities and beyond is similarly caught up in these relations. Bourdieu (1989) theorised that social spaces are constructed so that the closer the agents or groups are situated within a space, the more common properties they have, and the more distant the agents, the fewer.

This recognition alone is part of the solution, because there is still a contingent of educators, media commentators and the public who attribute literacy achievement solely to individual, psychological abilities and who fail to see literacy practices as a form of regionalised socialisation. Yet such awareness of the spatial injustice in the distribution of access to literacy achievement is important, but not enough. Rather, new geographical solutions are needed to provide more accessible networks of literacy resources to parents and communities beyond the metropolis, particularly in countries that have geographically dispersed populations.

A classic example of a study that uses socio-spatial principles to uncover literacy solutions is a published 4-year study by Nichols *et al.* (2012). This unique study of early literacy socialisation weaves '. . . places, texts, artifacts and narratives. . .' to locate the 'discursive' topography of literacy practices in the formative years (Nichols *et al.*, 2012: 159). The research examined networks and geographical connections between early literacy practices of participants observed in three local regions across two nations. An interesting feature of this work is that the reporting of literacy practices of young children and their caregivers is organised geospatially through a number of key early learning agencies. Social sites, such as homes, malls, clinics, churches and libraries emerged as significant in the lives of the participants. Applying socio-material and actor-network theories, the authors map in both discursive and geospatial ways the pathways of parents as they search for resources. The participant pathways were sometimes assisted by virtual networks, or through the everyday time-space movement of the participants (Mills & Comber, 2015).

The study demonstrates how these everyday institutions exert social power over children and their caregivers, and how participants respond to the texts produced by these agencies that operate in everyday life. The socio-spatial organisation of literate pathways is a distinctive feature of this early childhood research. Such findings would not have been possible if relevant practices were only observed in independent sites, and if the familial cartographies of accessing literacy resources were neither acknowledged nor mapped. This is a relevant example of how socio-spatial literacy research can provide solutions to socio-spatial literacy problems, identifying the literacies that are accessible to young children and their families in different regions, at a time when early socialisation is increasingly critical for schooling success.

Recent Developments in Socio-spatial Literacies

In this section, I discuss selected literacy studies that serve as counter-points to demonstrate and elaborate the new mobilities, deterritorialisation and social mediafication of relationships and literacy. I draw on illustrative examples of original spatialised literacy research to demonstrate the productive directions afforded by developing a unique spatial lens that also acknowledges a critical awareness of the politics and commodification of literacy practices and literate identities.

New mobilities of literacy practices

Literacy practices are clearly caught up in the recent changes to virtual geographies of children and youth that permit them to create trajectories of knowledge and relationships within vast online networks, with different starting and end points within these interactions. Children, young people and adults have always been a part of social networks of relations, but the new mobilities of technologies and communication in particular have intensified, accentuated, and enlarged the convolution of media networks, and the possibilities for increased speed, duration, ubiquity and quality of interactivity between textual users who are geographically disparate (see Leander *et al.*, 2010). Furthermore, the age groups of daily digital users are broadening, to include very young children, whose caregivers benefit from anywhere-any-time access to wireless mobile devices, such as tablets and smartphones laden with educational and recreational apps for children. This has raised new questions about the complex nexus of children, youth and the circuitry of literacies of the new mobilities that have emerged as a '...dominant form of social organisation' in Western societies (Wellman & Gulia, 1999: 228).

I define mobile literacies as literacies that are supported by portable digital devices with access to wireless platforms. Extending Bigum and Green's (1993) three-dimensional model of literacy to mobile literacies, researchers and educators need to consider the changed operational, cultural and critical dimensions of literacy practices. Mobile literacies are no longer centrally concerned with how online technologies transform literacy, but how mobile literacies have become an inseparable part of daily social life for children, youth and adults today. Mobile literacies travel with us so that we are constantly connected – at home, after school or work, on holidays, on public transport, in the mall, with friends continuously.

Mobile literacies require constantly upgraded operational knowledge to use multiple, synchronised platforms for hybrid communication and recreational purposes, whether to talk, read, view podcasts, plan a schedule, take photographs, email, text message, find directions, conduct financial transaction, use social media, listen to music or play games. There are changed cultural dimensions as users manage mobile literacy etiquette, as interactions with seemingly 'invisible' others online are carried out simultaneously with those in face-to-face encounters. Mobile literacies also require more sophisticated critical literacy skills, as online content becomes ubiquitously accessible and materially less bounded for children of increasingly younger ages.

The prevalence of mobile literacies has seen a surge of research interest and literacy activities to assist teachers to use mobile phones and tablets to achieve curriculum objectives. Teachers need new schematic frameworks for integrating technological knowledge with pedagogical and content knowledge (Mishra & Koehler, 2006). One such model is iPed for teaching digital media production, which I have outlined in detail elsewhere (see Mills & Levido, 2011). Teachers need to ensure that mobile literacies in the classroom are not limited by culturally reproductive models of education that reduce English pedagogy to basic skills repetition and fill-in-the-blank grammar and spelling exercises – whether in digital apps or print-based workbooks. In a media-saturated environment, children and youth are both cognitively and affectively connected with online and offline spaces, and narrow literacy research agendas are now a thing of the past (Nixon, 2003). New mobile literacies call for more than new digital devices couched in old pedagogies. New models of pedagogy, such as iPed, can make important contributions to transforming the print-based practices that have dominated Western schooling into digital practices that more closely reflect the authentic uses of mobile literacies beyond the classroom.

Deterritorialising literacy research: Social class, urban space and race

Here, I demonstrate how the concepts of deterritorialisation and reterritorialisation can be used in literacy research to describe the reclaiming of decentred literacy practices of marginalised communities as no less purposeful and valid than the literacy practices of the dominant white, middle class. Viewed in this way, patterns of literacy achievement that are taught and measured by the dominant culture, and which reproduce racial and social privilege, must be diversified to account for the broader repertoire of literacy practices that are found across different racial, economic and social groups.

The deterittorialisation of literacy practices is an implicit thread in sociospatial literacy research, perhaps owing in part to the influences of the ideological model of socio-cultural literacy studies that seeks to counter the autonomous versions of 'Standard English', with its recognition of the diverse language practices of local communities. For example, in Adelaide, Australia, Comber and colleagues conducted spatialised research of economically disadvantaged students in a school-based urban renewal project that involved children in a broad range of literacies as they redesigned features of the school with authentic interactions with the council, building developers and architects (Comber *et al.*, 2006). Such a spatial project involved more than mere critique of the literacies of schooling, but applied a radical re-envisioning of the material world through children's active and critical consciousness and citizenship. The primary school students were engaged in a process of transformative action in the local community and essentially gained a '... deepening awareness of the ... realities that shape their lives, and of their capacity to transform' the world (Freire, 1970b). In this way, the narrow band of literacy skills typically taught to working class children in school was deterritorialised to include powerful literacy practices that are necessary for social change and occupational success.

To illustrate the deterritorialising of urban spaces and literacy practices, I turn to a recent study of urban graffiti or street art. Graffiti can be interpreted as lived and material spaces of representation – where words, images and spatial meanings inscribed on walls, buildings and other architectonic features of the environment become stories of resistance within the cityscape. In Canada, in the Queen Street West district of Toronto, and Lilac Alley in the Mission district of San Francisco, Bowen (2013) researched graffiti as a countercultural, spatialised form of representation, typically taking place in urban sites, that is a literacy practice on the margins of society. Bowen borrows Soja's (1996: 11) principle of Third Space to denote the collision of social institutions and their attendant values, with the modes of lived experience. Graffiti, in this case, in socially sanctioned spaces for street art, involved the artists in a reimagining of urban spaces that sometimes involved for viewers and residents a 'radical restructuring' of how diverse artists inhabit the city and represent their experiences of such habitation (Soja, 1996: 2–3). Graffiti can be interpreted as a means to reconstruct the relations of power that are embedded in socio-spatial life in ways that produce transformed personal and political agency – deterritorialising the metropolis. This is just one example of how socio-spatial literacy research is suited to interpreting the material role of literacy practices in urban social spaces.

Spatial forms of analysis have been applied to the racial deterritorialisation of the classroom. For example, Leander (2002) demonstrated how Latanya, an economically marginalised African American student, successfully resisted the stigmatised black identity of 'ghetto' that other students used to label her, in the context of a Derogatory Terms Activity at school. In a destabilising and difficult conversation based on hegemonic and deprecating words emblazoned on a graffiti banner by the high school students, two teachers helped the students to deconstruct and challenge the racist undercurrents that existed like an unhealthy underlife among the class (Leander, 2002). These studies demonstrate how socio-spatial forms of analysis can be used to critically render visible, marginalising patterns of literacy practice, and more importantly, actively recognise or reconstruct liberating and deterritorialising forms of literacy and identity.

A lucid example of the territorialisation of racialised consumer spaces for enabling and constraining different literacy practices is illustrated by Moje (2011). As a participant observer, Moje would regularly spend quality time in public spaces with four Latino Youth. Moje describes how the social spaces of the mall provoked dominant racial enactments of identity, such as through the selection of consumer goods and restaurants. Conversely, when they walked through familiar Virnot street, the local Latino space '… shaped the texts that they consumed and produced' (Kop, 2011: 29). This was evident through the accessibility of Latino identity texts for purchase, such as t-shirts with Mexican slogans and Latino music DVDs, that became an economy of racial meanings of the city. The colour capital of Latino/Mexican identity was evident in the Spanish that was spoken in the street, converging with the ways the Latino youth chose to be recognised. While the sharp territorialisation of literacy practices was clearly demarcated – city as Mexican/Latino versus mall as mainstream popular culture – there was evidence of deterritorialisation as the group frequented the mall, and began to break down racial stigmas through their responsible interactions with shopkeepers (Mills & Comber, 2013). Over time, the mall became a more inclusive space to situate hybrid versions of Latina youth identity, and an '…economy of racial meanings…' was fluid and shifting in the lived moments of their performances (Hughey, 2012: 165).

These examples demonstrate how the organisation of spaces and literacy practices are clearly connected in material ways to class, geographical location and race. Socio-spatial research can be used to uncover the spatial ways in which social markers are reproduced in the interests of established racial and economic hierarchies. More importantly, these relations can be deconstructed and challenged; in Deleuze and Guattari's (1987: 423) terms, deterritorialised, just as the '…earth itself asserts its own powers of deterritorialisation, its lines of flight, its smooth places that live and blaze their way for a new earth'.

Spaces are not stable, homogenous entities, but are clearly implicated by complex relations of race, class, gender and other social dimensions. The socio-spatial dimensions of literacy practice are in the midst of reawakening to accommodate the transnational, globalised and technology-mediated networks, circulations and rhizomatic flights of new social media practices. Space-time compression, which concerns the lessening of social constraints due to receding geographical and cultural distances, is increasingly apparent in people's experiences of travel, synchronous online communication and so on. It has implications for thinking about the world, and about the way literacy is distributed and practiced globally and locally (Cope & Kalantzis, 2000b; Fenwick *et al.*, 2011). The implications of these global shifts have presented new directions of inquiry for socio-spatial literacy research to understand precisely how literacy practices that we observe are simultaneously influenced by both global and local places, and the flows and connections between them (Mills & Comber, 2015).

Social mediafication of relationships and rhizomes

An apparent spatial counterpoint to social mediafication of relationships, and its associated Web 2.0 literacies, such as tweets by tweeps (Twitter followers), pokes, widgets, tags, memes and selfies, is the spatial concept of the rhizome by philosophers Deleuze and Guattari:

A rhizome has no beginning or end; it is always in the middle, between things, interbeing, intermezzo...It is where things pick up speed...a transversal movement that sweeps one and the other away, a stream without beginning or end that undermines its banks and picks up speed in the middle. (Deleuze & Guattari, 1987: 25)

Rhizomes can be used to elaborate the features of networked sociality of literacy practices and the connections and unpredictable ruptures of practices. An example is Gibbs and Krause's (2006) application of rhizomes to hypertextual reading practices in the Web 2.0 world. Rhizomes can be used to explain multiplicities that extend in diverse trajectories of nodes or meeting points that can form vast networks, such as navigational pathways of internet users or in neural pathways. Rhizomes are not confined to predictable and static configurations, as are neither a tree's root system nor disciplinary knowledge, but rather can rupture at any point, extending across diverse lines of spontaneous flight.

Gibbs and Krause suggest that in social media-based practices, there is a renewed dominance of the spatial and visual, which is backgrounded by temporal and verbal dimensions in our listening, reading and viewing on the web. Social media users follow diverse hypertextual rhizomes or connected trajectories, entering in the middle rather than a beginning or end, and often generate unpredictable trajectories of flight in their interactions. Within these social grids, there are important 'nodes or points of structuration', such as when one tags an image, 'likes' another's profile, or retweets a post (Gibbs & Krause, 2006: 154). Rhizomes of practice can be traced using the digital data that map the sequences of sites traversed on the social web (see also Mills & Comber, 2015).

There are some early and new forays into rhizoanalytic literacy studies (Alvermann, 2000; Hagood, 2004; Kamberelis, 2004; Knight, 2009; Warner, 2013), each of which are elaborated here. They demonstrate methodological applications of rhizome analysis to literacy research with a social and spatial dimension. Together, these studies demonstrate the need to research literacy practices, not as confined to bounded spaces, such as homes or schools, but as fluid trajectories of connected meanings and social practices that are continually moving, changing and unfolding in spaces. They move as 'rhizomes...and multiplicities...defined by the outside: by the abstract line, the line of flight or deterritorialisation, according to which they change in nature and connect with other multiplicities' (Deleuze & Guattari, 1987: 9). As Leander interprets, rhizoanalytic approaches regard the production of social space and literacy practices as a set of assemblages that are part of an unfinished project. The general nature of the embryonic assemblage is 'critically significant for multiple readings' and 'emergent possibilities' (Leander et al., 2010: 13).

To ground rhizomes in original literacy research, consider an early example of rhizomatous map-making to analyse data about literacy practices. Alvermann (2000) applied rhizomatous map-making to re-analyse teen discussion transcripts, field notes and interviews with parents from a Read and Talk Club study. Alvermann's aim was to bring together diverse data 'fragments' to produce new linkages and 'reveal discontinuities' that had gone unnoticed in the original analysis (Alvermann, 2000: 118). She made connections between the data and at least five disparate published texts, including academic and popular texts, in order to map the 'proliferating shoots that have no central axis, no point of origin, and no endpoint...' in order to 'think differently' about adolescents' networks of literacy practices (Alvermann, 2000: 120). Accordingly, Alvermann avoids attempting to draw resolution to the seemingly limitless questions raised in this rhizomatic process; instead, identifying a number of connections, discontinuities and silences throughout the adolescents' readings, parental views, existing texts and her own sense-making. While one of the earliest examples of rhizome analysis in literacy studies, it illustrates how literacy practices and concepts are multifarious, connected and non-hierarchical, and can be studied in ways that push against reified descriptions of linear literacy practices with definite entry and exit points.

Observing that rhizomes have both affordances and limitations for capturing the complexity of literacy data, Warner (2013) recently applied rhizome analysis to juxtapose and make connections between the textual artefacts, access to technologies, and semiotic resources employed by five teens in poverty. For example, the teens in her study regularly self-initiated social media-composing practices, employing Tumblr, Instagram and Twitter. They recognised the benefits of interactivity between writers and readers in these platforms, and the ability to communicate with real audiences about their lives, as Aaliyah recounted, 'When I'm reading, I'm imagining it, but on Twitter, I'm in it' (Warner, 2013: 7). A striking difference was observed between the solitary nature of writing tasks in the English classroom and the dialogic nature of the teens' social media practices outside of school, such as 'retweeting' others' posts as endorsement. The use of rhizome analysis afforded Warner with a means to map some of the convergences and discontinuities among the teens' literacy activities, social purposes and use of digital tools by the youth across the varied social spaces of their daily lives.

Rhizomes are maps with multiple entry points, are heterogeneous rather than dichotomous, and are composed of a multiplicity of lines that extend in all directions while connecting to something else, yet have only surface features, rather than a deep structure (Deleuze & Guattari, 1987). While Deleuze and Guattari imply that deep structures are akin to received disciplinary knowledge and traditions (see Kamberelis, 2004), rhizomatic cartography can be used in complementary ways with traditional forms of analysis to map pathways and connections between texts, artefacts, people and places relevant to the study focus. For example, Hagood (2004) produced a basic rhizomatic cartography of two adolescents' constructions of their identities through interactions with popular texts, youth group events, school, peers, religious artefacts and beliefs.

Another more recent example is Knights' (2009) rhizomatic analysis that positioned young children as desiring machines. Early childhood drawing is entangled with desire and communication, and affective literacies. Knight expresses the need to subvert dominant early childhood education discourses that reduce curriculum to measurable outcomes, and that relegate drawing to the margins. Such discourses limit space for unexpected lines of flight in children's representational pathways to make connections and lines of reference to the world.

Related to these spatial metaphors are Deleuze and Guatarri's (1987) concepts of smooth and striated spaces, which could be productively applied to social-spatial literacy studies. These philosophers describe the sea as a smooth space, given its boundless continuity and its ability to be traversed.

Contrastingly, cities are essentially striated spaces, defined by economic structures, rules and architecture that are largely regulated by state apparatus. Yet as Deleuze and Guattari (1987: 474) acknowledge, 'the two spaces in fact only exist in mixture: smooth space is constantly being translated, traversed into a striated place; striated space is constantly being reversed, returned to a smooth space'. The notion of smooth and striated spaces has been taken up by Gibbs and Krause (2006) to interpret web spaces. They contend that the internet can be navigated and read in ways that give less attention to rule-governed or striated forms of literacy practice than other print-based forms, enabling greater democratic participation of users and freedom of public opinion in open forums. Yet they similarly observe that hypertextual documents are composed according to explicit and implicit rules, including linguistic, digital, spatial, visual or audio conventions.

All literacy practices, online or offline, are also somewhat striated, bounded by our prior knowledge, identities, histories, beliefs and social constraints (Mills & Comber, 2013). What rhizomatic analysis adds is a focus on the root-like networks and connections between literacy practices, mapping the extensions between them, rather than the linearity of texts or textual practices that are extracted from their wider social networks.

Deleuze and Guattari's (1987: 106) concepts of rhizomes and pack multiplicities has been taken up by Kamberelis (2004) in relation to the practices that play a central role in mobilising lines of flight or changes to legislation and other forms of political deterritorialising. 'Pack-multiplicities' refers to the powerful deterritorialising machines of collective action, such as political or social movements, which rise up to subvert mass multiplicities – the hierarchical assemblages of state apparatus, such as schools, labour unions, professional organisations and government agencies. Mass multiplicities exist to territorialise spaces through official forms of legislative power and stability. In contrast, pack multiplicities deterritorialise and reterritorialise arborescent structures, leading to social and political change, such as the antecedents of the civil rights movement or feminism (Kamberelis, 2004).

There are generative potentials for researching literacy as rhizomatic, socio-spatial practices that form, flow, connect and are mobilised efficiently in association with pack multiplicities. Many online literacy practices and texts circulating on the social web rise and rapidly proliferate, and may either diminish or continue, like a groundswell of pack multiplicities. Such informal socio-spatial practices have both convergences and discontinuities with the literacy practices of mass multiplicities that are taught and tested in schools as a function of the nation-state. A challenge for socio-spatial literacy research is to map the rhizomes of literacy practices and their pack multiliteracies and overlay these formations on the tracings or solidifications of official mass multiplicities, to identify ruptures, connections, disconnections and rhizomatic lines of flight, and in so doing, to continually resist the kinds of mass compartmentalising, homogenising and reproduction of literacy practices in schools that often works against a recognition of difference.

Intersections between Socio-spatial and Socio-cultural Literacy Paradigms

In mapping the distinctive features of socio-spatial literacy theory, it is acknowledged that there are connections, parallels, historical influences and divergences among socio-spatial and other literacy paradigms. In particular, attention to space and the spatiality of literacy practice has inspired novel ways of reconceiving socio-cultural research by asking different questions about the spatial networks, flows and connections between literacy practices across social spaces, such as schools, homes, public places and other social sites (Bulfin & North, 2007; Nespor, 1997; Pahl, 2001). For example, Leander and Sheehy's (2004) edited book, *Spatializing Literacy Research and Practice*, is grounded explicitly in socio-cultural literacy research, but with a particular emphasis upon how discourses and texts are produced and move across social spaces. The authors aim to 'recover the interpretive loss experienced when a context of literacy practice is considered to be background to the situated practices happening "within it"' (Leander & Sheehy, 2004: 3).

The interpretative loss of the backgrounded spatial dimension in other literacy studies, and conversely, the interpretive gain that might be realised if literacy researchers attended consciously to the spatial, is significant enough to warrant a distinctive socio-spatial research tradition in its own right. Therefore, I use the term 'socio-spatial approaches', because space is inherently social. Social space includes both individual and collective social action, which converges at specified times and places (Lefebvre, 1991). Socio-spatial approaches to literacy are grounded in a significant body of spatial theory within social and cultural geography that attends consistently to the social ordering of space, and to spatial dimensions and frames of social practice beyond contexts of education research.

There are many studies that address the socio-spatial dimensions of literacy without explicitly positioning research within a socio-cultural approach (e.g. Green et al., 2008; Mills, 2010a; Scollon & Scollon, 2003; Somerville, 2007). An example of such a spatial theory with its own theoretical origins is 'geosemiotics' outlined by Scollon and Scollon (2003: x). These theorists are focused on meaning-making systems and how they are specifically located in the material world. This shifts attention away from communities as the central units for understanding the social organisation of literacy practices (i.e. socio-cultural research), to understanding the indexing of sign, meanings and discourses by their material and geospatial contexts.

Theorists such as Leander (2004; Leander *et al.*, 2010) and colleagues, and more recently Mills and Comber (2015) have revisited Street and Heath's ethnographies to explicitly trace, defend or critique how spatial concepts are implicit or explicit in these accounts. Street's early analysis of literacy practices in Iran demonstrated clear connections between literacy practices and their position in the social space, such as to the national political agenda at that time, and to discourses that circulate in rural community life. The literacy practices he observed in local and material sites were also interpreted as being connected to the social world beyond it, such as the teachers who were '...in the village but not of the village' (Street, 1975: 299). Demonstrating an awareness of rural place and access to social mobility, Street observes:

> Education was an urban matter and ... those village youths who wanted to continue would have to leave.... Progress was outwards not upwards. (Street, 1975)

Conscious of the relations between local practices and the global, Street maintained that the life outcomes for those of the rural areas who gained education credentials were still uncertain due to fluctuating oil prices and economic downturns. In this account, socio-spatial and political arrangements, both material and immaterial, are seen to function powerfully in relation to local practices in the villages (Mills & Comber, 2015).

Heath's early and more recent ethnographic accounts in the Carolinas are similarly geographically, materially, economically and historically situated (Mills & Comber, 2015). Heath (1983: 344) observed that unlike the townspeople, the Roadville and Trackton children were 'geographically based and spatially limited' until they were old enough to attend school. The next generation, on the other hand, intended to move to the cities in search of employment. This account is one in which space is not the background for the action, or for literacy, but is constituted in the action. Mobility and social geography are also central to Heath's (2012) follow-on monograph, *Words at Work and Play*, which features maps representing the movement of the original families since the 1960s and 1970s, 20 and 30 years later. The tracing of community life are fluid – relocations and fragmentation of community related to the economy, work and changes to global migration over the passage of time (Mills & Comber, 2015).

Reinterpreting historical ethnographies through a spatial lens has led to overlaying recent developments and spatial concepts in social geography. Spatiality was somewhat backgrounded in these early accounts, appropriate to the requirements of ethnographic methodologies of the day. Yet from a socio-spatial perspective, all human actions, including forms of communication, are spatially produced, resisted or taken up in the social world, and find their meanings within specific contexts of use.

Leander *et al.* (2010: 334–335) state, while acknowledging learning as distributed and social, that many ethnographic studies focus on practices that possess a 'localist' vision that is '...packed rather tightly within local containers'. They observe that much of the fieldwork conducted within the earlier socio-cultural literacy studies tradition was small-scale ethnographies in local sites. Yet connections are typically made between practices across social sites – school, home, church, workplace, marketplace and recreational sites, and interpreted in relation to the wider historical, economic and political context of the times. These ethnographic studies of literacies form part of a long tradition in cultural anthropology, with the explicit goal to trace the 'limits and features of the situations in which such communication occurs' (Heath, 1983: 6, cited in Leander *et al.*, 2010). From a methodological point of view, ethnography incorporates a small number of sites in order to manage the scope of observational fieldwork.

Spatial literacy theorists, such as Sheehy and Leander (2004: 3) have sought '...to disrupt folk notions of how literacies are "situated"'. They critique that in literacy studies more broadly, '...context in literacy research has been overdetermined in its meaning...Space has been overmaterialised'. For example, classrooms are not bounded by bricks and mortar, but are connected to state policies, institutional documents, circulating media, discourses and texts within schools and society. Social space is relational and dynamic, connected to other spaces, involving continual meetings and partings and literacy practices are constantly moving, reproduced, remixed, modified, flowing, unbounded and potentially unlimited.

Implications of Socio-spatial Literacies for Practice

The implications of socio-spatial literacy research for classroom practices are numerous. By foregrounding the spatiality and connections between literacy practices, literacy practices in schools need not be seen as fixed, immobile and disconnected from the social domains of literacy practices outside of school. Teachers can harness the relevant mobilities in students' lives – iPads, tablets, digital cameras and smartphones – as resources to enhance the authenticity of literacy learning, both in and beyond the classroom site. Learning spaces can become expansive and reimagined worlds that are connected more strategically to the literacy practices that circulate in the students' out-of-school lives. Socio-spatial literacy research can identify ways for teachers to deterritorialise literacy practices in the curriculum and within educational institutions to better account for the literacy practices that are positioned peripherally to the mainstream. Such an approach can demonstrate ways for teachers to take up and modify literacy practices that are found in rhizomatic networks of social media practices to augment literacy practices in educational settings, adapting and aligning these practices with the purposes and credentialing power of schooling. Soja (2004: xi) states: 'When seen as a heterotopia or as fully lived space...the classroom becomes an encapsulation of everything and everywhere, a kind of hieroglyphic site that opens up a potentially endless realm of insightful reading and learning'.

New Directions for Socio-spatial Literacies

Socio-spatial approaches can remodel the shape of literacy research by emphasising the differing spatial dimensions of human relationships, texts and textual practices. Spatiality is central because how any text or textual practice is 'placed' or positioned 'in the world', influences part of its meaning (Scollon & Scollon, 2003: 205). Furthermore, all texts and textual practices operate in 'aggregate...a sign is never isolated from other signs in its environment' (Scollon & Scollon, 2003: 205). Such an approach can attend more systematically to a recalibrated awareness of the spatiality of the body, the tools, the texts, and the connections and networks of literacy activities (Mills & Comber, 2015). Literacy researchers and theorists need an expansive repertoire of conceptual and methodological tools to 'think spatially' (Ferrare & Apple, 2010: 216). Spatial approaches have the potential to uncover the complex relations between people, places and literacies as social practices. Given the social mediafication of literacy practice, a significant dimension of the future of socio-spatial literacy studies is to scope the multiplicity of 'activity spaces' – the '...spatial network of links and activities, spatial connections and locations, within which a particular agent operates' in a changing communication ecology (Massey, 2000: 54).

Research of literacy practices in the coming decades will continue to require transformed understandings of how literacy practices metamorphose in digital spaces. Flows of literacy practices will continue to involve a groundswell of conventional and hybrid literacy practices across local, national and transnational spaces. Furthermore, there will be modifications to the topography of the socio-material circulation of texts and practices, and the systems, rhizomes, and nodes that connect and divide literacy practices around the globe.

Most fundamentally, socio-spatial research of literacy practices acknowledges that all forms of communication and their associated spaces are socially produced. There is also an elemental consciousness of the politics of space and the distribution of literacy practices. If space really '... makes a difference in theory, culture and politics' (Soja & Hooper, 1993: 197), then it makes a difference to our knowledge of literacy practices that are intrinsically social, cultural and political.

6 Socio-material Literacies

Information only becomes knowledge when it is grounded quite concretely in the social, material world.
(Scollon & Scollon, 2003: 11)

There has been a recent upsurge of interest in the material dimensions of education, with the term 'material' referring to anything that possesses mass or matter, and which uses physical space (Haas, 1996). This includes the literacy practices and artefacts that cross between homes and communities. This interest stems from fields such as material culture studies and visual studies, and is associated with ethnographic and phenomenological approaches to inquiry. Within visual culture studies, there is an awareness that ethnographers need to attend not only to the visual content of local cultures, but also to their materiality (Pink, 2009). Social environments, classrooms, shopping malls, libraries, homes and workplaces, are inextricably tied to material culture. They are not culturally benign objects, but are '...active mechanisms for socialisation and enculturation' (Johnson, 1980: 174).

The material elements of classrooms, the books, pencils, desks, chairs, tablets, visual displays and other learning materials, often function as heuristics for learning, and the connections between materials, actors and knowledge in the classroom can be mapped and problematised in relation to their connections to the wider society (Bloome, 2012). Literacy, as socially and materially situated practice, involves tools for encoding and decoding, and is materialised in different ways using the resources at hand by cultural groups in specific social and historical contexts (Pahl & Burnett, 2013).

Theories of learning have long attended to tool use as central to social cognition, following Dewey, Vygotsky and Piaget. For example, applying Vygotskian principles of tool use, we have conducted research into students' use of Lego robots and programming software, which we regard as cultural tools (Mills *et al.*, 2013). A tool serves 'as the conductor of human influence' on goal-centred activity (Vygotsky, 1978: 55). We demonstrated that when children are confronted with new and challenging problems, they exhibit a range of responses to attain the goal, drawing on sophisticated technology tools and speech directed toward other persons to mediate their practical activity. Problem-solving activity involved mediating interactions with Lego robots, computer screens and actors, and those materials were inextricably connected to students' problem-solving (Mills *et al.*, 2013).

The mediating power of tools is tied to the accumulation of knowledge of prior generations that are embedded in the design of the artefact (Cole & Engeström, 1993). Examples of tool use in Vygotskian problem-solving experiments include everyday objects, such as string or sticks to extend a child's reach for a candy (Vygotsky, 1978). A learning material can be as simple as a stick or a piece of chalk, or as complex as a robot. From the design of school furniture, to the structure of the built environment, materials, including tools, have always played a vital part in the structuring of learning (Lawn & Grosvenor, 2005).

Materiality is vital to literacy learning. Socio-material approaches to literacy emphasise the active and dynamic role of the tangible materials, whether of pencils or policies, of paper or iPods, and their interplay with human elements in literacy learning. It is presented here as a way of researching social action, such as in the context of education or literacy practices, rather than a grand meta-narrative of society. At the outset, it is acknowledged that socio-material literacy research can be used not only to represent or understand literacy practice, but also to intercept or change the shape of socio-material relations that are observed. This concept of the agency of materials is consistent with certain socio-material approaches in education more broadly (Fenwick & Edwards, 2010).

Key Concepts of Socio-material Literacies

Within literacy studies, there are some early examples of research that attend to socio-material principles, such as object ethnography, which uses objects as the starting point for ethnographic inquiry (Carrington & Dowdall, 2013). Other approaches that prioritise materials in literacy practices are artifactual literacy (Pahl & Rowsell, 2010), and critical artifactual literacy (Pahl & Rowsell, 2011), which both regard artefacts and objects as life presences that actively reflect identities (Rowsell, 2011; Turkle, 2007). These theories are not explicitly named as socio-material approaches, but demonstrate the shift toward examining the role and meaning of materials in literacy events.

There are several defining principles of socio-material approaches in literacy research. The first is that socio-materiality does not privilege human consciousness in literacy or digital practices, because there is a central interest in the processes and relationships that emerge when material objects, actors or bodies and bodies of knowledge are brought together to create new knowledge. Unlike approaches that place a premium on the role of human consciousness in human social action, socio-material approaches do not consider independent human actors as the central focus of study. Literacy is seen as the process and product of material action and interaction, rather than as something that exists as abstract and cognitive processes in the minds of individuals.

Socio-material approaches do not position human actors as above the materials, but as among materials (Fenwick *et al.*, 2011). Due to the prevailing influence of human-orientated views of learners and education, socio-material approaches provide a theory of learning that does not necessarily begin with human aims, interests and needs (Sorenson, 2009).

Second, socio-material approaches trace the human and non-human elements of meaning making interactions, carefully mapping or untangling complex webs of elements that emerge or play a role in literacy practices. It is these relationships between entities that result in literacy practices, rather than the entities themselves.

Socio-material approaches to literacy investigate how bodies are formulated, stabilised, reproduced or transformed in particular social and material networks. Such bodies include bodies of knowledge about literacy practices, which also take a material form via texts, tools, actors and institutions. The emphasis is on understanding relationships between elements, and how they function together, rather than researching them independently. The research design must take into account that objects in the material world are integral to literacy and learning, rather than as a context or taken-for-granted background to thought and action.

Third, irrespective of the patch of social action or focus of socio-material analysis, the data is interpreted in relation to the wider system of networks and actors, as a whole societal system. Everything in natural and social worlds is interpreted as the continuous outcome of networks of relation, positioning the material and the social together (Law, 2008).

At the same time, the boundaries of the objects or systems of focus are also delineated, but systems of activity are not necessarily limited by their spatial or geographical regions (Lawn & Grosvenor, 2005). Questions are asked, such as:

- What literacy practices take place when particular objects of educational practices are brought together: particular technologies, books, pedagogies, students and policies?

- What kinds of literacy learning can be achieved, and what kinds of teachers and literacy users can be created in the context of these practices?
- What literacy practices are occurring within a system, and how are these practices formed and held together?

These questions can address issues such as how to integrate technologies into literacy curriculum in ways that interpret educational innovations with their socio-material relations. The materiality of literacy concerns how literacy practices connect to other entities, and the performance of the human and non-human in the social practices of literacy.

Theorists have categorised different forms of materiality, such as materials, bodies and texts (Law & Hetherington, 2003). Examples of materials in literacy practices include homes, libraries, classrooms, digital devices, stationery, furniture, offices and teacher education colleges. Bodies in schooled literacy practices include caregivers, teachers, children, school administrators, researchers, lecturers, policy makers, bloggers, journalists and other people, including their attributes, their clothing, their movements and postures, gestures and so on. Texts include materials that are encoded with meaning, such as books, internet sites, scrapbooks, photographs, digital stories and policies. While it is recognised that all objects communicate meaning, textual matter generally refers to objects that contain meaning. It is acknowledged that some objects or agents may straddle these categories. Other theorists, such as Fenwick and Edwards (2011), include abstract or immaterial entities, such as human memories or disciplines of knowledge.

Origins of Socio-material Literacies

Latour, Deleuze and Whitehead

A tenet of socio-material approaches is that humans are not regarded with greater attention than the object with which they interact. This concept can be traced to work of Bloor (1976), whose ideas were taken up and expanded by Latour:

I have sought to show researchers in the social sciences that sociology is not the science of human beings alone... Our collective is woven together out of speaking subjects, perhaps, but subjects to which poor objects, our inferior brothers, are attached at all points. (Latour, 1987: viii)

In relation to human interdependence or dependence on material objects, Latour continues, 'Without the non-human...humans would not last for a minute' (Latour, 2004: 91). Everyday things or parts of things, such as technologies, humans, policies, buildings, health and even memories, are seen as capable of coming together and exerting force on other elements.

For instance, think of video games of the trademark Skylanders, available across a range of technology platforms, and constituting a complex network of related materials, bodies and texts. There are marketing materials, collectable figures of the game characters, internet activities, stickers, DVD cases and licensed merchandise. There are networks of game stores or distributors, game reviewers, game censorship bodies, game producers and designers, salespeople, company employees and game users. There are system requirements, such as broadband internet connections, gaming console systems, copyright agencies, trademarks, groups of companies such as Microsoft and Activision, televisions, game controllers, system upgrades, headphones, modems and even the electrical power grids. There are connections to places and people, such as homes, afterschool and vacation care providers, community groups, parents and schools that bring peers together, and politicians who make decisions that either directly or indirectly influence the video game industry. On the internet, one can trace YouTube videos of Skylanders, animated parodies, fan sites and wikis, social media references and paid internet subscriptions. These assemblages and networks expand across time and space. It is the points of connection and association between these human and non-human elements, or the resistances and conflicts between them, that may focus the interest of socio-material researchers (Fenwick & Edwards, 2010).

The non-essentialist ontologies of Deleuze and Whitehead share a philosophy that attempts to explain the relations between human and nonhuman, or the subject and the object, while going beyond simplistic divisions between them. Deleuze and Whitehead, while writing separately, both understand a processural character of materiality and physicality, showing the interrelatedness between materiality and human subjectivity. The material world has often been assumed to be the domain and concern of science, while subjectivity and experiences of thinking humans has been largely the concern of the humanities and social theory.

The ontologies of Deleuze and Whitehead both point to the need to dissolve the conceptual wedge between the presumed physicality of objective worlds and the subjectivity of human experience. For example, Whitehead's ontological position conceives of process and becoming as the characterisations of being and materiality. He refers to 'stubborn fact' which is comprised of 'actual entities', which have both materiality and subjectivity, and which constitute '...the final real things of which the world is made up' (Whitehead, 1978: 19). Matter does not consist of 'self-contained particles', that are '...self-sufficient within its local habitation' (Whitehead, 1978: 19). Whitehead proposes a philosophy of the organism, in which actual entities have both materiality and subjectivity. Unlike philosophies of substance, that presuppose a subject that encounters a datum and reacts to the datum, a philosophy of organism presupposes a datum which meets feelings, and progressively becomes the unity of a feeling and knowing subject (Halewood, 2005). A philosophy of organism, like the socio-material, attends to materials and objects as an important part of human subjectivity. As Whitehead (1967: 206) explains, the world is a '...circumambient space of social physical activity'.

Actor Network Theory (ANT) and the socio-material

Socio-material approaches in educational research draw on some of the key principles of Actor Network Theory (ANT). The recent mapping of strands within socio-material research across disciplines beyond philosophy is a somewhat contested domain, with key works citing different amalgamations and conceptual differences of contributing theorists and theories. For example a significant contribution to material approaches in the study of organisations is Orlikowski's (2007) article, Socio-material Practices: Exploring Materials at work. Orlikowksi recounts that the constitution of humans and materials, particularly technologies, have been described as actor-networks (Callon, 1986; Latour, 1992), socio-technical ensembles (Bijker, 1995), a mangle of practice (Pickering, 1995), object-centred sociality (Knorr Cetina, 1997), relational materiality (Law, 2004) and material sociology (Beunza et al., 2006). However, these viewpoints share the rejection of a dualism or separation between the material and the social, and an emphasis on the intertwining of humans and material technologies in social practice.

At the most elementary level of Actor Network Theory is a foregrounding of materiality in learning and educational processes (Fenwick et al., 2011). Practical social activities are seen as the foci of activity theory, because social lives are ordered by activities in which we develop our consciousness, skills and orientation to the world (Sannino et al., 2009). There is also an insistence within actor network theory that non-human entities are of equal importance to human elements in social action.

Actor network theory has given rise to new conceptions of agency, which is seen as inextricably linked to the heterogeneity of actors, human and non-human, in tangled, networked relations. The material linkages of social action are traceable, and so are the politics through which the socio-material elements are connected (Fenwick *et al.*, 2011). Thus, the implications of this view of agency for literacy reforms, for example, moves from a focus on teacher knowledge about literacy, to seeking to transform a much broader set of relations between teachers, students, parents, educational systems, policies, learning materials and technologies, that collectively influence literacy learning. The literacy teacher's agency is caught up in a range of forces, including actions, desires, skills and connections to resources, as well as the mediating flow of texts and technologies available to the teacher, and the infrastructure and educational system within which teachers work.

Cultural Historical Activity Theory (CHAT) and the socio-material

Another cluster of key contributors to socio-material research in education is the development of principles within Cultural Historical Activity Theory (CHAT), beginning with certain concepts of Vygotsky (1978), Leontiev (1978), Luria (1976), Galperin (1992) and later Cole (1996) and Engeström (1999), among others. Like ANT, activity is central to CHAT. As Vygotsky (1987: 78) observed: 'Activity and practice – these are the new concepts that have allowed us to consider the function of egocentric speech from a new perspective, to consider it in its completeness'. Leontiev further explains the nature of the relations between individuals and social activity:

> The activity of individual people...depends on their social position, the conditions that fall to their lot, and an accumulation of idiosyncratic, individual factors. Human activity is not a relation between a person and a society that confronts him [or her]. (Leontiev, 1978: 10)

In other words, humans do not simply find themselves encountering external conditions to which they must adapt their activities, but in fact the social conditions contain the motives and goals of human activities (Leontiev, 1978).

Another central thesis of CHAT and the socio-material is that artefacts are the fundamental constituents of culture (White, 1998: xiv). Cole elucidates:

> An artifact is an aspect of the material world that has been modified over the history of its incorporation in goal-directed human action. By virtue of the changes wrought in the process of their creation and use, artifacts are simultaneously ideal (conceptual) and material. (Cole, 1996: 117)

In this view of artefacts, cultural mediation produces developmental change in which the accumulated knowledge and activities of previous generations are embedded in the present. The unseen people and things that have been built up around the individual, such as social rules and norms, cultural scripts and schemas, games and rituals, influence the social world and literacy practices. When the socio-material literacy theorist studies communication practices, he or she takes into account the manufactured and human objects that silently permeate intelligence into the apparatus of the world, whether of books, computers, ideas, machines, values, transportation systems or robots (White, 1998).

Within the CHAT tradition, Engeström (1999) has also contributed ideas to account for the transformation of socio-material relations, conceptualising activity systems as dynamic and open to change. When new tools or technologies are introduced to a system, there are modifications of the system rules, changing the roles of materials and influencing the division of labour (Edwards, 2011). Humans are seen to transform their social conditions through activity, resolve contradictions, generate new cultural artefacts, and to create new forms of life and the self.

Reading research and socio-material relations

When we consider socio-material reading research, there are models that have attempted to account for social, material and cultural contexts of learning processes since the 1980s. Earlier proponents of schema theory in the 1970s considered that meaning is stored in mental structures, which are activated and organised during the reading process. In this way, the situated nature of reading within a process of interaction between material texts and the schema were not central to this view. Meanings or mental structures were viewed as existing independently of particular embodied reading activities. The origin and development of the mental structures were not taken into account (McVee et al., 2005).

Research has recently revisited the schema theory of reading to better take into account the socio-material relations of practice. For example, McVee et al. (2005: 541) make a case that the origin of individual literacy knowledge is synchronically connected '...to the milieu's discourse practices, mediational tools and cultural artifacts, which have both a material and an ideational character'. Immaterial and material tools are value-laden, and shaped by relationships and established norms within and among people that govern the activity.

A revised understanding of the schema as a flexible rather than rigid structure, originating in relation to complex networks of social relations, materials and technologies, is necessary for understanding online reading environments in which authors engage with non-linear and hyperlinked textual pathways (Reinking et al., 1998).

Digital composition and socio-materiality

Within material approaches to literacy, there are references to the materiality of writing as early the late 1990s, such as Haas' (1996) volume, *Writing Technology: Studies of the Materiality of Writing*. Through original research, Haas demonstrated that the materiality of different computers and their software configurations are important to understanding how writers use technology to produce texts. As Haas (1996: 51) concludes: 'The computer is not an all-powerful monolith...'. Rather, findings about how writers use computers for both reading and writing were remarkably dissimilar for different computer systems and digital devices, and when used for different social purposes.

The interest in the materiality of writing may have arisen, in part, as a consequence of the role of rapid and continual changes to technologies to support textual practices. However, the relationship between writing and materiality is historically profound, and all '...writing is language made material' (Haas, 1996: 3). The physical nature of textual practices is an element that is not typically addressed in psychological or socio-linguistic approaches to literacy, calling for the need to revisit material approaches to the study of literacy practice in an era in which the materiality of writing is undergoing continual metamorphosis.

In particular, there is a need for new research of digital writing and composition that aims to understand the human-material interrelations without prioritising the human or the artefact. There is a need to understand the complex amalgamations and networks of human and non-human elements that collectively influence writing activity, taking into account the cultural constitution of socio-material activity, which is already embedded in the histories of the artefacts and agentive activities of literacy as socio-material practice.

Tensions for Socio-material Literacies

This section addresses some of the criticisms of socio-material theory, which is arguably in a germinal stage of application within literacy studies. I briefly consider the scope and limits of the socio-material, and provide examples of research questions that can and cannot be asked through this theory and its associated methodologies.

One potential problem with socio-material research of literacy practices concerns the difficulty of being able to find the boundaries of research enquiry. It may be difficult to trace the immaterial and material networks of textual practices that remain invisible and transitory in social settings or documents. As Smith theorised:

The appearance of meaning as a text detaches meaning from the lived processes of its transitory construction, made and remade at each moment of people's talk. The vesting of meaning in such permanent or semi-permanent forms is routine and commonplace, and has transformed our relations to language, meaning, and each other. (Smith,1990: 210–211)

Textual practices and their processes are often transient, involving many actors, unrecorded conversations, phone calls, meetings, memos, emails, curriculum documents, approvals, media releases, public perceptions, radio interviews, online news items, personal histories and pieces of information that are read moment by moment, that each contribute in almost untraceable ways to a text made permanent (Barton, 2001; Smith, 1990).

Our everyday lives are entangled in complex webs of textual practices – when we interpret the texts of others that are circulated via multiple modes and media, when we simultaneously read and write the web (e.g. blogging), and when we produce texts. Any mapping of these amalgamations of social and material relations will always be partial and incomplete, and need careful delimiters from the outset.

The second issue pertains to the rationale for attending to all objects, actions and bodies as important, especially once the human element is no longer privileged. Certainly, giving greater attention to the changing materiality of textual practices and the reconfiguring of language in these interactions would seem a worthy adaption of approaches that have previously neglected the role of texts as objects. However, while bringing materials to the fore, must we necessarily ignore the long-held focus in educational and literacy research on human actors?

We see the post-human argument in Fenwick and Landri's (2011) account of the socio-material, but not among all versions of material studies (see Pahl & Rowsell, 2010). When it comes to literacy studies, if there are no humans there are no textual practices. There is no human learning, no schools and no discipline of education to research. If the human element is no longer essential in the socio-material – decentred, as Fenwick and Landri (2012) assert, then why attend to the materials at all, which are by and large both created and used by humans? Clearly, a strength of the socio-material approach is to attend to the forgotten material or immaterial objects of social interaction – but in doing so, neither should the human dimension become forgotten, nor considered of lesser importance than matter.

A further issue is the potential problem of fragmentation in socio-material research, since certain proponents of socio-material literacy research have promoted the socio-material as above the socio-cultural. For example, Gourlay and Oliver (2013: 78) have explored the 'limitations of this theory [socio-cultural literacy] for theorising the materiality of the digitally-mediated textual engagements in particular'. Combining post-human studies on the human and the virtual, and socio-material approaches to educational research, they define digital literacies as collaboratively accomplished social practices that are achieved through human and non-human elements. They contend that socio-cultural literacy theory could be further enhanced by attending to the material, when in reality, the material nature of literacy practice has been acknowledged in much of the earlier theoretical work in the socio-cultural tradition (see Barton, 2001).

Again, Barton and Hamilton (2005) have critiqued Wenger's (1998) model of Communities of Practice, retheorising the role of material literacy artefacts that possess agentive power in the social process of reification. They draw attention to how non-human materials, as actors, play important roles in networks of literacy practices, drawing on work by Latour, Smith and Holland. For example, Smith (1999) sees that texts are agents in the solidification and reification of power. She sees the text in both its material and symbolic dimensions as a bridge between everyday living relations and the working of power. The text is seen as the material aspect that brings standardised forms of words and images, which once disseminated, can be read in multiple material and social contexts across time and space.

In adult literacy, one of the early applications of a socio-material approach was published by Hamilton (2001), who used Actor Network Theory to trace the life of a political artefact, the International Adult Literacy Survey. She traced the social processes involved in its creation, to the dispersion of its findings in policy, the media and educational practice. This literacy artefact served to maintain the distribution of English within the social order, and serves as an example of the useful work of examining the translation of research to policy and practice, with which literacy researchers should engage. Such socio-material work also demonstrates how literacy findings are translated through chains of events, actions and texts, demonstrating that the origins, caveats and complexities are erased or elided by its proponents in their own interests, and the distorted and reified common sense views are often relayed to teachers and students.

At the same time, Hamilton acknowledges the unpredictable nature of texts. Texts have power over social action only if someone is willing to disseminate them, if they are not ignored, and if there are people willing to spend time to read texts and order their lives accordingly (Law, 2008). Thus, the agency of materials, including texts, is acknowledged to be uncertain, and tied to networks of social entities, technologies and objects and their particular modes of interaction.

This example of relational materialism was theorised within New Literacy Studies perspectives, rather than presented as a contradictory, conflicting or alternative approach. While attention to the material dimension is not always apparent or overt in socio-cultural research, the consistency between socio-cultural and socio-material theories becomes clear in relation to the New Literacy Studies emphasis on the situatedness of textual practices that are inextricably tied to particular, tangible contexts of use, and never separated from social practices like an autonomous set of abstract skills. Hamilton (2001) sees that Actor Network Theory, in particular, can support socio-cultural literacy researchers to attend to the dissemination of literacy findings to the public sphere through building of strategic alliances with international policy makers, and contributing to international forums and debates.

A final concern for socio-material researchers pertains to methodology, and proponents of socio-material approaches in education more broadly have raised some of these questions that will likely have implications in literacy research (see Fenwick & Landri, 2012). These questions include the following:

- How can the networks of tangible materials, actors and practices be translated into symbolic representations and research reports?
- How does one avoid anthropomorphising objects in research accounts within human-centred disciplines of research?
- What materials and processes are highlighted, selected, hidden, shaped or inscribed in the report?
- How does one account for the pre-existing historical and cultural shaping of the materials that occurred prior to undertaking the research?
- If oppressive assemblages are identified, how are these reported to those who might have the power to change them?
- If assemblages are always changing, what stable features of the assemblages will maintain currency and value?

These are some of the complex issues that socio-material literacy researchers may encounter as they engage in this emerging approach. In short, socio-material theory has opened up new lines of inquiry and new vocabularies for reconceptualising literacy pedagogy, curriculum and assessment with an emphasis on relational effects beyond the immediate actor.

Recent Developments of Socio-material Literacies

Recent research of literacy and media practices has increasingly drawn attention to the socio-material networks and relationships of matter. Applying variants of actor-network theory, object ethnography and other similar approaches, the connections can be established between global media cultures, the meanings embedded in objects, and the way children and youth today do literacy. Beliefs about creativity, literacy and developmental play are embedded in educational artefacts themselves, and the media platforms that support the commercial circulation of these materials (Carrington & Dowdall, 2013).

When we consider early literacy learning in homes, kindergartens, libraries and schools, there are material cultures that play a vital role in this process, from tablets to toys (Nixon & Hately, 2013). In many capitalist societies today, digital media practices are cleverly connected to cultural and material objects for children and youth, creating a circulation of related artefacts, merchandise and digital literacy practices.

The role of materials in early learning has been theorised by Montessori-Pierson (1991), who outlined that pedagogical objects should be selected in the curriculum to enable three progressive learning aims. First, young children learn to identify attributes of materials and match similar attributes and objects. Once children can match objects or attributes of objects, they are able to identify differences and can distinguish between the properties of materials. Attributes can refer to properties that include the form, shape, colour, line, texture, length, height, weight, temperature, flavour, scent and sound of materials. This leads to the ability to distinguish between various gradients or degrees of attributes, such as seriating objects by precise shade of blue, hearing intervals of the tone of bells played as an octave, or articulating descriptors of precise movement.

Given the central role of language in learning, Montessori-Pierson also emphasises the need for adults to teach specialist language or vocabulary to denote gradients of attributes. Learners need a precise nomenclature for ordering mental frameworks to sort empirical or sensory differences among objects (Frierson, 2014). The role of language is central to these learning processes, to the mental identification, matching, differentiation, seriation and arranging of objects within the child's material world or learning environment.

The place of artefacts in literacy learning has gained some merited attention, with research demonstrating how objects that are valued by families in their homes are expressions of the immaterial, of subjectivities and values, and contribute to a sense of personhood and production of identity

(Hurdley, 2006). Recent research has demonstrated how students have engaged in storytelling using artefacts of significance in their lives, as companions to their lives and markers of events, emotions, memories and connections with others. Furthermore, various artefacts used in combination with multigenre writing have been used to develop intercultural understandings, with objects providing entry points for a more culturally accessible reading of a text (Varga-Dobai, 2014).

There is a strand of research within the socio-cultural literacy tradition that has drawn upon material culture studies to understand textual practices in relation to the material cultures in homes and communities (Pahl & Burnett, 2013). Researchers such as Pahl and Rowsell (2010: 134) use the term 'artifactual literacy' to describe their approach to literacy teaching that takes into account the socio-material dimension of meaning making:

Artifactual literacy ... allows for a much more collaborative and participatory mode of teaching and learning to come into literacy education. Artifactual literacy is about exchange; it is participatory and collaborative, visual and sensory. It is a radical understanding of meaning making in a human and embodied way. (Pahl & Rowsell, 2010)

Artefacts can provide an entry point for accessing memories, histories and values of research participants, which might otherwise not be uncovered through observations, document analysis, interviews (without artifactual prompts) or other repertoires of ethnographic methods (Rowsell, 2011). When we come to material literacy research since the digital turn, there are a growing number of useful examples of its application in multimodal contexts of use. A recent example is provided by Carrington and Dowdall (2013), who conducted an object ethnography of Lego. They adapted this approach based on Thing Theory seminar programs at Columbia University in spring 2006–2008, and examined Lego blocks as artefacts in the daily lives of two boys. They demonstrate how Lego minifigures have scripted features; particular affordances that influence what children do with the objects. They also demonstrate how Lego plays an active role in co-constructing the boys' identities in their literacy play. The object ethnography is also mapped to the history of Lego as a global media enterprise, tied to websites, movies and video games, and circulating discourses that operationalise and position Lego as a model of learning through play. They observe that children are being socialised into social, cultural and textual spaces that bring together online and offline objects and materials. In doing so, the object ethnography maps the intersections between everyday Lego artefacts, the children that play with Lego, and global media discourses (Carrington & Dowdall, 2013).

Original socio-material research has demonstrated that literacy operates as a means of maintaining social cohesion online, while being clearly located in the social, material and cultural structures of the children's offline worlds (Marsh, 2011). A study by Marsh (2011) examined the online and offline literacy practices of children aged 5–11 through surveying 175 children who engaged with virtual worlds both at school and home. The study included interviews with 26 children and detailed observations of three students interacting within the popular virtual world, Club Penguin. Children's literacy practices constituted the maintenance of an online interaction order. The children interacted with a wide range of actors, such as peers, who played together both online and offline. They also interacted with an array of related materials, such as mobile phones, digital toys, televisions and online games. The children's literacy practices were an amalgamation of cognate materials, entities and subjectivities that were entangled in the material and virtual worlds. The socio-material takes into account these germane relations in research of literacy practices.

Within the field of science and technology studies, Sorenson has compared the pedagogical uses of classroom materials that are old and new. Taking into account the embodied interactions between the classroom actors and the objects, Sorenson (2009) analyses the multiple forms of technology, knowledge and presence that are enacted in an online, three dimensional, virtual environment project with a fourth grade class. The learners' digital tool use was compared with the use of non-digital materials, such as textbooks, pencils and rulers. Sorenson provides a clear, empirical case in book-length detail to address an important set of cross-disciplinary issues, demonstrating how learning is dispersed across systems of people and objects. She positions material objects and process as vital components of children's cognitive activity.

Together, recent socio-material studies provide a burgeoning field of research that makes visible the micro-dynamics of literacy learning and the relational entanglement of human and non-human entities. In these accounts, any object or 'thing' that makes a difference to literacy practice or learning is an actor (Howes & Classen, 2006). Materials are no longer just matter, as conceived in science, but are matters of concern for social theory, literacy practice and education.

Intersections between Socio-material and Socio-cultural Approaches

Within socio-cultural approaches, the materiality of textual practices has been acknowledged as an important component from its incipience, as attested by Barton at the turn of the century:

The significance of the material existence of written language was apparent in the local literacies research, such disparate factors as the physical
existence of books on shelves, the displays on notice boards and texts on
clothing, were all acts of meaning. (Barton, 2001: 98–99)

This claim is supported by evidence from a number of socio-cultural literacy studies published around that period, including cultural artefact studies by Hall (2000) and also Graddol (1994), homework literacies by Ormerod
and Ivanic (2000) and prison literacies by Wilson (2000). Soon after, Pahl
(2001) examined map making by children, drawing attention to how textual
artefacts cross social sites. Some have examined the materiality of the book,
working at the nexus of materiality and its implications for reading processes
(Barton, 2001; Moylan & Stiles, 1996). Others have explored the networked
ecologies of literacy, tracing the circulation of linked practices and artefacts
across spaces (Neuman & Celano, 2006). The mapping of religious literacies,
also known as faith literacies (Gregory & Ruby, 2011) or liturgical literacies
(Rosowsky, 2008), has also included attention to the material circulation of
practices, such as religious artefacts that are used across religious meeting
places and homes.

   To demonstrate how socio-material and socio-cultural approaches can be
usefully blended, consider how Pahl and Rowsell (2010) see material artefacts as living sites of story making and community building (Vaughn, 2012).
These authors demonstrate how communities hold stories and values that
are instantiated in material objects. These objects can provide conduits for
the ebb and flow of literacy practices across social sites, such as between
home, community events and school.

   The fact that materiality of textual practices is a tributary within socio-
cultural research is interesting, given that socio-material approaches have
been promoted by some as an alternative to research of communities of
practice. For example, Fenwick and Landri (2012: 1) advance the view that
socio-material approaches '...attempt to move beyond overly simplistic
notions of participation and community of practice that have been so widely
critiqued'. Indeed, in socio-cultural literacy studies, there has been a long line
of researchers who have taken into account the role of texts as materials in
literacy learning within, rather than against, a view of communities of practice (e.g. Nichols *et al.*, 2012; Pahl, 2002). Socio-cultural theorists have
researched the movements of literacy artefacts across sites, demonstrating
that the socio-cultural and socio-material are not necessarily mutually exclusive approaches. They demonstrate that the inclusion of materials or artefacts is an important component of the situated practice of literacies, and an
outgrowth of pluralised approaches to multimodal literacy beyond written

words (Roe, 2012). However, within socio-cultural approaches more broadly, there has not been a distinctive movement away from the conventional framing of literacy as social practices, which is a terminology that does not capture the idea that the material relations are intrinsic to literacy practices in everyday life (Orlikowski, 2007). A distinctively socio-material approach is needed in studies of literacy in the digital age, as has occurred in philosophy, science, fashion design, engineering, information technology, organisational and management studies, in addition to education, that reinforces the idea of constitutive entanglement.

Intersections between Socio-material and Socio-spatial Approaches

The distinctive features and connections between the socio-material and socio-spatial approaches are also worth parsing. The book by Fenwick *et al.* (2011) traces the socio-material, devoting two chapters exclusively to spatial theory within this framing, positioning spatial theory alongside complexity theory, actor-network theory and cultural historical activity theory. Within spatial theory, they distinguish between four clusters of spatial thought, of which only the fourth is concerned with debates about the framing of matter and the material (Barad, 2007). This is based on Anderson and Wylie's (2009) view that there has been a recent shift from conceiving of space as abstract to a materialist turn in spatial framing. This newer view of the entangled nature of space and matter is associated with what they call an (im)mobilities paradigm of Urry (2007). They see that the primacy of human agency is not assumed, because as Urry (2007: 45) notes: '...human life ... is never just human'.

Interestingly, Fenwick and colleagues (2011: 129) define spatiality as '... the socio-material effects and relations of space', which is aligned to their purpose to research human-material interaction within educational systems. It is important to note that this definition is not generalisable to spatial theories more broadly. It is not certain in Fenwick and colleagues' (2011) reading of the spatial theories of Soja, Lefebvre and Massey, how these theorists are explicitly connected to a socio-material approach for educational research. Edward Soja's (1989) hugely influential book, *Postmodern Geographies*, provides a bird's eye perspective of the city of Los Angeles. A spatial thinker of huge influence, Soja's work has still been criticised for its lack of attention to human-material relations (a strength of the socio-material), presenting '...a morphology of landscape that...is rarely disturbed by human forms' (Gregory, 1994: 301).

Similarly, Lefebvre's (1991) central thesis is that geographical space is fundamentally social – space is socially produced. His theories focus on how spatial relations across territories, such as cities, landscapes and ownership of property, are given cultural meaning (Shields, 2011). These concerns are somewhat removed from the socio-material notions of assemblages of human-material relations.

Another key contribution to spatial theory, Massey's (2005) *For Space*, addresses regional questions, globalisation and identity formation, making powerful arguments for the connectedness of space, its multiplicity and its openness. She theorises that, 'The spatial is integral to the production of history, and thus, to the possibility of politics, just as the temporal is to geography' (Massey, 1994: 269). Her spatial thinking has contributed to understanding how industries make strategic use of regional differences in systems of gender relations, and to theorisations of space, regions and economic processes (Callard, 2011). Again, while there is a focus on entanglements of space, politics, gender, identity and so on, it is space rather than matter that really matters.

It is considered here that spatial theory historically embraces a much more heterogeneous collection of conceptualisations than those with socio-materialist ideals. For example, of the sixty *Key Thinkers of Space and Place*, the edited book by Hubbard and Kitchen (2011), the term 'material' is not given a position in the index. However, one spatial theorist whose work has more clearly contributed to both actor-network theory and socio-material understandings of social space is Latour, alongside Callon and Law (Laurier, 2011). For Latour and others associated with Actor Network Theory, space and time are effects of the socio-material relations between heterogeneous elements, thus shifting away from abstract Euclidean concepts of space and time as universal enablers or constrainers of social action (Latour, 1997). Latour describes the nature of space as topological, constituted of relations between its parts. So it is with Latour that we begin to see a significant synergy of the spatial and socio-material theory.

One of the more controversial elements of Latour's conceptualisations is the anti-anthropocentric idea of social actants, which can be human or non-human. Prior to Latour and other socio-material thinkers, the agency of things was often limited to debates about animal rights or artificial intelligence, not to seemingly sundry, inanimate objects (Laurier, 2011). For literacy, the relations between the policy makers, the circulation of texts, the media, the children, the teachers, the parents, the organisational structure of schools, the digital devices, the design of the interfaces, the networks of online practices, the text books markets, the digital infrastructure and so on, take on significance.

For the purpose of developing theoretical tools for generating knowledge of literacy practices in the present volume, socio-material and socio-spatial theories are given distinct attention with important conceptual differences. This is because socio-spatial literacy theories, as developed by theorists in the last 10 years, draw from spatial thinkers in social geography, who essentially examine the role of social space in shaping cultural, economic and political life. There are transformative potentials of socio-spatial literacy approaches because one's socio-spatial positioning in relation to literacy is not seen as immutable and fixed, but dynamic and open to transformation through collective action. The conceptual emphasis is on social space, not on examining relations between all forms of matter more broadly conceived. Yet questions about the materiality of space are still relevant to the spatial theorist. Sheehy and Leander (2004: 3) have contended that literacy spaces have sometimes been 'over-determined' by a 'seemingly natural interpretation' of space as a fixed material setting, container or place. In this respect, literacy spaces have sometimes been 'over-materialised', and yet at other times conceived as an abstract metaphor '...without material substance'.

The aims of socio-spatial literacy theory are clearly distinct from those of the socio-material, since spatial theory opens up new empirical insights about the dialectic between literacy practices and their distribution and movement across spaces and geographies – in cities, in suburbs, in rural areas, in the centres, in the margins and across borders. It can shed light on the socio-spatial construction of literacy and gender, ethnicity and class relations, lived spaces, identity formation, cultural hybridities and the political geography of literacy practices (Soja, 2004: x).

Conversely, socio-material literacy approaches stem from recent philosophical understandings of the dynamic relations between the human and non-human objects (see Orlikowski, 2007). In particular, there is a clear notion that materiality is not pre-formed substance, but is a recursive entanglement of the social and material, which emerge in ongoing relations and practices (see Latour, 2005). The emphasis is not on what space or place symbolises within social action, but on the agentive effects of networks of materials – human, non-human, tangible and intangible (see Pels et al., 2002). The major implication for literacy research is a very different emphasis on the nature of socio-material assemblages, whether of laptops, bodies, minds, regions, policies, markets, arrangements, infrastructure and texts – how the histories of those objects influence the present, and how they actively mediate literacy practices.

Socio-material literacy approaches are not concerned with techno-centric perspectives of literacy, such as how the material tools such as iPads or pencils leverage literacy practices. Neither are socio-material approaches interested in human-centred interpretations of literacy practices that focus exclusively on how learners use the affordances of the materials at hand. Rather, socio-material literacy approaches focus on how human-tool assemblages are constitutively entangled in everyday literacy practices. The materials of literacy, the realities of literacy, are interpreted as relational outcomes, rather than researched as existing in and of themselves (Law, 2004).

Implications of Socio-material Literacies for Practice

The application of socio-material approaches to classroom practice, such as through artifactual literacies, is about reimagining pedagogy and policy with a greater awareness of how objects or materials function in learning. It widens research of literacy practices to attend to the complex ecologies, or assemblages and arrangements of actors and objects, digital or non-digital. Socio-material literacy studies can help to answer questions, such as:

- What is the nature of the relationship between artefacts and stories?
- What role do materials play in literacy learning?
- How do materials represent identities, cultures and memories?
- How do the meanings embedded in textual materials connect communities?

The concept of community is understood here, not as reified, but as dynamic, contested and often viewed differently by children and adults (Pahl & Rowsell, 2010). The socio-materiality of literacy practices has the potential to highlight how classrooms or communities function as ecologies of literacy practices, how objects are circulated and involved in border crossing between social sites, and how they help to bridge understanding of family, community or cultural histories and heritage across time.

To apply socio-material theory to research, the researcher begins by asking questions about social practices and their material relations to objects and bodies. The researcher then attends, observationally and through dialogue with research participants, to how the literacy or classroom practice is being done or enacted in the particular social context. Whether of literacy practices at home, in public transport, in the mall, at school, at university, in a library or a workplace, social practice or action still matters.

The socio-material researcher attends to relations between objects and actors and their assemblages, including their location or position in the social sites. Rather than seeking to find and describe an independent, singular, coherent practice, one focuses on how the concert of practices and objects function and are held together. This includes the entanglement of materials, hardware, software, internet pages and actors that are brought together in particular digital literacy practices, and what are the temporal and spatial patterns of practice. Finally, one considers any contradictions, anomalies and paradoxes (Law, 2012).

Another approach is to begin with materials or artefacts that are central to literacy practice. A useful heuristic for interrogating the meanings of artefacts is provided by Pahl and Rowsell, who consider the following six trajectories of inquiry with questions I have adapted:

- Mode and Media: What combinations of modes and media are salient in the artefact, and what are their attendant meanings?
- Production: How was the artefact made and why? To what other materials or actors is the object connected?
- Time: How does the artefact relate to time? When was it created and how have its meanings changed over time?
- Space: What spaces has the artefact inhabited, and where has it travelled?
- Value: What is the value of the artefact and to whom is it valued?
- Power: How is the artefact implicated in power relations? (e.g. policies to regulate literacy practices, commercial products tied to global corporations)
- Role: What is the role of the artefact in social interactions, and to the culture in which it is embedded?

To elaborate on the role of artefacts in social interaction, we can consider the research on children's talk and its relation to drawing or other textual objects (Dyson, 1993). Children's talk in literacy learning is often referential to children's experiences, and to other texts, and there are important translations that occur between talk and semiotic objects. Objects are semiotic because they are bound up with the act of meaning making (Pahl & Rowsell, 2010). In my research of claymation movie making, I have demonstrated how the three dimensional plasticine figures were objects that embodied the identities of their makers through the materials, such as braiding wool for hair on the figures, to represent their own likeness (Mills, 2011c). Artefacts are often biographical, and can be an important springboard for children or adults to narrate the self, to recall emotions, and to mediate social and learning relationships.

New Directions for Socio-material Literacies

Mobile devices and other emerging platforms for online communication are part of the reconfigured social and material dimensions of literacy practices. Indeed, they constitute part of the modified socio-material assemblages that act upon literacy learning over the life course. Both the materials for the production of texts, and the range of cultural artefacts that constitute literacy, are altered (Graddol, 1994; Hall, 2000). Yet socio-material research is currently only marginal in literacy studies. This is despite its well-developed presence across a number of disciplines, such as material culture studies, science and technology studies, social geography, environmental studies and gender studies (Fenwick & Landri, 2012). Sorenson (2009: 2) believes that in education more broadly there has been an apparent '...blindness toward the question of how educational practice is affected by materials'.

The application of socio-material theory to literacy research, particularly in a digital age of traceable networks of textual practices, can potentially open up new trajectories of knowledge. While there are many methodological ways of doing socio-material research, the hallmark of socio-material inquiry is that everything, whether of the natural or social world, is regarded as continuously generated assemblages of relations. Nothing is researched as existing in a vacuum, or researched without recognising those relations (Law, 2008).

Future directions for socio-material research may involve mapping the processes through which literacy policies, media news and artefacts are produced, with a need to map less transparent objects of analysis than previous studies of published documents (Hamilton, 2001). These include the processes and social struggles in the production and implementation of literacy policies, curriculum documents and journalistic news in which literacy surfaces as a public agenda. Studies may document the struggles between actors and texts in meetings, conversations and back regions that are connected to processes of literacy research, classroom practice and literacy reform agendas in institutions of higher education. This may include the highly contested and often politically regulated arenas of college entrance requirements and pre-service teacher education.

The nature of the relationship between new digital technologies, literacy practices and other materials is always undergoing subtle and sometimes radical shifts. As Leander (2010: 202) sees, '...digital media and popular culture are not merely being "connected" to classrooms...not simply integrated (as a project of domestication), but are rather actively reshaping our assumed genres and roles concerning pedagogy and schooling'. Exponential intensities of change in the way we do literacy, in the seeming maturation of postmodernity, globalisation, neoliberal capitalist agendas, new mobilities, new risks and new interactional online orders, call for socio-material approaches to understand these phenomena.

And while researchers in postcolonial societies have investigated the effects of many material elements and digital and social practices within educational institutions, less is known about the materiality of schooling within developing countries (Fuller, 1987). Socio-material researchers are well positioned to ask: Under what social and material conditions and processes do children become literate in developing countries, and among marginalised groups (e.g. rural, poor, migrant) in postcolonial societies?

In conclusion, research on literacy must begin to examine and acknowledge the material bases of literacy practices. In the array of digital composition tools and interfaces available today, whether by tablet, smartphone, or smartpen, the materiality of the technology influences the social and cognitive processes through which texts are produced. As Haas (1996: 74) demonstrated through her interviews with digital composition authors: 'Spatial, visual and tactile elements of writing profoundly shape writers' experiences with different technologies...'. These can include constraints as well as affordances for different social purposes. In a world in which material technologies of encoding and decoding are more novel and varied than the past, ignoring the materiality of literacy practices is hardly possible (Haas, 1996).

7 Sensory Literacies

Without our bodies – our sensing abilities – we do not have a world...
(Arola & Wysocki, 2012: 3)

Key Concepts of Sensory Literacies

In this chapter I propose a new approach which I have coined 'sensory literacies'. I also highlight areas of intersection with other established approaches to literacy practice. The sensory literacies approach is a revitalised way of thinking about the multisensoriality of literacy and communication practices, including their technologies of mediation and production. Such a view is grounded in an established research tradition in the social sciences that has foregrounded the sensorial nature of human experience, perception, knowing and practising, and which draws from anthropology, sociology and philosophy of the senses (Pink, 2009). While there has been a recognised sensorial direction in the anthropology of the senses (Howes, 2003), I see the potential of theorising the sensoriality of literacy practice, that is, deriving from or relating to the senses, across a diversity of cultures (see Mills *et al.*, 2013; Ranker & Mills, 2014).

Theorists, such as Abram (1997) in his highly cited work, *The Spell of the Sensuous*, have awakened a paradigm shift that emphasises the body and its connections to the natural world in language, without renouncing rationality. There are now recognised versions of sensory scholarship, (Stoller, 1997), sensuous ethnography (Stoller, 2004), sensual methodology (Warren, 2008), and sensuous geographies of the body and place (Rodaway, 1994). The social sciences have given attention to the sensoriality of culture (Howes, 2005), the sensoriality of film (MacDougall, 2005), the sensoriality of architecture (Pallasmaa, 2005), the sociology of the senses (Simmel, 1997 [1907]), the sensoriality of teamwork in medical procedures (Hindmarsh & Pilnick, 2007), the sensoriality of laundering (Pink, 2005), the sensoriality of gardening (Tilley, 2006), the sensoriality of cooking and the sensoriality of memory (Sutton, 2006).

It is important to acknowledge at the outset that the corporeal acknowledgment of the bodily dimension of literacy practice does not conflict with established principles of socio-cultural literacy studies, outlined in Chapter 2 of this volume. Rather, by acknowledging different communities of practice and their diverse bodily ways of making meaning, socio-cultural views of literacy can support sensory approaches by illuminating cultural frames of reference for somatic literacy practices across culture, sub-cultures and social sites.

Senses and literacy practices

The sensoriality of literacy includes the aesthetic enjoyment of a film, curling up with a book on the sofa, and the entanglement of the body and senses in sensory walks with a camera (see Pink, 2009). In the context of a widened array of hybrid digital technologies affording heightened interactivity, increased mobility and convergence with multiple platforms, the sensoriality of literacy practices is constantly shifting. For example, the sensation of human movement and gestures is now fundamental to game playing with motion-sensing technologies. Full-body, three-dimensional, motion-capture technologies offer different sensory affordances in game consoles, such Xbox Kinect. Without touching the screen, players use gross motor skills, such as dancing, bending, jumping, kicking, turning, swaying, locomotion and motioning with the arms to compete in game play. Nintendo DS games held in the palm of the hand are frequently responsive to the players' verbal instructions and deliberate blowing of breath into the device, in addition to the continual movement of the stylus controlled by the user on the screen.

Haptics – pertaining to touch – is also central to the touch screen controls of iPad games, e-books and smartphone applications, and software platforms for drawing and writing are frequently responsive to a tilt or shake of the mobile device. Many game technologies are also visually responsive, with features of eye tracking or pinpointing the user's eye-movements to alleviate the need for haptic controls, such as mouse, touch screen or track pad. Users positioned correctly in front of the computer or device can simply gaze at screen commands to select program options. The recent changes to the purview of interactive technologies for responding to human movement, touch, breath, gaze and other sensory forms calls for new approaches to literacy research that go beyond disembodied views of texts and textual practices to foreground the body and the senses.

Clearly, our bodies and the bodies of others are central to the practical accomplishment of literacy in its many communication forms, requiring bodily interaction with material technologies, whether a book, paint, pen or digital device. It is not that the technologies of communication have made the senses matter for the first time to literacy practice. Even the most historically widespread forms of communication, such as oral language, depend upon the body – voice, posture, movement, gestures, gaze and so on. Rather, the rapid expansion of technical affordances of communication technologies, from predominantly typographic keyboard-controlled interfaces of static desk-top computers, to a broadened range of user interfaces with affordances for multisensorial interactivity, draws attention to the increasingly dynamic and indispensable role of the senses and the mobility of the body in human communication. A sensorial approach is needed to enable digital literacy researchers in the 21st century to interpret and theorise embodied literacy practice, particularly in the context of increased affordances of multisensory response technologies for communication.

The body and literacy

Approaches to the sensoriality of literacy practice currently exist as a growing collection of studies that acknowledge the role of the body and embodiment in encoding and decoding (Mills *et al.*, 2013; Nespor, 1997; Ranker & Mills, 2014). However, this emerging corpus of research currently lacks a systematic theoretical framework in literacy studies. The sensorial approach to literacy advanced here, first acknowledges that when humans communicate with one another, with or without digital technologies, the body is central to the practical enactment of the interaction. Therefore, the body should be explicitly foregrounded in any theory about the process of meaning making. As Scollon and Scollon interpret (2003: 45), 'Our bodies as humans cannot fail to anchor us in the real, physical world in which we are performing as social actors'. Thus, sensory approaches to literacy and digital practices focus on the embodied activity of human beings – a distinctive feature of sensory approaches to digital literacy practice.

At the same time, such approaches do not take for granted either the role of a knowing mind, nor that of the material technologies that support meaning-making (Haas, 1996). The mind is not separated from the body, nor the role of the body taken for granted; rather, both mind and body are seen as integral to literacy practice. Such a view repositions the body in the recognition of the primacy of active, sensing beings to all embodied social action. Literacy is an embodied activity, and the body plays a fundamental role in literacy practices across a wide range of technology-mediated forms.

At the same time, sensory approaches do not deify or exalt the body – they merely acknowledge the forgotten role of the senses in literacy practice.

Embodied acts in social life incorporate a plethora of social and cultural forms, from everyday skills, such as gardening, cooking or riding a bike, to specialised cultural performances such as dancing, sport, music and art. Embodied acts are also central to occupational duties, such as the surgical procedures of a doctor, the deftness with which a stylist cuts hair, or the embodied speech, gaze, gestures and movements of a seasoned public speaker. Social acts generate an enormous range of embodied knowledge, which are often systematised, and which include successfully accomplishing certain cultural conventions. These culturally and socially learned repertoires of action and uses of the body constitute social life (Mauss, 1979).

Tensions for Sensory Literacies

Key tensions within sensory approaches beyond literacy are addressed in this section. Debates about the senses in other fields have concerned the historical dominance of ocularcentrism, or privileging the visual over other senses such as audio, tactile, olfactory, taste and kinesis or movement, within the social sciences more broadly, and in semiotic theory more specifically. I also address debates concerning the dominance of words over other senses in theories of meaning making, arguing for a return to research that addresses the multisensoriality of literacy practice.

Dominance of the visual

There are many accounts in the social sciences of a long period of ocularcentrism – the dominance of the visual over other human forms of perception – across many disciplines (Howes, 1991; Porteous, 1990; Stoller, 1989). In modern Western societies there has been a widespread view that what is seen through the eyes is objective truth (empiricism). Theorists such as Ingold (2000) and Pink (2009) warn against the assumptions of visualism, holding that the visual dimensions of human action should be considered in interrelationship with other senses. This is because embodied practices, including literacy, are constituted and experienced multisensorially, including experiences of sight, sound, touch, posture, movement, smell, taste and other forms of bodily awareness (e.g. inner emotions, external temperature). In particular, some theorists have recently drawn attention to the neglect of haptics or tactility in technology research (Paterson, 2007). Pandya's (1993) work demonstrated the power of olfactory senses and identity in Ongee culture in which individual identity in Ongee society in the Little Andeman Islands can be defined by one's body odour (Pink, 2009). Similarly, Porteous (1990) researched the smellscapes and soundscapes involved in various human experiences. Still others, such as Ingold (2008), have demonstrated a case for understanding the world as perceived through the feet and human locomotion. While theorists sometimes focus on one sense or another, they are generally united by the view that: 'We need to encourage a democracy of the senses, rather than a hegemony of sight' (Arola & Wysocki, 2012: 7).

The implications of these historical developments within sensory theories is that sensorial approaches to literacy may become subject to similar criticisms, that is, a hegemony of sight, if attention is not given to the interplay of more than one human sense. Sensory approaches account for the aggregation of more than one sense, and the interrelationships between them in meaning making. Such approaches to literacy explicitly need to account for the central role of the senses and the body in meaning making, extending these beyond the visual.

Dominance of words

Within academic accounts of human experience, there has also historically been a dominance of words over the senses (Howes, 1991). Referred to as 'verbocentric' accounts of experience, theorists suggest that researchers have not given enough attention to understanding the role of the senses in the generation of knowledge, and within relationships between the researchers and participants (Bendix, 2000; Pink, 2009). More recently, there has been a surge of ethnographic research that extends beyond purely written accounts of the lives of research participants to include corporeal elements of the researcher-researched relationship, exploring questions about the culture and the senses in human experience (Pink, 2009).

Within the field of semiotics, Kress and Bezemer (2008) maintain that writing is no longer the central mode of representation in educational contexts. For example, web-based educational sites, videos, media and textbooks are typically multimodal, with many combining visual, audio, spatial, gestural and linguistic elements (Kress, 2000b). They draw attention to two key trends influencing semiotics: (i) digital media are becoming more prevalent than printed books as sites of textual display, and (ii) image is displacing writing as the dominant mode of representation. Kress and Bezemer call for greater attention to be given to visual and other modes, particularly given the rapid convergence of technologies for multimodal design.

I envisage that while recent decades have seen a shift from the dominance of words to dominance of the image, and later to focus on multimodal meanings, there will be a renewed interest in the multisensorial nature of human experience, particularly literacy practices that are mediated by sensory-attuned technologies. The increasing affordances of digital technologies to capture the corporeal engagement of the whole body in communication necessitate a shift in the current emphases of literacy theories.

Recent Developments in Sensory Literacies

Power and sensory literacies

Examining the intersection of power and the body in sites of social discipline can strengthen research that prioritises the role of the body and the senses in literacy practices (e.g. Luke, 1992). For example, Foucault (1980) postulates that power influences society at the deep-seated level of desire, and also in relation to knowledge. Power permeates the minutiae of elementary existence and social life, and the relations that govern our bodies, including gestures, and which influence our behaviours (Foucault, 1980). Foucault recognised the embodied ways in which power influences humans '...who are gradually...and materially constituted through a multiplicity of organisms, forces, energies, materials, desires, [and] thoughts...' (Foucault, 1980: 97). From Foucault's perspective, power and the body are central to the enactment of social life.

Embodiment theory and power are implicated in the making of class, gender and racial divides. Corporeal performances of the body are constantly evolving as people conform to naturalised ways of being, constituted by the intersection of political and economic relations (Hubbard & Kitchen, 2011). Oppressive or enabling institutional forces and social relationships shape our sensorial experiences. For example, in Luke's (1992) article, 'The Body Literate', he demonstrates how literacy practices are inscribed on the literate body of students in a Year 1 classroom engaged in a whole-class reading time. Luke elaborates Bourdieu's (1973) description of language acquisition, where the emphasis is on the institutional and class-based shaping of body habitus (Luke, 1992). Bourdieu (1977: 660) posits that, 'Language learning is one dimension of the learning of a total body schema...'. The habitus is the unifying principle at the foundation of linguistic practices, which becomes a 'marker and proscription' of one's class position and relation to the language market (Luke, 1992: 113).

The body and power both figure prominently in Foucault's (1977b: 148) understanding of the body as an 'inscribed surface of events'. Discourses are forms of power that '...literally and metaphorically inscribe the collective and individual social body' (Luke, 1992: 112). Similarly, power and the body are central to Bourdieu's theorisation of the hexis of the body in class based patterns of language and literacy acquisition that begin even before the start of formal schooling. This is because 'the body is an instrument that records its previous uses, and which, although continuously modified by them, gives greater weight to the earlier of them; it contains...the trace and memory of the social events' (Bourdieu, 1977: 660).

Literacy and digital practices in any social site involve the body, and as Luke expresses aptly: 'teachers inscribe and read the student body as the surface of the mind' (Luke, 1992: 118). Teachers observe the children's bodily movements, postures, gestures, direction of gaze, voice and so on, like a window to gauge their investment in learning. Power is central to sensorial approaches to literacy and digital practices of communication, given the centrality of bodily hexis, and the traces and memories of literate and digital media practices inscribed in the bodies of social actors. For example, children typically learn the directionality of reading, correct pencil hold, written letter and number formation, and keyboard skills, through bodily control and repetition in the early years of schooling. In essence, the '...regulated body remembers' (Luke, 1992: 114). Literacy practices, whether using paper or pixels, become inscribed in our bodily memory.

Place in sensorial approaches

Sensorial approaches to literacy may foreground the role of place and its connection with the senses in human experience and learning. There is an emplaced nature of sensory experiences, and also of meaning making. For example, everyday literacy experiences are seen to influence, and be influenced by, one's sensory experience of place, whether filming one's experiences of visits to different places, deriving writing inspiration from being in a certain place, or being socialised in the literacy practices that belong to a place.

The connections between the senses and place have been examined in cultural geography as early as the 1990s, but have not yet been systematically applied to literacy studies. For example, Rodaway (1994) saw the senses as an important means of structuring or defining spaces and places. Without the senses we cannot truly know or understand places. Theorists of embodiment, such as Coffey (1999) and Shilling (1991), also began to account for the situated nature of the knowledgeable body as humans negotiate the spatial context of social action. Knowledge is not based on abstract formulations in the mind, but is contingent on the sensing, corporeal body in places. Similarly, Howes (2005) has put forward the idea of emplacement to draw attention to the multisensory relationship between body, mind and place.

Literacy is an emplaced practice. The idea of being emplaced is extended by Pink (2009) to explain the foundations of sensory ethnography. This is to adequately account for the relationship between bodies, minds and the materially of space as ethnographers and participants of research. Aligning her methodology with Ingold's (2000) view of emplacement, Pink sees that any skilled activity is the outworking of a complex set of relations between people, their minds and whole bodies, and richly structured social environments. Pink observes that there is a focused engagement with the substance we work with in many situations, involving emplaced engagement with objects and other human beings. While these understanding of the sensoriality of the body in place have burgeoned in social geography and anthropology, I see that there is potential for these to be extended to understanding literacy practices, and continually emerging literacy practices that are mediated by digital technologies. Literacy practices cannot be performed without the body and mind, or without interaction with the tangible materials and skills that are part of a social field, contextualised, and enacted in particular places.

A significant application of ideas about the entanglement of the body, the senses and place in theories of meaning making is Scollon and Scollon's (2003) theory of geosemiotics. An essential argument of geosemiotics is that humans live and communicate in a world of real places. For example, their volume on geosemiotics – *Discourses in Place: Language in the Material World* – says more about the connections between place and meaning in a material world than about the multisensoriality of meaning making, but nevertheless touches on emplaced and embodied meanings of signs. Scollon and Scollon explore the connections between the body, senses and place in sign making. For example, they discuss the semiotics of street performers who take on the role of 'human statues' in public places, who stand lifeless and motionless as part of the built environment, while simultaneously being a social actor. Such scenes of social action blur the distinction between place and action, since such social performances very much emplace meanings, which are contingent on being part of a place.

To understand the connections between space and the senses consider how Hall (1969) categorises five types of sensorial or perceptual space: visual space, auditory space, olfactory space, thermal space and haptic space. Each of these refers to the spatial boundaries or limits of what an individual can perceive. For example, one can see to the next wall or building, hear the airplane several kilometres away, smell a neighbour's dinner cooking, touch within arm's reach, and feel, in terms of temperature, the distance to a fireplace to sense warmth. We often selectively give more attention to visual and auditory spatial meanings, while giving less attention to olfactory, thermal and haptic semiotic zones. The potentials of sensory approaches to literacy are grounded in the realisation that literacy activities are performed and limited by these sensory and spatial zones. Even though words can transport one's mind to another world, and technologies can enable one to interact with others who are spatially distant, these interactions are still limited in various ways by one's corporeal body within one's perceptual space. Sensorial literacies give attention to the interaction of multiple senses in one's perceptual space in literacy practices.

Embodiment and literacy practice

The centrality of the body has been largely under emphasised in literacy studies (Haas, 1996), yet embodied social practices have been theorised in relation to the discourses of professional firefighting (Lloyd, 2007), jazz music playing (Wilf, 2010), learning physics through augmented reality experiments (Enyedy et al., 2012), early childhood learning (Clark, 2011), bike riding to participate in town-planning (Headrick Taylor & Hall, 2013), doll-making (Stein, 2006) and modelling claymation figures to be digitally filmed (Mills, 2010a). Embodiment theory has been usefully applied to domestic arts, such as the literacies of artisans as they preserve recipes, which is a type of knowledge gained not by reading, but by experience and labour (Wall, 2010).

In this section, I propose that literacy as digital practices can also be usefully theorised in terms of the sensorial, tangible and corporeal nature of both human experience and communication. I draw on research that specifically illuminates the sensorial nature of literacy practices. By acknowledging the inextricable relations between literacy and the body in context, we can give attention to the corporeal foundations of all forms of literacy practices, from speech that is produced by the body, to the central role of the body in the production and distribution of textual products.

We can theorise embodiment in literacy practices in very concrete and obvious ways. As Haas (1996: 226) posits: 'Certainly writing can be understood as embodied practice... the body is the mechanism by which the mediation of the mental and the material occurs'. Haas (1996: 226) contends that a writer's bodily movements and interactions, particularly movement of the hands and eyes, are evident in the conduct of everyday literacy activities. Yet she notes that the whole body is necessary for writing:

> Writers pick up and chew their pencils, they rest their hands on keyboards, they hunch over manuscript... stretch out with books under trees... and move through on-line texts by pushing keys or clicking buttons. (Haas, 1996)

Writers' relationships to their texts are embodied in the most intimate of ways, because writers have no other way of producing text or interacting with it than through their bodies (Haas, 1996). Yet embodiment theory is more than a simple acknowledgement that our interaction with texts involves tangible bodies and materials. More importantly, it acknowledges that the complex socialisation of individuals into different communities of literacy and digital practice fundamentally constitutes a process of embodiment.

While the reading of novels and other literature often requires a linear reading from beginning to end, theorists of writing composition have described how the writing process is messy, dynamic and embodied. Until recently, the role of the body in writing has received little attention in research and theory, as if writing processes are independent of the body. Dolmage (2012: 121) identifies this oversight: 'As a discipline, broadly speaking, we in composition and rhetoric have not acknowledged that we have a body, bodies; we cannot admit that…our work has material, corporeal bases, effects and affects'.

In arguing for a recognition of the body in the writing process, Dolmage (2012), who approaches writing processes from disability studies, warns against normative assumptions of the body that writes – of marginalising those whose bodies do not conform. Arguably, a good proportion of writing pedagogies tend to focus on able bodies, rather than all bodies. This is not surprising since '…dominant pedagogies privilege those who can most easily ignore their bodies' (Dolmage, 2012: 111).

Pedagogies for teaching writing, where the body is concerned, centre on the need to control and discipline the writing body – on standards of correct and streamlined writing, rather than the real fissures, gaps and messiness of the writing processes. Anyone who writes knows that writing rarely occurs as a linear process, from left-to-right, and at an even pace from beginning to end, without revisions or variable patterns of entering, engaging with, reviewing, modifying or forgetting the text (Emig, 1971). However, as Dolmage (2012: 211) contends, 'The desire to impede this messiness is the desire to ignore the body, its attachments, its ennoblements and limitations'. This leads to a focus instead on a venerated and flawless final written product, while bodily and material means of production are seemingly invisible and forgotten.

Literacy practices, including their digitally mediated forms, are ways of communicating with others through situated, embodied, social and material contexts. The body is a vital locus of information that possesses its own narrative (Lloyd, 2007). Embodied literacy learning foregrounds the role of the body in social contexts in which there is a flow of knowledge between members of the practice, shared discourses and stories, and socialisation of the whole person into situated ways of being with textual practices. This view takes into account Wenger's (1998: 125) idea of 'communities of practice' to describe how sensory learning occurs. It is through meaningful corporeal connections and meetings between people, texts and technologies, rather than through the development of skills and minds alone, that individuals can transition from novices to expert members of the community of literacy practice.

Gee (2005) uses the notion of affinity spaces to emphasise the shared configuration of virtual spaces in which people interact, as opposed to membership in a geographically proximal community. An example of this is multiplayer online games, such as Minecraft, and its associated networks of gaming tip wikis and YouTube videos of Minecraft players enjoying the game. These online affinity spaces support shared discourses, knowledge and particular ways of being in the online gaming community that socialise newcomers into the play space. Gergen (1999: 237) observes, 'Individuals mentally construct the world, but they do so largely with categories supplied by social relationships'. These social relationships, whether online or offline, are embodied interactions within shared and collective affinity spaces.

The concept of embodiment draws on understandings of situated practice and culturally based systems of learning and communicating. Embodiment theory, drawing on situated learning developed by learning theorists, such as Connerton (1989), Johnson (1987), Lave (1993) and Lave and Wenger (1991), emphasises that '...an embodied practice is a culturally sanctioned, culturally learned activity that is accomplished by individual human beings moving through time and space' (Haas, 1996: 225).

A more widespread corporeal or somatic move toward embodiment in the social sciences can be identified as early as the late 1970s in selected works of Foucault (1977a), which shifted thinking from abstract and 'disembodied' views of social phenomena to give attention to the body. Literacy has similarly been viewed as a set of abstract skills in the 1950s (Mills, 2005), and later as largely contingent upon mental schemas by cognitive theorists of reading comprehension (Anstey & Bull, 2004). Functional grammar and genre theorists following Halliday (1989) influenced the teaching of written genres in Australia and Britain and drew attention to the metalanguages – naming the text structure and grammatical features of genres for different purposes. These approaches have contributed complementary understandings of literacy practice, but need to be coupled with an acknowledgment of the embodied ways of interacting with print and digital texts that play a taken-for-granted role in digital communications with different media.

The senses matter because the nature of our bodily interactions with screen-based texts are changing more quickly than in the past. No longer are writing bodies always seated upright at a desk with pen and paper, or at a desktop computer. Writers are frequently mobile bodies. Using mobile devices, such as smartphones and tablets, writing can be done anywhere and anytime, and potentially shared instantly with worldwide audiences of other stationary or mobile bodies. Any digitally-mediated literacy practice is essentially an embodied practice that is a 'culturally sanctioned, culturally learned activity, accomplished by individual human beings moving through time and space' (Haas, 1996: 225).

An embodied view of literacy, and writing in particular, extends Ingold's phenomenological view of the senses which follows in the existential phenomenology of Merleau-Ponty (2002). However, it is important to note that a sensory literacies approach differs from Merleau-Ponty's view of the equivalence of seeing and hearing, which is also reflected in Ingold's (2000) theories of the senses. The emphasis on the whole, immediately experiencing and perceiving body, can become decontextualised from sociological and anthropological understandings. It can obscure research on the history and anthropology of the senses that demonstrates the differential elaboration of the senses throughout different cultures and across time (see Howes & Classen, 2014). This is an important point of difference between Howes' (2014) and Ingold's approaches to understanding the senses, which was foregrounded in Howes' opening chapter of this volume. The social significance of particular individual senses is well supported by ethnographic evidence demonstrating that across varied cultural contexts, sensory experiences and categories take on different meanings. An example is the significance of smelling one's own bodily odour among the Ongee in the Andaman Islands (Classen, 1993b: 113), which contrasts the suppression of natural bodily odours in other societies.

The concept of embodiment in sensory literacies also extends Bourdieu's concept of habitus (1985), which has been theorised in relation to broader interdisciplinary, phenomenological emphasis on the senses across a range of domains of social practice. The concept of embodiment and literacy practice is one that allows for the human agency of the text user, and is active rather than passive. It also takes into account later work in the somatic turn that promotes a more active and dynamic view of habitus than Bourdieu. For example, Williams' (1982) semasiology, that is, theory of human body language, brought together ideals of action, discourse and embodiment. Williams built on earlier theories of embodiment to give greater attention to embodied social action, repositioning the body as moving, dynamic and active, rather than proscriptive and based largely on one's early socialisation (Farnell, 2012).

Interest and the mediation of the senses

The senses are the immediate source of human knowledge, and as some have theorised, can include innate awareness and impressions

(Montessori-Pierson, 1991). A key issue regarding the role of the senses in children's knowledge formation is the concept of 'interest' – that is, the selective attention that humans give to certain aspects of their environment. Interest is vital in understanding the role of the senses in literacy learning because readers and writers attend to the sensory information in their environment actively, selectively and discerningly. As Montessori describes:

> In the world around us, we do not see everything...only some things that suit us... We do not concentrate our attention haphazardly, but according to an inner drive. (Montessori, 1913: 185)

Theorists such as Locke (1690) and Hume (1975) have similarly reasoned that direct sensation and reflection upon those sensory experiences is the origin of ideas and knowledge, providing a fundamental basis for learning throughout the life course. Montessori extends this knowledge of the role of the senses by highlighting the active work of the senses – the highly selective work of the learner to focus attention on particular sensory stimuli. Shifting one's attention to prioritise certain sensations over others can typically be learned. Certain sensory knowledge becomes relevant experience to the learner through the learner's interests, who attunes their focus on particular sensory information in discerning, organised, classificatory and discriminate ways. It is the learner's interest that gives shape and direction to knowledge. To Montessori, these are not a priori structures of cognition, but innate tendencies or drives that are demonstrated in sensitive periods of attunement or privileging of certain sensory experiences over others (Frierson, 2014).

Central to sensory literacies is the recognition that sensory experiences are mediated through mental frameworks, which enable sensory experiences to be both interpreted and extended to abstractions beyond the material world, and which can bring coherence to identify and organise the relations among experiences. Learning through the senses also involves interest-driven cultivation, because new interests can be developed and directed by others, leading to active engagement. In other words, the way humans exercise their senses is not static or fixed, but is dynamic and malleable.

Intersections between Sensory and Multimodal Literacy Paradigms

The convergences and divergences between sensory and multimodal literacies are given priority here, as these paradigms have shared characteristics, and more importantly, unique orientations. Given that sensory literacies is an emergent formulation, attention to the key concepts of power, place and the body in the previous section has already alluded to points of concord with critical, spatial and material literacies. I have also indicated at the outset of this chapter how socio-cultural understandings provide a foundation for sensory literacies. At an elemental level, the socio-cultural differentiation of literacy practices across cultures and communities is the same basis upon which the sensorial dimensions of perception and communication may be researched. In addition, sensory literacy theorists share a resistance toward privileging words over other forms of communication, a view that is maintained by socio-cultural and multimodal literacy theorists.

The following two central assumptions are shared by sensory and multimodal literacy theories: (a) meaning making occurs through multiple representational and interpretative modes that are co-present and interactive; and (b) communication acts are fundamentally social, and shaped by cultural, political and historical use.

To elaborate, the first principle is an acknowledgement of the multiple ways of perceiving and communicating in the world. Both sensory and multimodal theories emphasise the whole body in meaning making (Kress, 2000b), even though multimodal approaches have been critiqued for emphasising some modes over others, as I discuss further below. The second is an emphasis on the socially, culturally and historically situated dimension of perception and communication that diverges across time and space in important ways, while similarly involving the immediacy and engagement of the individual in experiences of the world.

While multimodal theorists have not described meaning making precisely in this way (see for example Jewitt, 2011a), communication acts are seen as recursive in that every language event recreates meaning, contributing in some way to the continuation of those meanings while recasting meaning in somewhat new ways. These meanings are always reflexively shaped and monitored by users in the daily flow of language and perceptions within the power relations that operate in the social context of those communicating. Abram, an ecologist, philosopher and sleight of hand magician, describes:

> The enigma, that is language, constituted as much by silence as by sounds, is not an inert or static structure, but an evolving bodily field. It is like a vast, living fabric continually being woven. (Abram, 1997: 83)

To Abram, language is dynamic and constantly changing, likened to the weaving of a living fabric. Multimodal theorists also see that language is constantly transformed and continued through moments of use (New London Group, 2000).

However, there are some key divergences between multimodal and sensory literacy approaches. The most salient distinction is that sensorial literacy approaches draw from theories of human sensorium in cultural anthropology and philosophy, attending to perception and communication beyond the analysis of multimodal texts. In contrast, multimodal semiotics explicitly deals with systematic 'principles of composition' (e.g. Kress & Bezemer, 2008, 167), and multimodal metalanguages (see Kress, 2000a).

Sensorial approaches attend to the changing nature and role of the senses and the body in the social process of meaning making. The body, the senses and their entanglement in the social and material spaces of culture are highly important, as are their relations to the materials and forms of literacy practice. Sensorial approaches begin by understanding the forgotten and changing role of the body and human experience in relation to literacy practices and texts. Multimodal literacy has often given more attention to images of bodies in texts than to understanding the role of the body, the mind and the senses in multimodal textual practices.

Another distinction between sensory and multimodal literacies is an emphasis on Western forms of text encoding in multimodal approaches. Sensory theorists describe a broader culturally, ecologically and anthropologically informed appreciation of sensorium across cultures and based on the relationship between the mind, body and the world. As Kress and van Leeuwen concede regarding their Western approach to multimodality in *Reading Images: The Grammar of Visual Design*:

...we would say that 'our' grammar is a quite general grammar of contemporary visual design in 'Western' cultures, an account of the explicit and implicit knowledge and practice around a resource, consistent with the elements and rules underlying a culture-specific form of visual communication. (Kress & van Leeuwen, 2006: 3)

Sensory theories in cultural anthropology are quite different in focus, preferring to take into account the 'social significance' of the sensory features of cultures and societies (Howes, 2003: 43). There is ethnographic evidence that in specific cultural contexts humans use particular and differentiated sensory categories with different meanings. Thus, a sensory approach observes how sensory literacy practices are differentiated across social groups. It is worth noting that despite Kress and van Leeuwen's (2006: 3) stated emphasis on Western cultures, multimodal approaches have been applied across a growing number of social and cultural contexts that clearly extend this earlier work.

Pink (2009) has examined the role of the senses in Kress' earlier definitions of multimodality – the senses are fundamental to the way we perceive the world (e.g. Kress, 2000b). However, Pink (2009: 102) sees that her view of the senses in ethnography has 'fundamental differences' to multimodal approaches. A key difference, Pink explains, concerns the priority given to the visual mode in semiotic theories (Kress *et al.*, 2001) over other important senses, such as taste, touch, smell and somatics. For example, Ingold (2000: 268) upholds the view that: '...the eyes and ears should not be understood as separate keyboards for the registration of sensation, but as organs of the body as a whole'. Ingold's statement is not dissimilar to arguments by Kress and the New London Group that consistently draw attention to the whole body in meaning making. Multimodal forms of meaning, theorised by Kress (2000a) and the New London Group (2000), explicitly describe the complexity and interrelationship of more than one mode of meaning, combining linguistic, visual, auditory, gestural or spatial modes. Multimodal design differs from independent modes because it interconnects the modes in dynamic relationships and involves more than the visual in making meaning.

In practice, multimodal analysis has given attention to describing individual modes, and well as analysing intermodal relations. Yet concurring with Pink (2009), at the present time, the formulation of grammars for different modes has frequently given more significant attention to outlining visual and audio grammars than say, grammars of smell, taste, touch, locomotion and so on (see for example Kress & van Leeuwen, 2006; van Leeuwen & Jewitt, 2001). The grammar of multimodality is indeed a broader view of meaning making than one solely based on spoken and written words, as Norris (2004: 3), a multimodal theorist, confirms, '...multimodality steps away from the notion that language [spoken and written words] always plays a central role in interaction, without denying that it often does'. The interesting point here is the disclaimer that words are often attributed a central role in interaction, which positions other modes at the margins.

However, with the current emergent formulations of sensory literacies begun in Australia since 2013 (see Mills *et al.*, 2013), and cross-disciplinary sensory theories, such as the work of Howes (2014a), Pink (2009), and Ingold (2000), one would expect to see a new emphasis on haptics (touch), taste, smell and somatics by theorists of multimodality situated in the field of social semiotics. Ultimately, this may result in sensory literacy and multimodal theories appearing more similar than they did originally.

Theorists of multimodality, such as van Leeuwen, have also developed grammars of sound which have been usefully applied to the analysis of film and other digital forms of audio design (see for example van Leeuwen, 1985, 1999). It is interesting to consider that the New London Group's (1996) articulation of multimodal design includes gestural design, even though their elaboration of gestural grammars was not comprehensive, and intended to be indicative only.

It is important to remember that the aims of sensory and multimodal approaches are distinctive by way of emphasis because sensory appro- aches find their origins in cultural geography, cultural anthropology, phi- losophy and ecology, focused on the perceptive and embodied relations between humans, each other, the ecology and their environment. In con- trast, multimodal approaches originate in applied linguistics and communi- cation studies.

In spite of these distinctions, social semiotic approaches to multimodal analysis forged by Kress, van Leeuwen, and Jewitt can be usefully applied to studies of sensoriality in meaning making. For example, I have previously analysed the classroom as a multimodal text, seeing learning environments as a complex ecology of social actors, discourses, symbolic systems and tech- nologies (Mills, 2010a). In my analysis of upper elementary students' clay- mation movie-making, multisensorial meanings – such as the direction of their gaze, bodily movements, postures and gestures – both transformed, and were transformed by, the classroom space. These elements of multi- modal meaning making are featured in Jewitt's (2006) reworking of a mul- timodal approach. These examples illustrate how multimodal approaches can be extended to understand embodied or multisensorial meanings in complementary ways. At the same time, sensorial approaches maintain a distinctive focus on the body and sensorium in the social practices of liter- acy, with potentials for illuminating the transformed relations between the body and the world in culturally situated experiences of digitally mediated communication.

Implications of Sensory Literacies for Practice

Embodied sensory experiences in tangible places and movement across different social spaces can be seen as rich resources for representational work in the classroom. For example, my research with colleagues in Australia has involved primary students filming in different local places of significance during sensory walks in the local area (Mills et al., 2013; Sunderland et al., 2012). We took our cameras into the local neighbourhood, pausing at various locations to become attuned to our senses and what we could feel in each place. For example, we conducted sensitising activities, such as sitting in a circle in an outdoor environment to close our eyes, focusing our attention on near sounds, sounds that were far away, dominant sounds and back grounded sounds, human sounds, mechanical sounds and sounds of nature.

We allowed the children to take video cameras home to film life in their homes and communities, and walked with cameras in the local area beyond the school for the students to understand the world perceived through their sensing bodies. Filming, as a literacy experience, was embodied because the students represented their sensory experiences of the places they visited in tangible ways. Physical experiences were central to their story. The filmmakers' bodies and the bodies of their peers were not peripheral, but central to their knowing and representing the world to others. When filming, the students concerned themselves with the positioning of their bodies in places of significance, making visible the connections between their bodies and the environment (Mills *et al.*, 2013).

The children used camera techniques, such as filming while gliding down a playground slide, to invoke an embodied reading of their sensed experience and subjectivities. They wanted viewers to understand what it felt like to be in this place, and to empathise with their multisensorial experiences. The senses play a role in geographical understanding because our senses indicate our bodily relationship to the immediate world (Gibson, 1979). A continuous pattern in the children's documentaries was the development of a multisensory realisation of the body in places, because 'as place is sensed, senses are placed; as places make sense, senses make place' (Feld & Basso, 1996: 91). More importantly, senses function to structure place (Gibson, 1979).

When the children as photographers created their films, they often attempted to capture the movement of their own bodies 'behind the camera' (MacDougall, 2005: 3). For example, Figure 7.1 below shows a still frame from a video of a child's feet balancing along a wall, filming downwards to give viewers a sense of their locomotion and bodily position relative to other objects.

At other times, the children stopped the movement of the camera to help focus the viewer on the natural or ambient sounds to create a sense of place, such as live bird sounds at the recreation reserve, or the sound of motor vehicles at a shopping centre car park. They sought to represent what they had experienced through their ears attuned to the ecology. The mode of video production enabled them to represent their multisensorial experiences, such as the heat and brightness of the sun, and the seeds of a dandelion blowing in the airflow of a child's breath (see Figure 7.2).

These examples of text production with video in places clearly illustrate the role of the body and the senses in meaning making, based on direct

Figure 7.1 Locomotion and walking on a wall

physical and sensory connections and contact with the world. Our video projects, which have been published in greater detail elsewhere (see for example Mills *et al.*, 2013), demonstrate how film production enables the children to represent their embodied connections to their world. As philosopher Merleau-Ponty (2002), wrote, the body is one's primary medium – both between and in the middle.

Walking with the camera can also mediate empathetic understandings of others' perceptions of their environments, such as by talking to local residents who inhabit their world (Pink, 2007). For example, the children in our research conducted street interviews and recorded them using their video cameras to represent the world by socialising with others who belong to the

Figure 7.2 Blowing dandelion seeds

places we visit (Mills *et al.*, 2013). The video camera was used to encourage students to engage physically with their sensory and material ecologies, representing their emplaced experiences and ideas corporeally.

Embodied memories of school life have been explored in video practice by children, such as Potter's (2010) study of students' curatorship of themselves through video production. Potter undertook an analysis, scene by scene, of a commemorative video about two girls and their embodied memories of school. Potter's analysis draws on interpretive themes, such as habitus, to interpret the children's depictions of themselves in different physical locations around the school environment. Their embodied memories of school life were emplaced in the very architectonic features of the school building, such as the bench upon which they sat together whenever they felt deep emotions.

What is important is that studies of filmmaking are beginning to acknowledge the centrality of the body as filmmakers re-author themselves and the bodies of others. Film is certainly not the only medium that involves embodied engagement with the world and others. There is potential to reconsider the role of the body in all literacy practices, from the emplaced meanings when children read environmental print, to children's first experimental marks on the page using pencils or crayons, to their embodied engagement with books or touch-screen technologies such as tablets. Embodiment theory can help us to reconsider the oft-forgotten bodily dimension of literacy practice.

New Directions for Sensory Literacies

There are two silences in literacy research that pertain to the senses. The first concerns the relations between kinesics or movement and literacy, particularly with the advent of mobile technologies for the moving, literate body. A second issue for future research is the current neglect of haptics in the context of digital practice, since many new digital devices for inscription require different physical uses of the hands in literacy learning.

Kinaesthesia in literacy practice

Kinaesthesia – sensory awareness of the position and movement of the body – has been rarely regarded in theories of literacy learning. The absence of kinaesthesia in Western thought more broadly, particularly our taxonomy of the five senses, has been recognised by a number of scholars, from Descartes to Dewey, and from Gibson to Merleau-Ponty (Farnell, 2012).

More recently, Ingold (2000: 242) has forged a number of studies that draw attention to kinaesthesia in human action because: 'The world of our experience is a world that is suspended in movement, that is continually coming into being as we – through our own movement – contribute to its formation'. Without bodily movement, we can experience very little of the world first-hand.

Here, I extend Ingold's ideas about the movement inherent in human action, to the analysis of kinesis involved in literacy and digital text creation. Creating digital texts can involve significant kinesis or movement, which is illustrated in the process of filmmaking in different locations. Whether it involves walking with the camera to different filming locations, or filming other people moving in different ways, kinesis is often inherent in video representation. The media production process is a way in which the movement of people, things and sensory experiences can be drawn together to understand the world (Pink, 2007).

In Figure 7.3 above, the student placed the camera on the ground to film her feet walking along the pavement, stopping momentarily to tie her shoelace as the voiceover appeals: 'If I was a community leader I would make more green spaces and areas for kids to play, but they have to be safe areas'. There is sense here that the locomotion of the body is salient to the children's sense of safe places (Butler, 2006). Similarly, in Figure 7.4, a student filmed her peer walking along the wall.

We cannot separate our sense of vision from our bodies that move and touch the ground to locate our viewpoint (Lund, 2005). Rather than attempting to develop a sense of place making through cognition alone, locomotion provides a portal for accessing memories and understandings of place and 'culture on the ground' (Ingold, 2004: 166).

Figure 7.3 Child walking in a safe place

Figure 7.4 Locomotion and balance on a wall

In the students' videos described earlier, there was a consistent focus on the moving body, whether walking, climbing the playground, spinning or sliding, which allows a view of the sensing and living body in motion, in place (Lund, 2005). For example, the students filmed younger children playing on the rotating playground equipment (Figure 7.5).

There was an apparent sense throughout the children's films that the world can be perceived, not only through the mind, but kinaesthetically through the movement of the hands and feet (Ingold, 2004). It demonstrates that literacy using digital technologies, such as film, directly involve '... active participation through practical bodily engagement...' with the world (Ingold, 2000: 260).

Figure 7.5 Movement on rotating playground equipment

Figure 7.6 Movement on the slide

In another example, a student filmed himself descending the playground slide, video camera in hand, to capture the kinaesthetic sensation of movement while creating a digital record of this experience (see Figure 7.6). There are devices such as digital video cameras that are attached to the body and designed for skateboarding or when engaged in other physical activities, to capture the feeling of movement when creating films.

Kinesics of play, particularly embodied, socio-dramatic play where children use their bodies and movements to enact a scene or situation, is familiar to young children and is closely tied to the development of symbolic representation (Nicolopoulou, 1993; Piaget, 1952b). Most play in early learning environments is naturally embodied, and has been described as the leading activity of childhood responsible for promoting development during the preschool years (Griffin & Cole, 1984). The role of movement in representational play, such as through video games, needs to be taken more seriously for understanding literacy and digital media practices beyond the early years.

To demonstrate the central role of kinesis in literacy practices, I revisit another classroom study of literacy in which kinesics was central to literacy practice. The study of the use of KidPad storymaking software in the United Kingdom involved Stanton *et al.* (2001) in designing a magic carpet – a tangible interface for groups of students to collaboratively navigate a story using their whole bodies. The magic carpet involved a series of pressure mats on the floor with video-tracked and bar-coded physical props to jointly construct the story. The design helped to overcome the problems the children encountered with a laptop with keyboard and mouse controls for multiple users. Designed, implemented and refined iteratively with 6–7 year old children and teachers in a school, the magic carpet enabled embodied and sensory engagement with others in storytelling. The magic carpet extended the original design of The University of Maryland's KidPad Shared 2D Drawing Tool, which allows students to create stories by designing story objects using paintbrush or other drawing tools and linking elements to sequence the story events. The use of pressure mats on a large floor area allowed children to work side-by-side to fill the drawing space simultaneously. The children's interaction with the magic carpet was based on kinesics or movement, and the manipulation of tangible, corporeal objects and materials is central to the children's collaborative story creation. Simple changes to the design of the interface resulted in radically different changes to the kinds of social and sensorimotor engagements possible with the technology.

For over a decade, other researchers have been examining interfaces that involve students in movement-based literacy practices, including Curlybot (Frei *et al.*, 2000), Triangles and Strings (Gorbet *et al.*, 1998), StoryRooms (Alborzi *et al.*, 2000) and StoryMat (Ryokai & Cassel, 1999) and MIT's KidsRoom (Bobick *et al.*, 2000). While software platforms are quickly superseded by other technologies, motion-sensing technologies are becoming more widespread for recreational and learning uses within and beyond classrooms (e.g. Xbox Kinect, Nintendo Wii). With technical affordances enabling kinaesthetic, gestural and sensorimotor literacy practices, a theory of sensorial or sensory literacies is a timely approach that recognises and seeks to understand the changing role of the body and movement in literacy practices.

Haptics in literacy practice

A related argument to kinesics or movement, is that that literacy teachers and researchers need to embrace the possibility of attending more consciously to haptics or touch in literacy and media production. There are relevant precursors to the notion of haptics in literacy, as found in art history and aesthetics. For example, Paterson observes distinction between the haptic and the optic, the role of touch in Renaissance art, and the complexity of the senses in aesthetic experiences (Paterson, 2007). Haptics continues to be an important dimension of the arts, philosophy and aesthetics, while few have considered how literacy, including new digital practices, enables us to touch the world and the world to touch us. The increasing availability and popularity of touch sensitive technologies, such as electronic toys, smartphones, iPads, tablets and other mobile media for children's literacy learning has opened up unexamined changes to the role of haptics and sensorimotor elements in communication, education and recreation.

We need only to look at the evidence around us to observe the growing use of touch-sensitive technologies for reading, writing and play. A key finding of the Common Sense Media Research Study (2011) of children ages 0–8 years, surveyed in the United States, was that children are increasingly accessing internet sites using mobile platforms that use touch screen technologies. More than half (52%) of children surveyed have access to one of the newer mobile devices at home, which includes smartphones (41%), iPods (21%), or an iPad or other tablets (8%). Of course, not all young children are accessing apps, with a definitive 'app gap'. Only 62% of lower-income parents knew the meaning of the shorthand term 'app' compared to 97% of higher income parents. Toddlers are able to access their favourite apps using their multi-touch gestures or a stylus at earlier stages of sensor-motor development than in the era of the keyboard and mouse. The popularity and widespread use of touch screen technologies has prompted libraries to offer Toddler Tech sessions for parents and toddlers to use their mobile devices for literacy and other educational purposes.

What I perceive as a multisensorial revolution in digital practice has not only led to different kinds of corporeal ways of interacting with digital texts, but has sparked a renewed attention to the physicality of the book, such as books with different textiles, flaps, buttons, music and dials. The sensorial nature of literacy practices extends across all textual forms. Taking Bourdieu's concept of the habitus, sensorial practices of literacy can be seen as modified by daily interactions with new technologies that generate different internalised dispositions and meaningful practices and meaning-giving sensory perceptions with textual practices. These transposable dispositions are carried out across other systematic and universal practices, along with a heightened sensorial awareness of literacy practice that can be applied beyond the limits of what has been directly learnt with a particular platform, and based on the fundamental corporeality inherent in the changing learning conditions across the life course (Bourdieu, 1986a: 170). The sensoriality of literacy practices becomes part of our daily interactions with texts, and over time, will become as taken for granted as the tactility of using pencil and paper for writing, or of turning the material pages of an inspiring book. Literacy practices are undergoing important sensorial adaptations, and the potentials of those sensorial dimensions of the digital turn are only just beginning to emerge in literacy research.

Beyond literacy and the mind

This chapter has provided an essential background to the origins of the somatic or bodily turn in digitally mediated approaches to literacy practice and research, which had formerly focused on the skills of the mind, and also of the social practices of communities. Significant shifts in anthropology, philosophy and sociology have foregrounded the need to consider the body in human social action, and have implications for researching literacy practices in the digital turn. I have identified a disembodied view of human beings that permeated the social sciences, prior to a corporeal shift toward embodiment theory of the 1970s, and the implications for semiotic and literacy theory.

Turning to recent developments in literacy, I provided evidence that the scope of literacy practice, mediated by digital technologies within and beyond classroom, constitute dynamically embodied acts. This is a timely reawakening of the forgotten somatic dimensions of learning and of literacy practice – timely in the context of an extended range of affordances of interactive digital technologies for responding to human voice, breath, touch, gestures and locomotion. Arola and Wysocki (2012: 4) recommend that those who teach literacy: '... need to consider media that use the alphabet, and to ask how such media engage with our senses, and contribute to our embodiment'.

There is a plethora of embodied knowledge across many domains of learning, which becomes systematised in various ways according to sociocultural criteria and conventions (Mauss, 1979). Even the most elemental human actions, such as talking, gesturing, posturing, dressing and moving, are imbued with social and relational significance, and have embodied intentionality and unintentionality (Gibson, 1979). Some forms of embodied action are acquired from birth, such as gestures or the timbre of the voice, and become taken for granted or invisible to social actors. Embodied literacy practices may vary according to axes of race, ethnicity, gender, age, class, kin, tribe, social context and no doubt others. Literary acts involve embodied socialisation into shared systems of meaning, just as there are rule-governed sign systems in sacred and secular rituals, sporting groups and theatrical, musical and other performance traditions (Farnell, 2012). Literacy practices require knowledge, not only of a conceptual kind, but also corporeal.

It is undeniable that '... without our bodies – our sensing abilities – we do not have a world...' (Arola & Wysocki, 2012: 3). An expanded range of affordances of digital devices, such as iPads, motion sensing game technologies, and many other encoding and decoding processes, makes it more difficult, and more erroneous, to ignore the full array of sensorial dimensions of practice, such as touch, breath, movement, gaze and locomotion. New technologies can provide the impetus and means for representing the sensoriality of life. Sensory literacies are an acknowledgement that literacy practice, as embodiment, is '... contextual, enmeshed within the specifics of place, time, physiology and culture, which together compose enactment' (Hayles, 1999: 196). Without our sensing bodies, we do not have literacy practices.

References

Abram, D. (1997) *The Spell of the Sensuous: Perception and Language in a More-Than-Human World*. New York: Random House.

ACARA (2012) *My School*. See http://www.myschool.edu.au (accessed 1 May 2015).

ACARA (2014) *Australian Curriculum*. See http://www.acara.edu.au/curriculum.html (accessed 1 May 2015).

Ackerman, J.M. (1993) The promise of writing to learn. *Written Communication* 10 (3), 334–370.

Adey, P. (2011) John Urry. In P. Hubbard and R. Kitchen (eds) *Key Thinkers on Space and Place* (pp. 432–439). Thousand Oaks, California: Sage.

Ajayi, L. (2009) English as a Second Language learners' exploration of multimodal texts in a junior high school. *Journal of Adolescent & Adult Literacy* 52 (7), 585–595.

Alborzi, H., Druin, A., Montemayor, J., Sherman, L., Taxen, G., Best, J., Hammer, J., Kruskal, A., Lal, A., Schwenn, T., Sumida, L., Wagner, R. and Hendler, J. (2000) Designing StoryRooms: Interactive storytellng spaces for children. Paper presented at Designing Interactive Systems (DIS) Brooklyn.

Alvermann, D.E. (2000) Researching libraries, literacies, and lives: A rhizoanalysis. In E.A. St Pierre and W. Pillow (eds) *Working the Ruins: Feminist Poststructural Theory and Methods in Education* (pp. 114–129). New York: Routledge.

Anderson, B. and Wylie, J. (2009) On geography and materiality. *Environment and Planning A* 41, 318–335.

Anderson, G.L. and Irvine, P. (1993) Informing critical literacy with ethnography. In C. Lankshear and P. McLaren (eds) *Critical Literacy: Politics, Praxis, and the Postmodern* (pp. 81–104). Albany, NY: Suny Press.

Anstey, M. and Bull, G. (2004) *The Literacy Labyrinth* (2nd edn). Frenchs Forest, NSW: Pearson.

Apple, M. (1996) *Cultural Politics and Education*. New York: Teachers College Press.

Apple, M.W. (1982) Reproduction and contradiction in education. In M.W. Apple (ed.) *Cultural and Economic Reproduction in Education* (pp. 1–31). Boston, MA: Routledge & Kegan Paul.

Apple, M.W., Au, W. and Gandin, L.A. (2009) Mapping critical education. In M.W. Apple, W. Au and L. Armando Gandin (eds) *The Routledge International Handbook of Critical Education* (pp. 3–19). New York: Routledge.

Applebee, A. and Langer, J. (2009) What is happening in the teaching of writing. *English Journal* 98 (5), 18–28.

Arola, K.L. and Wysocki, A. (2012) *Composing (Media) = Composing (Embodiment)*. Logan, Utah: Utah State University Press.

Ascher, M. and Ascher, R. (1981) *The Code of the Quipu: A Study in Media, Mathematics and Culture*. Ann Arbor, MI: University of Michigan Press.

Ascher, R. (2002) Inka writing. In J. Quilter and G. Urton (eds) *Narrative Threads: Accounting and Recounting in Andean Khipu* (pp. 103–115). Austin: University of Texas Press.

Au, W. (2009) Fighting with the text: Contextualising and recontextualising Freire's critical pedagogy. In M.A. Apple, W. Au and L.A. Gandin (eds) *The Routledge International Handbook of Critical Education* (pp. 221–239). New York: Routlege.

Au, W. and Apple, M.A. (2009) Rethinking reproduction: Neo-Marxism in critical education theory. In M.A. Apple, W. Au and L.A. Gandin (eds) *The Routledge International Handbook of Critical Education*. New York: Routledge.

Auerbach, E. (1997) Reading between the lines. In D. Taylor (ed.) *Many Families, Many Literacies*. Portsmouth, NH: Heinemann.

Barab, S., Thomas, M., Dodge, T., Carteaux, R. and Tuzun, H. (2005) Making learning fun: Quest Atlantis, a game without guns. *Educational Technology Research and Development* 53 (1), 86–107.

Barad, K. (2007) *Meeting the Universe Halfway*. Durham, NC: Duke University Press.

Barthes, R. (1967) *Elements of Semiology*. London: Cape.

Barthes, R. (1984) *Camera Lucida*. London: Fontana.

Barton, D. (2001) Directions for literacy research: Analysing language and social practices in a textually mediated world. *Language and Education* 15 (2 & 3), 92–104.

Barton, D. and Hamilton, M. (1998) *Local Literacies: Reading and Writing in One Community*. London: Routledge.

Barton, D. and Hamilton, M. (2005) Literacy, reification and the dynamic of social interaction. In D. Barton and K. Trustin (eds) *Beyond Communities of Practice: Language and Social Context*. Cambridge: Cambridge University Press.

Barton, D., Hamilton, M. and Ivanic, R. (2000) *Situated Literacies: Reading and Writing in Context*. London: Routledge.

Beach, R. (2000) Using media ethnographies to study response to media as activity. In A. Watts Pailliotet and P. Mosentha (eds) *Reconceptualizing Literacy in the Media Age* (pp. 3–39). Stamford, CT: JAI Press.

Beach, R. and Myers, J. (2001) *Inquiry-Based English Instruction: Engaging Students in Literature and Life*. New York: Teachers College Press.

Beavis, C., Apperley, T., Bradford, C., O'Mara, J. and Walsh, C. (2009) *Digital Games: Literacy in Action*. Adelaide: Wakefield Press.

Beck, U. (1992) *Risk Society: Towards a New Modernity*. London: SAGE.

Bendix, R. (2000) The pleasures of the ear: Toward an ethnography of listening. *Cultural Analysis* 1, 33–50.

Bernstein, B. (2000) *Pedagogy, Symbolic Control and Identity: Theory, Research, and Critique*. Oxford: Rowman & Littlefield.

Beunza, D., Hardie, I. and Mackenzie, D. (2006) A price is a social thing: Towards a material sociology of arbitrage. *Organisational Studies* 27 (5), 721–745.

Bigum, C. and Green, B. (1993) Technologising literacy or interrupting the dream of reason. In A. Luke and P. Gilbert (eds) *Literacy in Context: Australian Perspectives and Issues* (pp. 4–28). St Leonards, NSW: Allen and Unwin.

Bijker, W.E. (1995) *Of Bicyles, Brakelites and Bulbs: Toward a Theory of Sociotechnical Change*. Cambridge, MA: MIT Press.

Birdwhistell, R. (1952) *Introduction to Kinesics: An Annotation System for Analysis of Body Motion and Gesture*. Louisville, KY: University of Louisville.

Bishop, R. (2003) Changing power relations in education: Kaupapa Maori messages for 'mainstream' education in Aotearoa/New Zealand. *Comparative Education* 39 (2), 221–238.

Bissell, D. (2009) Conceptualising differently-mobile passengers: Geographies of everyday encumbrance in the railway station. *Social and Cultural Geography* 10 (2), 173–195.

Black, A. (2005) Access and affiliation: The literacy and composition practices of English-language learners in an online fanfiction community. *Journal of Adolescent & Adult Literacy* 49 (2), 118–128.

Black, R.W. (2009) Online fanfiction, global identities, and imagination. *Research in the Teaching of English* 43 (4), 397–425.

Bloome, D. (2012) Classroom ethnography. In M. Grenfell, D. Bloome, C. Hardy, K. Pahl, J. Rowsell and B. Street (eds) *Language, Ethnography and Education: Bridging New Literacy Studies and Bourdieu*. New York: Routledge.

Bloor, D. (1976) *Knowledge and Social Imagery*. London: Routledge and Kegan Paul.

Bobick, A., Intille, S., Davis, J., Baird, F., Pinhanez, C., Campbell, L., Ivanov, Y., Schutte, A. and Wilson, A. (2000) The KidsRoom: A perceptually-based interactive and immersive story environment. *Presence: Teleoperators and Virtual Environments* 8 (4), 367–391.

Bogatyrev, P. (1976) Costume as a sign. *Semiotics of Art*, 12–20.

Bourdieu, P. (1973) Cultural reproduction and social reproduction. In R. Brown (ed.) *Knowledge, Education and Cultural Change* (pp. 100–104). London: Tavistock.

Bourdieu, P. (1977) The economics of linguistic exchanges. *Social Sciences Information* 16, 645–668.

Bourdieu, P. (1985) The genesis of the concepts of habitus and field. *Sociocriticism* 2, 11–24.

Bourdieu, P. (1986a) *Distinction: A Social Critique of the Judgement of Taste* (R. Nice, trans.). London: Routledge & Kegan Paul.

Bourdieu, P. (1986b) The forms of capital (R. Nice, trans.). In J.E. Richardson (ed.) *Handbook of Theory of Research for the Sociology of Education* (pp. 241–258). Westport, CT: Greenwood Press.

Bourdieu, P. (1989) Social space and symbolic power. *Sociological Theory* 7 (1), 14–25.

Bowen, T. (2013) Graffiti as spatializing practice and performance. *Rhizomes* 25, 1.

Boyd, D. (2009) The public nature of mediated breakups. In M. Ito (ed.) *Hanging Out, Messing Round, Geeking Out: Living and Learning with New Media* (pp. 111–117). Cambridge, MA: MIT Press.

Brandt, D. and Clinton, K. (2002) Limits of the local: Expanding perspectives on literacy as a social practice. *Journal of Literacy Research* 34 (3), 337–356.

Brass, J. (2008) Local knowledge and digital movie composing in an after-school literacy program. *Journal of Adolescent and Adult Literacy* 51 (6), 464–478.

Brown, A. (1994) The advancement of learning. *Educational Researcher* 23 (8), 4–12.

Brown, A. and Campione, J. (1994) Guided discovery in a community of learners. In K. McGilly (ed.) *Classroom Lessons: Integrating Cognitive Theory and Classroom Practice* (pp. 229–270). Cambridge: MIT Press.

Brown, A., Ash, D., Rutherford, M., Nakagawa, K., Gordon, A. and Campione, J. (1993) Distributed expertise in the classroom. In G. Salomon (ed.) *Distributed Cognitions: Psychological and Educational Considerations* (pp. 188–228). New York: Cambridge University Press.

Brown, A., Collins, J. and Duguid, P. (1989) Situated cognition and the culture of learning. *Educational Researcher* 18 (1), 32–42.

Bruner, J. (1986) *Actual Minds, Possible Worlds*. Cambridge, MA: Harvard University Press.

Buchanan, M. (2002) *Nexus: Small Words and The Groundbreaking Science of Networks*. London: WW Norton.

Buckingham, D. (2007) Digital media literacies: Rethinking media education in the age of the internet. *Research in Comparative and International Education* 2 (1), 43–55.

Bulfin, S. and North, S. (2007) Negotiating digital literacy practices across school and home: Case studies of young people in Australia. *Language and Education* 21 (3), 247–263.

Burbules, N. and Callister, T. (1996) Knowledge at the cross-roads: Some alternative futures of hypertext learning environments. *Educational Theory* 46 (1), 23–50.

Burn, A. and Parker, D. (2003) Tiger's big plan: Multimodality and the moving image. In C. Jewitt and G. Kress (eds) *Multimodal Literacy* (pp. 56–72). New York: Peter Lang.

Butler, K. (2006) A walk of art: The potential of the sound walk as practice in cultural geography. *Social and Cultural Geography* 7 (6), 889–908.

Callard, F. (2011). John Urry. In P. Hubbard and R. Kitchen (eds) *Key Thinkers of Space and Place* (2nd edn, pp. 299–306). London: Sage.

Callon, M. (1986) Some elements of a sociology of translation: Domestication of the scallops and the fishermen of Saint Brieuc Bay. In J. Law (ed.) *Power, Action and Belief: A New Sociology of Knowledge?* (pp. 196–233). London: Routledge.

Cameron, D. (2000) Book review: Multiliteracies: Literacy learning and the design of social futures. By Bill Cope, Mary Kalantzis (eds) (2000), Routledge, London. *Changing English* 7 (2), 203–207.

Campbell, M.A. (2005) Cyber bullying: An old problem in a new guise? *Australian Journal of Guidance and Counselling* 15 (1), 66–76.

Carrington, V. and Dowdall, C. (2013) This is a job for Hazmat Guy: Global media cultures and children's everyday lives. In K. Hall, T. Cremin, B. Comber and L.C. Moll (eds) *International Handbook of Research on Children's Literacy, Learning, and Culture* (pp. 96–107). Oxford: John Wiley and Sons.

Carspecken, P. (1996) *Critical Ethnography in Educational Research: A Theoretical and Practical Guide*. New York: Routledge.

Castells, M. (2000a) Materials for an explanatory theory of the network society. *British Journal of Sociology* 53 (1), 1–18.

Castells, M. (2000b) *The Rise of the Network Society* (2nd edn). Malden, MA: Blackwell.

Cazden, C.B. (1988) *Classroom Discourse: The Language of Teaching and Learning*. Portsmith, NH: Heinemann.

Cazden, C.B., John, V.P. and Hymes, D. (eds) (1972) *Functions Of Language in the Classroom*. London: Teachers College Press.

Chandler-Olcott, K. and Mahar, D. (2003) Tech-savviness meets multiliteracies: Exploring adolescent girls' technology-mediated literacy practices. *Reading Research Quarterly* 38 (3), 356–385.

Charlesworth, R. (2014) *Understanding Child Development* (9th edn). Belmont, CA: Wadsworth.

Cho, B. (2013) Adolescents' constructively responsive reading strategy use in a critical internet reading task. *Reading Research Quarterly* 48 (4), 329–332.

Christie, F. and Martin, J.R. (1997) *Genre and Institutions: Social Processes in the Workplace and School*. New York, NY: Continuum.

Clancy, S. and Lowrie, T. (2002) Researching multimodal texts: Applying a dynamic model. Paper presented at the Annual Meeting of the Australian Association for Research in Education, Brisbane.

Clark, A. (2011) Multimodal map making with young children: Exploring ethnographic and participatory methods. *Qualitative Research* 11 (3), 311–330.

Classen, C. (1993a) *Worlds of Sense: Exploring the Senses in History and Across Cultures.* London: Routledge.

Classen, C. (1993b) *Inca Cosmology and the Human Body.* Salt Lake City: University of Utah Press.

Classen, C. (1997) Foundations for an anthropology of the senses. *International Social Sciences Journal* 49 (153), 401–412.

Classen, C. (1999) Other ways to wisdom: Learning through the senses across cultures. *International Review of Education* 45 (3/4), 269–280.

Cobb, P., Confrey, J., diSessa, A., Lehrer, R. and Schauble, L. (2003) Design experiments in educational research. *Educational Researcher* 32 (1), 9–13.

Coffey, A. (1999) *The Ethnographic Self: Fieldwork and the Representation of Identity.* London: Sage.

Coiro, J., Knobel, M., Lankshear, C. and Leu, D.J. (eds) (2008) *Handbook of Research on New Literacies.* New York: Routledge, Taylor and Francis Group.

Cole, M. (1996) *Cultural Psychology: A Once and Future Discipline.* Cambridge: Cambridge University Press.

Cole, M. and Engeström, Y. (1993) A cultural-historical approach to distributed cognition. In G. Salomon (ed.) *Distributed Cognitions: Psychological and Educational Considerations* (pp. 1–46). New York: Cambridge University Press.

Collins, J. and Blot, R. (2002) *Literacy and Literacies: Texts, Power, and Identity.* Cambridge: Cambridge University Press.

Comber, B. (1997) Literacy, poverty and schooling. *English in Australia* 119–120 (20), 22–34.

Comber, B. and Simpson, A. (eds) (2001) *Negotiating Critical Literacies in Classrooms.* Mahwah, NJ: Erlbaum Associates.

Comber, B., Thompson, P. and Wells, M. (2001) Critical literacy finds a place: Writing and social action in a low-income Australian grade 2/3 classroom. *The Elementary School Journal* 101 (4), 451–464.

Comber, B., Nixon, H., Ashmore, L., Loo, S. and Cook, J. (2006) Urban renewal from the inside out: Spatial and critical literacies in a low socioeconomic school community. *Mind, Culture and Activity* 13 (3), 228–246.

Common Sense Media Research Study (2011) Zero to Eight: Children's Media Use in America. See http://www.commonsensemedia.org/sites/default/files/research/zerotoeightfinal2011.pdf (accessed 31 May 2015).

Connerton, P. (1989) *How Societies Remember.* New York: Cambridge University Press.

Cook-Gumperz, J. (ed.) (1986) *The Social Construction of Literacy: Studies in Interactional Socio-Linguistics* (Vol. 3). Cambridge: Cambridge University Press.

Cook-Gumperz, J. (ed.) (2006) *The Social Construction of Literacy: Studies in Interactional Socio-Linguistics* (2nd edn, Vol. 3). Cambridge: Cambridge University Press.

Cope, B. and Kalantzis, M. (1993) Introduction: How a genre approach to literacy can transform the way writing is taught. In B. Cope and M. Kalantzis (eds) *The Powers of Literacy: A Genre Approach to Teaching Writing* (pp. 1–21). London: Falmer Press.

Cope, B. and Kalantzis, M. (1999) *Teaching and Learning in the New World of Literacy: A Professional Development Program and Classroom Research Project: Participants' Resource Book.* Melbourne: RMIT University: Faculty of Education, Language and Community Services.

Cope, B. and Kalantzis, M. (2000a) Designs for social futures. In B. Cope and M. Kalantzis (eds) *Multiliteracies: Literacy Learning and the Design of Social Futures* (pp. 203–234). South Yarra, Australia: Macmillan.

Cope, B. and Kalantzis, M. (2000b) *Multiliteracies: Literacy Learning and the Design of Social Futures*. South Yarra, Australia: Macmillan.

Cope, B. and Kalantzis, M. (2014) New learning: Transformational designs for learning and assessment. See http://newlearningonline.com (accessed 20 Jan 2014).

Council of Chief State School Officers & National Governors Association (2013) *Common Core State Standards for English Language Arts*. See www.corestandards.org/the-standards (accessed 1 May 2015).

Courtland, M. and Paddington, D. (2008) Digital literacy in a grade eight classroom: An e-zine webquest. *Language and Literacy: A Canadian E-Journal* 10 (1).

Coyne, R. (2012) Mosaics and multiples: Online digital photography and the framing of heritage. In E. Giaccardi (ed.) *Heritage and Social Media: Understanding Heritage in a Participatory Culture* (pp. 161–178). Routledge: London.

Crafton, L.K., Brennan, M. and Silvers, P. (2007) Critical inquiry and multiliteracies in a first-grade classroom. *Language and Education* 84 (6), 510–518.

Dalton, B., Proctor, C., Uccelli, P., Mo, E. and Snow, C.E. (2011) Designing for diversity: The role of reading strategies in interactive vocabulary in a digital reading environment for fifth-grade monolingual English and bilingual students. *Journal of Adolescent and Adult Literacy* 43 (1), 68–100.

Damico, J. and Riddle, R. (2006) Exploring freedom and leaving a legacy: Enacting new literacies with digital texts in the elementary classroom. *Language Arts* 84 (1), 34–44.

Dank-McGhee, K. and Slutsky, R. (2007) *The Impact of Early Art Experiences on Literacy Development*. Reston, VA: National Art Education Association.

Darcy, R. and Auld, G. (2008) The production and distribution of Burarra talking books. *Australian Educational Computing* 23 (1), 19–23.

Davidse, K. (1987) M.A.K Halliday's functional grammar and the Prague school. In R. Dirven and V. Fried (eds) *Functionalism in Linguistics* (pp. 39–79). Netherlands: John Benjamin's Publishing Company.

Davies, J. and Merchant, G. (2007) Looking from the inside out: Academic blogging as new literacy. In C. Lankshear and M. Knobel (eds) *A New Literacies Sampler* (pp. 167–198). New York: Peter Lang.

Davis, J. (2012) Community connections in education: Community Durithunga yarning. In P. Phillips and J. Lampert (eds) *Introductory Indigenous Studies in Education: Reflection and the Importance of Knowing* (2nd edn, pp. 149–177). Frenchs Forest, NSW: Pearson.

Debes, J. (1969) The loom of visual literacy: An overview. *Audiovisual Instruction* 14 (8), 25–27.

Deleuze, G. and Guattari, F. (1987) *A Thousand Plateaus: Capitalism and Schizophrenia* (B. Massumi, trans.). Minneapolis and London: University of Minnesota Press.

Dewey, J. (1971) *The School and Society*. Chicago: University of Chicago Press.

Dirven, R. and Fried, V. (1987) M.A.K Halliday's functional grammar and the Prague school. In K. Davidse (ed.) *Functionalism in Linguistics* (pp. 39–80). Netherlands: John Benjamin's Publishing.

Dixon, K. (2011) *Literacy, Power, and the Schooled Body: Learning in Time and Space*. New York and London: Routledge.

Dolmage, J. (2012) Writing against normal: Navigating a corporeal turn. In K.L. Arola and A. Wysoki (eds) *Composing Media Composing Embodiment*. Logan, UT: Utah State University Press.

Domico, J. (2006) Exploring freedom and leaving a legacy: Enacting new literacies with digital texts in the elementary classroom. *Language Arts* 84 (1), 34–44.

Dyson, A. (1993) *Social Worlds of Children Learning to Write in an Urban Primary School*. New York: Teachers College Press.

Edwards, A. (2011). Cultural historical activity theory. *British Educational Research Association on-line resource*. See https://www.bera.ac.uk/wp-content/uploads/2014/03/Cultural-Historical-Activity-Theory-CHAT.pdf (accessed 24 May 2015).

Elliotte, A. and Urry, J. (2010) *Mobile Lives*. Abingdon, Oxon: Routlege.

Emig, J. (1971) *The Composing Processes of Twelfth Graders*. New York: NCTE Press.

Engeström, Y. (1999) Activity theory and individual and social transformation. In Y. Engeström, R. Miettinen and R.L. Punamäki (eds) *Perspectives on Activity Theory* (pp. 19–38). Cambridge: Cambridge University Press.

Engeström, Y., Miettinen, R. and Punamäki, R.L. (1999) *Perspectives on Activity Theory*. New York: Cambridge University Press.

Enyedy, N., Danish, J.A., Delacruz, G. and Kumar, M. (2012) Learning physics through play in an augmented reality environment. *Computer-Supported Collaborative Learning*, 347–378.

Ernst-Slavit, G. (1997) Different words, different worlds: Language use, power, and authorized language in a bilingual classroom. *Linguistics and Education* 9 (1), 25–48.

Fairclough, N. (1989) *Language and Power*. London: Longman.

Faraclas, N. (1997) Critical literacy and control in the New World Order. In S. Muspratt, P. Luke and P. Freebody (eds) *Constructing Critical Literacies: Teaching and Learning Textual Practice*. Allen & Unwin: Melbourne.

Farnell, B. (2012) *Dynamic Embodiment for Social Theory*. UK: Taylor and Francis.

Feenberg, A. (1991) *Critical Theory of Technology*. Oxford: Oxford University Press.

Feld, S. and Basso, K. (1996) *Sense of Place*. Santa Fe, NM: School of American Research Press.

Fenwick, T. and Edwards, R. (2010) *Actor Network Theory in Education*. London: Routledge.

Fenwick, T. and Landri, P. (2012) Materialities, textures and pedagogies: socio-material assemblages in education. *Pedagogy, Culture and Society* 21 (1), 1–7.

Fenwick, T., Edwards, R. and Sawchuck, P. (eds) (2011) *Emerging Approaches for Educational Research: Tracing the Sociomaterial*. London: Routledge.

Ferrare, J.J. and Apple, M.W. (2010) Spatializing critical education: Progress and cautions. *Critical Studies in Education* 51 (2), 209–221.

Flewitt, R., Melanie, N. and Payler, J.J. (2009) 'If she's left with books she'll just eat them': Considering inclusive multimodal literacy practices. *Journal of Early Childhood Literacy* 9 (2), 211–233.

Flewitt, R., Hampel, R., Hauck, M. and Lancaster, L. (2011) What are multimodal data and transcription? In C. Jewitt (ed.) *The Routledge Handbook of Multimodal Analysis* (pp. 40–53). London: Routledge.

Forceville, C. (1999) Review: Educating the eye? Kress and Van Leeuwen's reading images: The grammar of visual design. *Language and Literature* 8 (2), 163–178.

Foster, E., Thomas, I. and Fraser, L. (1989) Appendix B: Computer access for English classes. In C. Selfe, D. Rodrigues and W. Oates (eds) *Computers in English and the Language Arts: The Challenge of Teacher Education* (pp. 287–289). Urbana, IL: National Council of Teachers of English.

Foucault, M. (1977a) *Discipline and Punish: The Birth of the Prison* (A. Sheridan, trans.). London: Penguin Books.

Foucault, M. (1977b) *Language, Counter Memory, Practice* (D. Bouchard, trans.). Oxford: Basil Blackwell.

Foucault, M. (1980) Power/Knowledge: Selected Interviews and Other Writings, 1972–77. Brighton: Harvester Press.

Foucault, M. (1986) Of other spaces. *Diacritics* 16, 22–27.

Foucault, M. (1988) *Technologies of the Self: A Seminar with Michel Foucault*. Amherst: University of Massachusettes Press.

Fowler, B., Hodge, G., Kress, G. and Trew, T. (1979) *Language and Control*. Kegan Paul: Routledge.

Fowler, R. and Hodge, B. (1979) Critical linguistics. In R. Fowler (ed.) *Language and Control* (pp. 185–213). London: Routledge and Keegan Paul.

Frei, P., Su, V., Mikhak, B. and Ishii, H. (2000) Curlybot: Designing a new class of computational toys. Paper presented at the CHI.

Freire, P. (1970a) Cultural action and conscientization. *Harvard Educational Review* 40 (3), 452–477.

Freire, P. (1970b) *Pedagogy of the Oppressed* (M. B. Ramos, trans.). New York: Continuum.

Freire, P. (1982) Education as the practice of freedom (M. B. Ramos, trans.). In P. Freire (ed.) *Education for Critical Consciousness* (pp. 1–84). New York: The Continuum Publishing Company.

Freire, P. (1985) *The Politics of Education: Culture, Power, and Liberation*. South Hadley, MA: Bergin and Garvey.

Freire, P. (1998) *Teachers as Cultural Workers: Letters to Those Who Dare Teach*. Boulder, CO: Westview Press.

Freire, P. and Macedo, D. (1987) *Literacy: Reading the Word and the World*. Hadley, MA: Bergin and Garvey.

Frierson, P.R. (2014) Maria Montessori's epistemology. *British Journal for the History of Philosophy* 22 (4), 767–791.

Fuller, B. (1987) What school factors raise achievement in the third world? *Review of Educational Research* 57 (3), 255–292.

Galperin, P. (1992) The problem of activity in Soviet psychology. *Journal of Russian and East European Psychology* 30 (4), 37–59.

Gee, J. (1992) *The Social Mind: Language, Ideology, and Social Practice*. New York: Bergin and Garvey.

Gee, J. (2005) Semiotic social spaces and affinity spaces. In D. Barton and K. Tusting (eds) *Beyond Communities of Practice: Language Power and Social Context* (pp. 214–232). New York: Cambridge.

Gee, J. (2007) *What Video Games Have to Teach us about Learning and Literacy* (2nd edn). New York: Palgrave, Macmillan.

Gee, J. (2009) A situated sociocultural approach to literacy and technology. See http://www.jamespaulgee.com/node/6 (accessed 24th June).

Gee, J. (2012) *Social Linguistics and Literacies: Ideology in Discourses* (4th edn). NY: Routledge

Gee, J.P. (1999) Critical issues: Reading and the new literacy studies: Reframing the National Academy of Sciences report on reading. *Journal of Literacy Research* September.

Gergen, K. (1999) *An Invitation to Social Construction*. Thousand Oaks, CA: SAGE.

Giaccardi, E. (2012) *Heritage and Social Media: Understanding Heritage in a Participatory Culture*. London and New York: Routledge.

Gibbs, D. and Krause, K.-L. (2006) *Cyberlines 2.0: Languages and Cultures of the Internet*. Albert Park, VIC: James Nicholas.

Gibson, J.J. (1979) *The Ecological Approach to Visual Perception*. Boston: Houghton Mifflin.
Giddens, A. (2002) *Runaway Word: How Globalisation is Reshaping our Lives*. London: Profile Books.
Giroux, H. (1988) *Schooling and the Struggle for Public Life: Critical Pedagogy in the Modern Age*. Minneapolis: University of Minnesota Press.
Goffman, E. (1959) *The Presentation of Self in Everyday Life*. New York: Doubleday.
Goffman, E. (1993) The Interaction Order. *American Sociological Review* 48 (1), 1–17.
Goodfellow, R. and Lea, M.R. (2005) Supporting writing for assessment in online learning. *Assessment and Evaluation in Higher Education* 30 (3), 261–271.
Gorbet, M., Orth, M. and Ishii, H. (1998) Triangles: Tangible interface for manipulation and exploration of digital information topography, (pp. 49–56): ACM.
Gore, J.M. (1988) Disciplining bodies: On the continuity of power relations in pedagogy. In J.M. Gore (ed.) *Foucault's Challenge: Discourse, Knowledge and Power in Education* (pp. 231–254). New York: Teachers College Columbia University.
Gourlay, L. and Oliver, M. (2013) Beyond 'the social': Digital literacies as sociomaterial practice. In R. Goodfellow and M.R. Lea (eds) *Literacy in the Digital University: Learning as Social Practice in a Digital Age* (pp. 79–94). London: Routledge.
Graddol, D. (1994) What is a text? In D. Graddol and O. Boyd-Barrett (eds) *Media Texts: Authors and Readers* (Vol. 40–50). Clevedon: Multilingual Matters.
Graff, H. (1987) *The Legacies of Literacy: Continuities and Contradictions in Western Culture and Society*. Bloomington, IN: Indiana University Press.
Graff, H.J. (1979) *The Literacy Myth: Literacy and Social Structure in the 19th Century City*. Waltham, Massachusettes: Academic Press.
Graff, H.J. (1995) *The Labyrinth of Literacy: Reflections on Literacy Past and Present*. Pittsburg, PA: University of Pittsburgh Press.
Gramsci, A. (1971) *Selections from the Prison Notebooks* (Q. Hoare & G. N. Smith, trans.). New York International Publishers.
Grant, L. (2006) *Using Wikis in School: A Case Study*. London: Future Lab.
Green, B. (1993) *The Insistence of the Letter: Literacy Studies and Curriculum Theorising*. London: The Falmer Press.
Green, B. (1995) *On Compos(IT)ing: Writing Differently in the Post-Age*. Geelong: VIC: Deakin University Centre for Education and Change.
Green, B. (1997) Reading with an attitude: Or deconstructing 'critical literacies'. In S. Muspratt, A. Luke and P. Freebody (eds) *Constructing Critical Literacies: Teaching and Learning Textual Practice* (pp. 227–242). St. Leonards, NSW: Allen and Unwin.
Green, B. and Corbett, M. (2013) *Rethinking Rural Literacies: Transnational Perspectives*. New York: Palgrave MacMillan.
Green, B. and Letts, W. (2007) Space, equity, and rural education: A trialectical account. In K. Gulson and C. Symes (eds) *Spatial Theories of Education: Policy and Geography Matters* (pp. 57–76). New York and London: Routledge.
Green, B., Cormack, P. and Reid, J. (2008) River literacies: Discursive constructions of place and environment in children's writing about the Murray-Darling Basin. In F. Vanclay, J. Malpas, M. Higgins and A. Blackshaw (eds) *Making Sense of Place: Exploring Concepts and Expressions of Place Through Different Senses and Lenses*. Canberra: National Museum of Australia.
Gregory, D. (1994) *Geographical Imaginations*. Oxford: Blackwell.
Gregory, E. and Ruby, M. (2011) The insider/outsider dilemma of ethnography: Working with young children and their families in cross-cultural contexts. *Journal of Early Childhood Research* 9 (2), 162–174.

Grenfell, M. (2012) Introduction. In M. Grenfell, D. Bloome, C. Hardy, K. Pahl, J. Rowsell and B. Street (eds) *Language, Ethnography and Education: Bridging New Literacy Studies and Bourdieu*. New York: Routledge.

Griffin, P. and Cole, M. (1984) Current activity for the future. The zo-ped. *New Directions for Child Development* 23, 45–64.

Grisham, D.L. and Wolsey, T.D. (2006) Recentering the middle school classroom as a vibrant learning community: Students, literacy and technology intersect. *Journal of Adolescent & Adult Literacy* 49 (8), 648–660.

Gross, E. (2004) Adolescent internet use: What we expect, what teens report. *Applied Developmental Psychology* 25, 633–649.

Gruszczynska, A., Merchant, G. and Pountney, R. (2013) 'Digital futures in teacher education': Exploring open approaches towards digital literacy. *The Electronic Journal of e-Learning* 11 (3), 193–206.

Gulson, K. and Symes, C. (2007) Knowing one's place: Educational theory, policy and the spatial turn. *Spatial Theories of Education: Policy and Geography Matters* (pp. 1–16). New York: Routledge.

Gumperz, J. and Hymes, D. (1972) *Directions in Sociolinguistics: The Ethnography of Communication*. New York Holt Rinehart and Winston.

Gutierrez, K. (2013) Foreword. In T. Cremin, K. Hall, B. Comber and L. Moll (eds) *International Handbook of Research on Children's Literacy, Learning and Culture*. Oxford: Wiley-Blackwell.

Gutierrez, K., Rymes, B. and Larson, J. (1995) Script, counterscript and underlife in the classroom: James Brown versus Brown versus Board of Education. *Harvard Educational Review* 65 (3), 445–471.

Gutierrez, K.D. and Larson, J. (2007) Discussing expanded spaces for learning. *Language Arts* 85 (1), 69–77.

Guzzetti, B.J. and Gamboa, M. (2005) Online journaling: The informal writings of two adolescent girls. *Research in the Teaching of English* 40, 168–206.

Haas, C. (1996) *Writing Technology: Studies on the Materiality of Literacy*. New Jersey: Laurence Erlbaum Associates.

Hagood, M. (2004) A rhizomatic cartography of adolescents, popular culture and constructions of self. In K. Leander and M. Sheehy (eds) *Spatializing Literacy Research and Practice* (pp. 143–160). New York, NY: Peter Lang.

Hague, B.N. and Loader, B.D. (eds) (1999) *Digital Democracy: Discourse and Decision Making in the Information Age*. Routledge: London.

Halewood, M. (2005) On Whitehead and Deleuze: The process of materiality. *Configurations* 13 (1), 57–76.

Hall, E.T. (1959) *The Silent Language*. Garden City, NY: Doubleday.

Hall, J.K. (1969) *The Hidden Dimension*. Garden City, NY: Doubleday.

Hall, N. (2000) The materiality of letter writing: A nineteenth century perspective. In D. Barton and N. Hall (eds) *Letter Writing as a Social Practice* (pp. 83–108). Amsterdam: John Benjamins.

Halliday, M. (1978) *Language as Social Semiotic: The Social Interpretation of Language and Meaning*. London: Edward Arnold.

Halliday, M. (1985) *An Introduction to Functional Grammar*. London: Edward Arnold.

Halliday, M. (2002) A personal perspective. *On Grammar* (Vol. 1, p. 6). London: Equinox.

Halliday, M.A.K. and Hasan, R. (1989) *Language, Context, Text: Aspects of Language in a Social, Semiotic Perspective*. Oxford: Oxford University Press.

Hamilton, M. (2001) Priviledged literacies: Policy, institutional processes, and the life of the IALS. *Language and Education* 15 (2/3), 178–196.

Hammond, J. (2001) Literacies in school education in Australia: Disjunctions between policy and research. *Language and Education* 15 (2 & 3), 162–173.

Hamston, J. (2006) Pathways to multiliteracies: Student teachers' critical reflections on a multimodal text. *The Australian Journal of Language and Literacy* 29 (1), 38–51.

Harvey, D. (1996) *Justice, Nature and the Geography of Difference*. Cambridge, MA: Blackwell Publishers.

Hawkins, M.R. (2004) Researching english language and literacy development in schools. *Educational Researcher* 33 (3), 14–25.

Hayles, N.K. (1999) *How We Became Posthuman: Virtual Bodies in Cybernetics, Literature, and Informatics*. Chicago: University of Chicago Press.

Headrick Taylor, K. and Hall, R. (2013) Counter-mapping the neighborhood on bicycles: Mobilizing youth to reimagine the city. *Technology, Knowledge and Learning* 18 (1–2), 65–93.

Heath, S. (1983) *Ways with Words: Language, Life and Work in Communities and Classrooms*. Cambridge: Cambridge University Press.

Heath, S.B. (2012) *Words at Work and Play*. Cambridge: Cambridge University Press.

Heath, S.B. (2013) The hand of play in literacy learning. In K. Hall, T. Cremin, B. Comber and L. Moll (eds) *International Handbook of Research in Children's Literacy, Learning and Culture*. West Sussex: Wiley-Blackwell.

Hegel, G.W.F. and di Geovanni, D. (2010) *The Science of Logic*. Cambridge: Cambridge University Press.

Helgøy, I., Homme, A. and Gewirtz, S. (2007) Introduction to special issue local autonomy or state control? Exploring the effects of new forms of regulation in education. *Eurpoean Educational Research Journal* 6 (3), 198–202.

Henshaw, J.M. (2012) *A Tour of the Senses: How Your Brain Interprets the World*. Baltimore, MD: Johns Hopkins University Press.

Hildyard, A. and Olson, D. (1978) Literacy and the Specialisation of Language. Ontario Institute of Studies in Education.

Hindmarsh, J. and Pilnick, A. (2007) Knowing bodies at work: Embodiment and ephemeral teamwork in anaesthesia. *Organisation Studies* 28 (9), 1395–1416.

Hodge, B. and Kress, G. (1988) *Social Semiotics*. London: Polity Press.

Hodge, R.I.V. and Kress, G.R. (1979) *Language as Ideology* (2nd edn). London: Routledge.

Hoijer, H. (1956) Review: Language in relation to a unified theory of the structure of human behaviour. *Language* 32 (3), 477–479.

Honzl, J. (1976) Dynamics of the sign in the theater. *Semiotics of Art*, 74–93.

Horst, H.A. (2009) From MySpace to Facebook: Coming of age in networked public culture. In M. Ito, S. Baumer, M. Bittanti, D. Boyd, R. Cody, B. Herr, H.A. Horst, P. Lange, D. Mahendran, K. Martinez, C.J. Pascoe, D. Perkel, L. Robinson, C. Sims and L. Tripp (eds) *Hanging Out, Messing Around, Geeking Out: Living and Learning with New Media* (pp. 83–99). Cambridge, MA: MIT Press.

Howes, D. (1991) *The Varieties of Sensory Experience: A Sourcebook in the Anthropology of the Senses*. Toronto: University of Toronto Press.

Howes, D. (2003) *Sensual Relations: Engaging the Senses in Culture and Social Theory*. Ann Arbor, MI: The University of Michigan Press.

Howes, D. (2014a) Multimodality and anthropology: The conjugation of the senses. In C. Jewitt (ed.) *The Routledge Handbook of Multimodal Analysis* (2nd edn., pp. 225–235). London: Routledge.

Howes, D. (2014b) The secret of aesthetics lies in the conjugation of the senses: Rethinking the museum as a sensory gymnasium. In N. Levent and A. Pascual-Leone (eds) *The Multisensory Museum: Cross-Disciplinary Perspectives on Touch, Sound, Smell, Memory and Space* (pp. 285–300). New York: Rowman and Littlefield.

Howes, D. (ed.) (2005) *Empire of the Senses: The Sensual Cultural Reader*. Oxford Berg.

Howes, D. and Classen, C. (2006) The museum as sensescape: Western sensibilities and Indigenous artifacts. In E. Edwards, C. Gosden and R.B. Phillips (eds) *Sensible Objects: Colonialism, Museums and Material Culture* (pp. 199–220). Oxford: Berg Publishers.

Howes, D. and Classen, C. (2014) *Ways of Sensing: Understanding the Senses in Society*. London and New York: Routledgte.

Hubbard, P. and Kitchen, R. (2011) *Key Thinkers on Space and Place* (2nd edn). London: SAGE.

Hughey, M. (2012) *White Bound: Nationalists, Antiracists, and the Shared Meanings of Race*. Standford, CA: Standford University Press.

Hughs, P. and Macnaughton, G. (2001) Fractured or manufactured: Gendered identities and culture in the early years. In S. Grieshaber and G. Cannella (eds) *Embracing Identities in Early Childhood Education: Diversity and Possibilities* (pp. 114–130). New York: Teachers College Press.

Hull, G. and Nelson, M. (2005) Locating the semiotic power of multimodality. *Written Communication* 22 (2), 224–261.

Hull, G.A. (2003) At last: Youth culture and digital media: New literacies for new times. *Research in the Teaching of English* 38 (2), 229–233.

Hull, G.A. and Stornaiuolo, A. (2010) Literate arts in a global world: Reframing social networking as cosmopolitan practice. *Journal of Adolescent and Adult Literacy* 54 (2), 85–97.

Hume, D.A. (1975) *Treatise of Human Nature* (2nd edn). Oxford: Clarendon Press.

Hurdley, R. (2006) Dismantling mantelpieces: Narrating identities and materialising culture in the home. *Sociology* 40 (4), 717–733.

Iedema, R. (2001) Resemiotization. *Semiotica* 137 (1), 4.

Ingold, T. (2000) *The Perpection of the Environment: Essays in Livelihood, Dwelling and Skill*. London: Routledge.

Ingold, T. (2004) Culture on the ground: The world perceived through the feet. *Journal of Material Culture* 9 (3), 315–340.

Ingold, T. and Howes, D. (2011) Worlds of sense and sensing the world: A reply to Sarah Pink and David Howes. *Social Anthropology* 19 (3), 313–331.

Ingold, T. and Vergunst, L. (2008) *Ways of Walking: Ethnography and Practice on Foot*. Aldershot: Ashgate.

Ito, M., Horst, H.A., Bittanti, M., Boyd, D., Herr-Stevenson, B., Lange, P. *et al.* (2008) *White Paper: Living and Learning with New Media: Summary of Findings from the Digital Youth Project*. Chicago, IL.

Ito, M., Baumer, S., Bittanti, M., Boyd, D., Cody, R., Herr, B., Horst, H.A., Lange, P., Mahendran, D., Martinez, K., Pascoe, C.J., Perkel, D., Robinson, L., Sims, C. and Tripp, L. (2009) *Hanging Out, Messing Around, Geeking Out: Living and Learning with New Media*. Cambridge, MA: MIT Press.

Iyer, R., Kettle, M., Luke, A. and Mills, K.A. (2014) Critical applied linguistics. In B. Street and C. Leung (eds) *The Routledge Companion to English Studies* (pp. 188–196). London: Routledge.

Jacobs, C. (2005) On being an insider on the outside: New spaces for integrating academic literacies. *Teaching in Higher Education* 10 (4), 475–487.

Jacobs, G.E. (2004) Complicating contexts: Issues of methodology in researching the language and literacies of instant messaging. *Reading Research Quarterly* 39 (4), 394–406.

Janks, H. (2010a) Language, power and pedagogies. In N.H. Hornberger and S.L. McKay (eds) *Sociolinguistics and Language Education*. Bristol: Multilingual Matters.

Janks, H. (2010b) *Literacy and Power*. New York and London: Routledge.

Janks, H. and Comber, B. (2006) Critical literacy across the continents. In K. Pahl and J. Rowsell (eds) *Travel Notes from the New Literacy Studies* (pp. 95–117). Clevedon: Multilingual Matters.

Jenkins, H., Puroshotma, R., Clinton, K., Weigel, M. and Robson, A.J. (2006) *Confronting The Challenges of Participatory Culture: Media Education for the 21st Century*. Chicago, Illinois: The MacArthur Foundation.

Jenkins, H., Ravi, P., Weigel, M., Clinton, K. and Robison, A.J. (2009) *Confronting the Challenges of Participatory Culture: Media Education for the 21st Century*. Cambridge, MA: MIT Press.

Jewitt, C. (2006) *Technology, Literacy and Learning: A Multimodal Approach*. Abingdon: Routledge.

Jewitt, C. (2011a) An introduction to multimodality. In C. Jewitt (ed.) *The Routledge Handbook of Multimodal Analysis*. London: Routledge.

Jewitt, C. (2011b) *The Routledge Handbook of Multimodal Analysis*. London: Routledge.

Johnson, M. (1987) *The Body in the Mind*. Chicago: University of Chicago Press.

Johnson, N.B. (1980) The material culture of public school classrooms: The symbolic integration of local schools and national culture. *Anthropology and Education Quarterly* 9 (3), 173–190.

Jones, C.A. (ed.) (2006) *Sensorium: Embodied Experience, Technology and Contemporary Art*. Cambridge, MA: MIT Press.

Jones Diaz, C., Beecher, B. and Arther, L. (2007) Children's worlds: Globalisation and critical literacy. In L. Makin, C. Jones Diaz and C. McLachlan (eds) *Literacies in Childhood: Changing Views Challenging Practices* (2nd edn., pp. 71–86). Marrickville, NSW: Elsevier.

Junquiera, E.S. (2008) Challenging the boundaries between standard and popular language situated in historical contexts: The communicative practices of high-school Brazilian students crafting hybrid multi-modal ways with words. *Language and Education* 26 (6), 393–410.

Kalantzis, M. and Cope, B. (eds) (2005) *Learning By Design*. Melbourne, VIC: Victorian Schools Innovation Commission and Common Ground.

Kalantzis, M. and Cope, B. (2008) *New learning: Elements of a Science of Education*. Port Melbourne, Vic: Cambridge Uni Press.

Kalantzis, M. and Cope, B. (2012) *Literacies*. Port Melbourne, Victoria: Cambridge University Press.

Kamberelis, G. (2004) A rhizome and the pack: Liminal literacy formations with political teeth. In K. Leander and M. Sheehey (eds) *Spatializing Literacy Research and Practice* (pp. 161–197). New York: Peter Lang.

Kenway, J. and Bullen, E. (2001) *Consuming Children: Education-Entertainment-Advertising*. Buckingham: Open University Press.

Kietzmann, J., Hermkens, K. and McCarthy, I. (2011) Social media? Get serious! Understanding the functional building blocks of social media. *Business Horizons* 54 (3), 241–251.

Kincheloe, J. and McLaren, P. (1994) Rethinking critical theory and qualitative research. In N. Denzin and Y. Lincoln (eds) *Handbook of Qualitative Research* (pp. 138–157). New York: SAGE.

Kincheloe, J.L. (2007) Critical pedagogy in the twenty-first century: Evolution for survival. In P. McLaren and J. L. Kincheloe (eds) *Critical Pedagogy: Where Are We Now?* (pp. 9–42). New York: Peter Lang Publishing.

Kincheloe, J.L. (2008) *Critical Pedagogy* (2nd edn). New York: Peter Lang.

Kinder, B. (1991) *Playing With Power in Movies: Television and Video Games from Muppet Babies to Teenage Mutant Ninja Turtles.* Berkley: University of California Press.

Knight, L. (2009) Chapter 4: Desire and rhizome. In D. Masny and M. Cole (eds) *Multiple Literacies Theory: A Deleuzian Perspective* (pp. 51–62). Rotterdam, The Netherlands: Sense Publishers.

Knobel, M. and Healy, A. (1998) Critical literacies: An introduction. In M. Knobel and A. Healy (ed.) *Critical Literacies in the Primary Classroom* (pp. 1–12). Arizona, USA: Zephyr Press.

Knobel, M. and Lankshear, C. (eds) (2007) *A New Literacies Sampler* (Vol. 29). New York, NY: Peter Lang Publishing.

Knobel, M., Stone, L. and Warschauer, M. (2002) *Technology and Academic Preparation: A Comparative Study.* California: Department of Education, University of California.

Knoester, M. (2009) Inquiry into urban adolescent independent reading habits: Can Gee's theory of discourses provide insight? *Journal of Adolescent & Adult Literacy* 52 (8), 676–685.

Knorr Cetina, K. (1997) Sociality with objects: Social relations in postsocial knowledge societies. *Theory, Culture and Society* 14 (4), 1–30.

Kop, R. (2011) The challenges to connectivist learning on open online networks: Learning experiences during a Massive Open Online Course. *International Review of Research in Open and Distance Learning* 12 (3), 2–38.

Koskos, K., Boehlen, S. and Walker, B.J. (2000) Learning the art of instructional conversation: The influence of self-assessment on teachers' instructional discourse in a reading clinic. *The Elementary School Journal* 100 (3), 229–252.

Kress, G. (1985) *Linguistic Processes in Sociocultural Practice.* Victoria: Deakin University.

Kress, G. (1990) Critical discourse analysis. *Annual Review of Applied Linguistics* 11, 84–99.

Kress, G. (1993) Genre as social process. In B. Cope and M. Kalantzis (eds) *The Powers of Literacy: A Genre Approach to Teaching Writing* (pp. 1–21). London: Falmer Press.

Kress, G. (1997) *Before Writing: Rethinking the Paths to Literacy.* London: Routledge.

Kress, G. (2000a) Design and transformation: New theories of meaning. In B. Cope and M. Kalantzis (eds) *Multiliteracies: Literacy Learning and the Design of Social Futures* (pp. 153–161). South Yarra, VIC: Macmillan.

Kress, G. (2000b) Multimodality. In B. Cope and M. Kalantzis (eds) *Multiliteracies: Literacy Learning and the Design of Social Futures* (pp. 182–202). South Yarra, VIC: Macmillan.

Kress, G. (2005) *Literacy in the New Media Age.* London: Routledge.

Kress, G. and van Leeuwen, T. (2001) *Multimodal Discourse: The Modes and Media of Contemporary Communication.* London: Arnold

Kress, G. and van Leeuwen, T. (2006) *Reading Images: The Grammar of Visual Design* (2nd edn). London: Routledge.

Kress, G. and Bezemer, J. (2008) Writing in multimodal texts: A social semiotic account of designs for learning. *Written Communication* 25 (2), 166–195.

Kress, G., Jewitt, C., Ogborn, J. and Tsatsarelis, C. (2001) *Multimodal Teaching and Learning: The Rhetorics of the Science Classroom.* London: Continuum.

Kristien, Z. and Harmon, J. (2009) Picturing a writing process: Photovoice and teaching writing to urban youth. *Journal of Adolescent & Adult Literacy* 52 (7), 575–584.

Labov, W. (1966) *The Social Stratification of English in New York City*. Washington DC: Centre for Applied Linguistics.

Labov, W. (1969) *The Logic of Non-Standard English* (Vol. 22). Georgetown, Washington DC, USA: Georgetown University School of Languages and Linguistics.

Labov, W. (1970) The logic of non-standard English. In J.E. Alatis (ed.) *Linguistics and the Teaching of Standard English to Speakers of Other Languages or Dialects* (pp. 1–44). Washington, DC, Georgetown: Georgetown University Press.

Labov, W. (1972) *Sociolinguistic Patterns*. Philadelphia, PA: University of Pennsylvania Press.

Ladson-Billings (2009) Race still matters: Critical race theory in education. In M.W. Apple, W. Au and L.A. Gandin (eds) *The Routledge International Handbook of Critical Education* (pp. 110–123). New York: Routledge.

Lam, E.W.S. (2000) L2 Literacy and the design of the self: A case-study of a teenager writing on the Internet. *TESOL Quarterly* 34 (3), 427–482.

Lam, E.W.S. (2009) Multiliteracies on instant messaging in negotiating local, translocal, and transnational affiliations: A case of an adolescent immigrant. *Reading Research Quarterly* 44 (4), 377–397.

Landow, G. and Delany, P. (1991) Hypertext, hypermedia and literary studies: The state of the art. In P. Delany and G. Landow (eds) *Hypermedia and Literary Studies* (pp. 3–50). London: MIT Press.

Lankshear, C. and Knobel, M. (2005) Paulo Freire and digital youth in marginal spaces. In G.E. Fischman, P. McLaren, H. Sunker and C. Lankshear (eds) *Critical Theories, Radical Pedagogies, and Global Conflicts* (pp. 293–306). Oxford: Rowman and Littlefield.

Lankshear, C. and Knobel, M. (2008) Digital literacy and participation in online networking spaces. In M. Knobel and C. Lankshear (eds) *Digital Literacies: Concepts, Policies and Practices*. New York: Peter Lang Publishing.

Lankshear, C., McLaren, P. and Greene, M. (eds) (1993) *Critical Literacy: Politics, Praxis, and the Postmodern*. New York: State University of New York Press.

Lankshear, C., Gee, J., Knobel, M. and Searle, C. (1997) *Changing Literacies*. Philadelphia: PA: Open University Press.

Lash, S. and Urry, J. (1994) *Economies of Signs and Space*. London: SAGE.

Latour, B. (1987) *Science in Action*. Cambridge, MA: Harvard University Press.

Latour, B. (1992) Where are the missing masses? Sociology of a few mundane artefacts. In W. Bijker and J. Law (eds) *Shaping Technology, Building Society: Studies in Sociotechnical Change* (pp. 225–258). MA: Cambridge, MIT Press.

Latour, B. (1997) Trains of thought: Piaget, formalism, and the fifth dimension. *Common Knowledge* 6, 170–191.

Latour, B. (2004) *Politics of Nature*. Cambridge, MA: Harvard University Press.

Latour, B. (2005) *Reassembling the Social: An Introduction to Actor-Network Theory*. Oxford: Oxford University Press.

Laurier, E. (2011) Bruno Latour. In P. Hubbard and R. Kitchen (eds) *Key Thinkers on Space and Place* (2nd edn., pp. 272–278). London: Sage.

Lave, J. (1988) *Cognition in Practice: Mind, Mathematics, and Culture in Everyday Life*. Cambridge: Cambridge University Press.

Lave, J. (1993) The practice of learning. In S. Chaiklin and J. Lave (eds) *Understanding Practice: Persepctives on Activity and Context* (pp. 3–32). Cambridge: Cambridge University Press.

Lave, J. and Wenger, E. (1991) *Situated Learning: Legitimate Peripheral Participation*. Cambridge: Cambridge University Press.

Law, J. (2004) *After Method: Mess in Social Science Research.* Abingdon: Routledge.

Law, J. (2008) Actor network theory and material semiotics. In B.S. Turner (ed.) *The New Blackwell Companion to Social Theory* (3rd edn., pp. 141–158). Chichester: Wiley-Blackwell.

Law, J. (2012) Collateral realities. In F. Rubio and P. Baert (eds) *The Politics of Knowledge* (pp. 156–178). London: Routledge.

Law, J. and Hetherington, K. (2003) Materialities, spatialities, and globalities. In M. Dear and S. Flusty (eds) *The Spaces of Postmodernism: Reading in Human Geography* (pp. 390–401). Oxford: Blackwell Publishing.

Lawn, M. and Grosvenor, I. (2005) *Materialities of Schooling.* Oxford Symposium Books.

Leadbeater, C. (2010) *Cloud Culture: The Future of Global Cultural Relations.* London: Counterpoint.

Leander, K. and Sheehy, M. (eds) (2004) *Spatializing Literacy Research.* New York, NY: Peter Lang.

Leander, K.M. (2002) Locating Latanya: The situated production of identity artifacts in classroom interaction. *Research in the Teaching of English* 37, 198–250.

Leander, K.M. (2003) Writing travellers' tales on new literacyscapes. *Reading Research Quarterly* 38 (3), 392–397.

Leander, K.M., Phillips, N.C. and Headrick Taylor, K. (2010) The changing social spaces of learning: Mapping new mobilities. *Review of Research in Education* 34, 329–394.

Lee, C. (2007) Affordances and text-making practices in online instant messaging. *Written Communication* 24 (3), 223–249.

Leeds-Hurwitz, W. (2005) The natural history approach: A Bateson legacy. *Cybernetics and Human Knowing* 12 (1–2), 137–146.

Lefebvre, H. (1968) *Le Droit a la Ville.* Paris: Anthropos.

Lefebvre, H. (1991) *The Production of Space* (D. Nicholson-Smith, trans.). London: Blackwell.

Lemke, J. (1998) Multiplying meaning: Visual and verbal semiotics in scientific text *Reading Science: Critical and Functional Perspectives on Discourses of Science.* London: Routledge.

Lemke, J. (2002) Travels in hypermodality. *Visual Communication* 1 (3), 299–325.

Lemke, J., Lecusay, R., Cole, M. and Michalchick, V. (2015) *Documenting and Assessing Learning in Media-Rich Environments.* Cambridge, MA: MIT Press and MacArthur Foundation.

Leontiev, A.N. (1978) *Activity, Consciousness, and Personality.* Englewood Cliffs, NJ: Prentice Hall.

Leu, D. (1996) Sarah's secret: Social aspects of literacy and learning in a digital information age. *The Reading Teacher* 50 (2), 162.

Leu, D.J. (2009) The New Literacies: Research on reading instruction with the internet and other digital technologies In S.J. Samuels and A.E. Farstrup (eds) *What Research Has to Say About Reading Instruction.* Newark, DE: International Reading Association.

Leu, D.J., Reinking, D., Carter, A., Castek, J., Coiro, J. and Henry, L.A. (2007) *Defining Online Reading Comprehension: Using Think Aloud Verbal Protocols to Refine A Preliminary Model of Internet Reading Comprehension Processes.* Paper presented at American Educational Research Association Annual Meeting.

Lewis, C. and Fabos, B. (2000) But will it work in the heartland? A response and illustration. *Journal of Adolescent & Adult Literacy* 43 (5), 462–469.

Lewis, C. and Fabos, B. (2005) Instant messaging, literacies, and social identities. *Reading Research Quarterly* 40 (4), 470–501.

Lipman, P. (2007) Education and the spatialization of urban equality: A case study of Chicago's Renaissance 2010. In K. Gulson and C. Symes (eds) *Spatial Theories of Education: Policy and Geography Matters* (pp. 155–174). London: Routledge.

Lloyd, A. (2007) Learning to put out the red stuff: Becoming information literate through discursive practice. *The Library Quarterly* 77 (2), 181–191.

Locke, J. (1690) *An Essay Concerning Human Understanding*. London: Taylor.

Lopez-Gopar, M.E. (2007) Beyond alienating alphabetic literacy: Multiliteracies in Indigenous education in Mexico. *Diaspora, Indigenous, and Minority Education* 1 (3), 159–174.

Luke, A. (1988) *Literacy, Textbooks and Ideology: Postwar Literacy Instruction and the Mythology of Dick and Jane*. London: Falmer Press.

Luke, A. (1992) The body literate. *Linguistics and Education* 4, 107–129.

Luke, A. (1994) *The Social Construction of Literacy in the Primary School*. Melbourne: Macmillan Education Australia.

Luke, A. (1998) Critical approaches to literacy. In V. Edwards and D. Corson (eds) *Encyclopedia of Language and Education* (Vol. 2). Dordrecht: Kluwer.

Luke, A. (2008) Digital Innovation in Schooling: Policy Efficacy, Youth Cultures and Pedagogical Change. Brisbane, Australia: Queensland University of Technology.

Luke, A. and Freebody, P. (1997) Shaping the social practices of reading. In S. Muspratt, A. Luke and P. Freebody (eds) *Constructing Critical Literacies: Teaching and Learning Textual Practice* (pp. 185–225). Sydney, Australia: Allen & Unwin.

Luke, A., Comber, B. and Grant, H. (2003) Critical literacies and cultural studies. In M. Anstey and G. Bull (eds) *The Literacy Lexicon* (2nd edn., pp. 15–35). Frenchs Forest: NSW.

Lund, K. (2005) Seeing in motion and the touching eye: Walking over Scotland's mountains. *Etnofoor Athropological Journal* 18 (1), 27–42.

Luria, A.R. (1976) *Cognitive Development: Its Cultural and Social Foundations*. Cambridge, MA: Harvard University Press.

Lynch, T.L. (2008) Rereadings and literacy: How students' second readings might open third spaces. *Journal of Adolescent and Adult Literacy* 52 (4), 334–341.

MacDougall, D. (2005) *The Corporeal Image: Film, Ethnography, and the Senses*. Princeton, NJ: Princeton University Press.

Makin, L. and Whiteman, P. (2007) Literacies in childhood: Changing views, challenging practice. In L. Makin, C. Diaz and C. McLachlan (eds) *Multiliteracies and the Arts* (pp. 168–182). Marrickville: MacLennan and Petty, Elsevier.

Marsh, J. (2003) Connections between literacy practices at home and in the nursery. *British Education Research Journal* 29 (3), 369–382.

Marsh, J. (2011) Young children's literacy practices in a virtual world: Establishing an online interaction order. *Reading Research Quarterly* 46 (2), 101–118.

Martin, J. and Rothery, J. (1980) *Writing Project Report Number 1: Working Papers in Linguistics*. Sydney: University of Sydney.

Martin, J. and Rothery, J. (1981) *Writing Project Report Number 2: Working Papers in Linguistics*. Sydney: University of Sydney.

Martin, J. and Rothery, J. (1986) *Writing Project Report Number 4: Working Papers in Linguistics*. Sydney: University of Sydney.

Martinec, R. (1996) *Rhythm in Multimodal Texts*. London: The London Institute.

Martínez, K., Z. (2009) Sharing snapshots of teen friendship and love. In M. Ito, S. Baumer, M. Bittanti, D. Boyd, R. Cody, B. Herr, H.A. Horst, P. Lange, D. Mahendran, K. Martinez, C.J. Pascoe, D. Perkel, L. Robinson, C. Sims and L. Tripp (eds) *Hanging Out, Messing Around, Geeking Out: Living and Learning with New Media* (pp. 78–80). Cambridge: MIT Press.

Marx, K. (1970) *Preface to a Contribution to the Critique of Political Economy*. New York: International Publishers.

Marx, K. and Engels, F. (1968) Selected Works. London: Lawrence and Wishart.

Massey, D. (1991) A global sense of place. *Marxism Today* June, 24–29.

Massey, D. (ed.) (1994) *Space, Place, and Gender*. Cambridge: Polity Press.

Massey, D. and Allen, L. (1984) *Spatial Divisions of Labour: Social Structure and the Geography of Production*. London and Basingstoke: Macmillan.

Massey, D.B. (2000) The conceptualization of place. In D. Massey and P. Jess (eds) *A Place in the World? Places, Cultures, Globalization*. New York: Oxford University Press.

Massey, D.B. (2005) *For Space*. London: Sage.

Mauss, M. (1979) Techniques of the body (B. Brewster, trans.) *Sociology and Psychology: Essays by Marcel Mauss* (pp. 95–135). London: Routledge and Kegan Paul.

Mavers, D. (2009) Image in the multimodal ensemble: Children's drawing. In C. Jewitt (ed.) *The Routledge Handbook of Multimodal Analysis*. Abingdon, Oxen Routledge.

McCarthy, C., Pitton, V., Soochul, K. and Monje, D. (2009) Movement and stasis in the neoliberal reorientation of schooling. In M.W. Apple, W. Au and L.A. Gandin (eds) *The Routledge International Handbook of Critical Education* (pp. 36–50). New York: Routlege.

McGuinnis (2007) Khmer rap boys, X-Men, Asia's fruits, and Dragonball Z: Creating multilingual and multimodal classroom contexts. *Journal of Adolescent & Adult Literacy* 50 (7), 570–579.

McKenna, M., Reinking, D., Labbo, L. and Kieffer, R. (1999) The electronic transformation of literacy and its implications for the struggling reader. *Reading and Writing Quarterly* 15, 111–126.

McLaren, P. (1989) *Life in Schools: An Introduction to Critical Pedagogy in the Foundations of Education*. New York: Longman.

McLaren, P. (1993) *Schooling as Ritual Performance: Towards a Political Economy of Educational Symbols and Gestures* (2nd edn). London: Routledge.

McLaren, P. (1994) *Life in Schools: An Introduction to Critical Pedagogy in the Foundations of Education* (2nd edn). White Plains, NY: Longman.

McLaren, P. (1995) *Critical Pedagogy and Predatory Culture: Oppositional Politics in a Postmodern Era*. London and New York: Routlege.

McLuhan, M. and Powers, B.R. (1989) *The Global Village: Transformations in World Life and Media in the 21st Century*. Oxford: Oxford University Press.

McNeil, D. (1992) *Hand and Mind: What Gestures Reveal About Thought*. London: The University of Chicago Press.

McVee, M.B., Dunsmore, K. and Gavelek, J.R. (2005) Schema theory revisited. *Review of Educational Research* 75 (4), 531–566.

Menezes de Souza, L. (2004) The ecology of writing among the Kashinowa: Indigenous multimodality in Brazil. In S. Canagarajah (ed.) *Reclaiming the Local in Language Policy and Practice* (pp. 73–98). New York: Psychology Press.

Merchant, G. (2001) Teenagers in cyberspace: An investigation of language use and language change in internet chatrooms. *Journal of Research in Reading* 24 (3), 293–306.

Merchant, G. and Burnette, C. (2013) Points of view: Reconceptualising literacies through an exploration of adult and child interactions in a virtual world. *Journal of Research in Reading* 37 (1), 36–50.

Merchant, G. and Schamroth Abrams, S. (2013) The digital challenge. In K. Hall, T. Cremin, B. Comber and L. Moll (eds) *International Handbook of Research on Children's Literacy, Learning and Culture* (pp. 319–332). West Sussex: Wiley-Blackwell.

Merleau-Ponty, M. (2002) *The Phenomenology of Perception*. London: Routledge.

Metz, C. (1974) Film Language. New York: Oxford Press.

Michaels, S. (1985) Hearing the connections in children's oral and written discourse. *Journal of Education* 167, 36–56.

Miller, S.M. and McVee, M.B. (2012) *Multimodal Composing in Classrooms: Learning and Teaching for the Digital World*. New York: Routledge.

Mills, K.A. (2005) Deconstructing binary oppositions in literacy discourse and pedagogy. *Australian Journal of Language and Literacy* 28 (1), 67–82.

Mills, K.A. (2006a) Mr. Travelling-at-will Ted Doyle: Discourses in a multiliteracies classroom. *Australian Journal of Language and Literacy* 28 (2), 132–149.

Mills, K.A. (2006b) Multiliteracies: A critical ethnography: Pedagogy, power, discourse and access to multiliteracies. Unpublished PhD thesis, Queensland University of Technology, Brisbane.

Mills, K.A. (2006c) We've been wastin' a whole million watchin' her doin' her shoes: Situated practice within a pedagogy of multiliteracies. *The Australian Educational Researcher* 33 (3), 13–34.

Mills, K.A. (2007) Have you seen Lord of the Rings? Power, pedagogy and discourses in a multiliteracies classroom. *Journal of Language, Identity, and Education* 6 (3), 221–241.

Mills, K.A. (2008a) Transformed practice in a pedagogy of multiliteracies. *Pedagogies: An International Journal* 3 (2), 109–128.

Mills, K.A. (2008b) Will large-scale assessments raise literacy standards in Australian schools? *Australian Journal of Language and Literacy* 31 (3), 211–226.

Mills, K.A. (2009) Multiliteracies: Interrogating competing discourses. *Language and Education* 23 (2), 103–116.

Mills, K.A. (2010a) Filming in progress: New spaces for multimodal designing. *Linguistics and Education* 21 (1), 14–28.

Mills, K.A. (2010b) A review of the digital turn in the New Literacy Studies. *Review of Educational Research* 80 (2), 246–271.

Mills, K.A. (2010c) Shrek meets Vygotsky: Rethinking adolescents' multimodal literacy practicies in schools. *Journal of Adolescent and Adult Literacy* 54 (1), 35–45.

Mills, K.A. (2010d) What learners 'know' in digital text production: Learning by Design. *E-Learning and Digital Media* 7 (3), 223–236.

Mills, K.A. (2011a) 'I'm making it different to the book': Transmediation in young children's print and digital practices. *Australasian Journal of Early Childhood Education* 36 (3), 56–65.

Mills, K.A. (2011b) Inciting the social imagination to realising the dream: A unfolding story of transformative action in a low-socioeconomic school. Paper presented at the AERA 2011 Annual Meeting, Published Proceedings, April 8–12 New Orleans, Louisiana.

Mills, K.A. (2011c) *The Multiliteracies Classroom*. Bristol: Multilingual Matters.

Mills, K.A. (2011d) 'Now I understand their secrets': Kineikonic texts in the literacy classroom. *Australian Journal of Language and Literacy* 34 (1), 24–37.

Mills, K.A. (2013a) CUOL - See you online. *Screen Education* 70, 52–57.

Mills, K.A. (2013b) Multimodal and monomodal discourses of marketization in higher education: power, ideology, and the absence of the image. Paper presented at Education and Poverty: Theory, Research, Policy and Praxis : Proceedings of AERA Annual Meeting 2013.

Mills, K.A. and Chandra, V. (2011) Microblogging as a literacy practice for educational communities. *Journal of Adolescent and Adult Literacy* 55 (1), 35–45.

Mills, K.A. and Comber, B. (2013) Space, place, and power: A spatial turn in literacy research. In K. Hall, T. Cremin, B. Comber and L. Moll (eds) *International Handbook of Research on Children's Literacy, Learning and Culture* (pp. 412–423). Oxford: Wiley Blackwell.

Mills, K.A. and Comber, B. (2015) Socio-spatial approaches to Literacy Studies: Rethinking the social constitution and politics of space. In K. Pahl and J. Rowsell (eds) *Handbook of Literacy Studies*. London: Routledge.

Mills, K.A. and Exley, B. (2014a) Narrative and multimodality in English language arts curricula: A tale of two nations. *Language Arts* 92 (2), 136–143.

Mills, K.A. and Exley, B. (2014b) Time, space, and text in the elementary school digital writing classroom. *Written Communication* 31 (4), 368–398.

Mills, K.A. and Levido, A. (2011) iPed: Pedagogy for digital text production. *The Reading Teacher* 65 (1), 85–91.

Mills, K.A., Chandra, V. and Park, J. (2013) The architecture of children's use of language and tools when problem solving collaboratively with robotics. *Australian Education Researcher* 40 (3), 315–337.

Mills, K.A., Comber, B. and Kelly, P. (2013) Sensing place: Embodiment, sensoriality, kinesis, and children behind the camera. *English Teaching: Practice and Critique* 12 (2), 11–27.

Mills, K.A., Davis-Warra, J., Sewell, M. and Anderson M. (2015) Indigenous ways with literacies: Transgenerational, multimodal, placed, and collective. *Language and Education*, Online first. DOI: 10.1080109500782.2015.1069836

Mills, K.A., Sunderland, N., Davis, J., Darrah, J., Bristed, H., Wilson, G. and Hertslet, T. (2012) If I were a community leader: Knowing the world by changing it. *Queensland Teachers' Union Professional Magazine* November, 10–11.

Mills, K.A., Unsworth, L., Bellocchi, A., Park, J. and Ritchie, S.M. (2014) Children's multimodal appraisal of places: Walking with the camera. *Australian Journal of Language and Literacy* 37 (3), 171–181.

Mishra, P. and Koehler, M.J. (2006) Technological pedagogical content knowledge: A framework for integrating technology in teacher knowledge. *Teachers College Record* 108 (6), 1017–1054.

Mitchell, R. (1999a) Catching literature in the 'net'. *Primary English Teaching Association* 117, 1–8.

Mitchell, W. (1999b) *Iconology: Image, Text, Ideology*. Chicago, IL: University of Chicago Press.

Mitsikopoulou, B. (2007) The interplay of the global and the local in English language learning and electronic communication discourses and practices in Greece. *Language and Education* 21 (3), 232–246.

Moja, E.B. (2004) Tracing the out-of-school literacy spaces of Latino/a Youth. In K. Leander and M. Sheehy (eds) *Spatializing Literacy Research and Practice*. New York: Peter Lang.

Moje, E. (2013) Hybrid literacies in a post-hybrid world. In K. Hall, T. Cremin, B. Comber and L. Moll (eds) *International Handbook of Research on Children's Literacy, Learning and Culture*. West Sussex: Wiley-Blackwell.

Monaghan, J.E. and Saul, E.W. (1987) The reader, the scribe, the thinker: A critical look at the history of American reading instruction. In T.S. Popkewitz (ed.) *The Formation of the Schooled Subject* (pp. 85–122). New York: Falmer Press.

Montessori-Pierson, M. (1913) *The 1913 Rome lectures: First International Training Course*. Amsterdam.

Montessori-Pierson, M. (1991) *Spontaneous Activity in Education* Oxford, Clio Pres.

Morley , D. and Robins, K. (1995) *Spaces of Identity: Global Media, Electronic Landscapes and Cultural Boundaries.* London Routledge.

Morrell, E. (2002) Toward a critical pedagogy of popular culture: Literacy development among urban youth. *Journal of Adolescent & Adult Literacy* 46, 72–77.

Moss, G. (2000) Informal literacies and pedagogic discourse. *Linguistics and Education* 11 (1), 47–64.

Moss, G. (2003) Putting the text back into practice: Junior-age non-fiction as objects of design. In C. Jewitt and G. Kress (eds) *Multimodal Literacy* (pp. 73–87). New York: Peter Lang.

Moylan, M. and Stiles, L. (1996) *Reading Books: Essays on the Material Text and Literature in America.* Amherst: University of Massachusetts Press.

Mukama, E. and Andersson, S.B. (2008) Coping with change in ICT-based learning environments: Newly qualified Rwandan teachers' reflections. *Journal of Computer Assisted Learning* 24, 156–166.

Mukarovsky, J. (1976) Art as semiotic fact. *Semiotics of Art,* 3–9.

Nattiez, J.J. (1976) *Fondements Dune Semiologie Musicale.* Paris: Uge.

Nespor, J. (1997) *Tangled Up in School: Politics, Space, Bodies, and Signs in the Educational Process.* London: Falmer.

Nespor, J. (2008) Education and place: A review essay. *Educational Theory* 58, 475–489.

Neuman, S.B. and Celano, D. (2006) Access to print in a low-income and middle income communities: An ecological study of four neighbourhoods. *Reading Research Quarterly* 36 (1), 8–26.

Neumann, M.M. and Neumann, D.L. (2014) Touch screen tablets and emergent literacy. *Early Childhood Education Journal* 42 (4), 231–239.

New London Group (1996) A pedagogy of multiliteracies: Designing social futures. *Harvard Educational Review* 66 (1), 60–92.

New London Group (2000) A pedagogy of multiliteracies: Designing social futures. In B. Cope and M. Kalantzis (eds) *Multiliteracies: Literacy Learning and the Design of Social Futures* (pp. 9–38). South Yarra, Australia: Macmillan.

Nichols, S., Rowsell, J., Nixon, H. and Rainbird, S. (2012) *Resourcing Early Learners: New Networks, New Actors.* London: Routledge.

Nicolopoulou, A. (1993) Play, cognitive development, and the social world: Piaget, Vygotsky, and beyond. *Human Development* 36 (1), 1–23.

Nixon, H. (2003) New research literacies for contemporary research into literacy and new media. *Reading Research Quarterly* 38 (3), 407–413.

Nixon, H. and Hately, E. (2013) Books, toys, and tablets: Playing and learning in the age of digital media. In K. Hall, T. Cremin, B. Comber and L. Moss (eds) *InternationalHandbook of Research on Children's Literacy, Learning and Culture* (pp. 28–41). Malden, MA: Wiley and Sons Ltd.

Norris, S. (2004) *Analysing Multimodal Interaction.* London: Routledge Falmer.

Norris, S. (2011) Modal density and modal configurations: Multimodal actions. In C. Jewitt (ed.) *The Routledge Handbook of Multimodal Analysis* (pp. 78–90). London Routledge.

O'Dowd, R. (2005) Negotiating sociocultural and institutional contexts: The case of Spanish-American telecollaboration. *Language and Intercultural Communication* 5 (1), 40–56.

O'Halloran, K. (2004) *Multimodal Discourse Analysis: Systemic-Functional Perspectives.* London, NY: Continuum.

O'Halloran, K.L. (1999) Interdependence, interaction and metaphor in multisemiotic texts. *Social Semiotics* 9 (3), 317–354.

O'Halloran, K.L. (2009) Historical changes in the semiotic landscape: From calculation to computation. In C. Jewitt (ed.) *The Routledge Handbook of Multimodal Analysis* (pp. 98–113). London and New York: Routledge.

O'Reilly, T. (2005). What is web 2.0? Design patterns and business models for the next generation of software. See http://www.oreillynet.com/pub/a/oreilly/tim/news/2005/09/30/what-is-web-20.html (accessed 30 Sept 2005).

Orlikowski, W. (2007) Sociomaterial practices: Exploring technology at work. *Organization Studies* 28 (9), 1435–1448.

Ormerod, F. and Ivanic, R. (2000) Texts in practices: Interpreting the physical characteristics of children's project work. In D. Barton, M. Hamilton and R. Ivanic (eds) *Situated Literacies: Reading and Writing in Context* (pp. 91–107). London: Routledge.

Pahl, K. (2001) Texts as artefacts crossing sites: Map making at home and school. *Reading: Literacy and Language* 35 (3), 120–125.

Pahl, K. (2002) Ephemera, mess and miscellaneous piles: Texts and practices in families. *Journal of Early Childhood Literacy* 11 (2), 114–140.

Pahl, K. (2003) Children's text-making at home: Transforming meaning across modes. In J. Carey and G. Kress (eds) *Multimodal Literacy* (pp. 139–154). New York: Peter Lang.

Pahl, K. (2014) The New Literacy Studies. In B. Street and C. Leung (eds) *The Routledge Companion to English Studies* (pp. 435–448). London: Routlege.

Pahl, K. and Burnett, C. (2013) Literacies in homes and communities. In K. Hall, T. Cremin, B. Comber and L. Moll (eds) *International Handbook of Research on Children's Literacy, Learning and Culture*. West Sussex: John Wiley and Sons.

Pahl, K. and Rowsell, J. (2005) *Literacy and Education: Understanding the New Literacy Studies in the Classroom*. London: Chapman.

Pahl, K. and Rowsell, J. (2006) *Travel Notes from New Literacy Studies: Instances of Practice*. Clevedon: Multilingual Matters.

Pahl, K. and Rowsell, J. (2010) *Artifactual Literacies: Every Object Tells a Story*. New York: Teachers College Press.

Pahl, K.H. and Rowsell, J. (2011) Artifactual critical literacy: A new perspective for literacy education. *Berkeley Review of Education* 2 (3), 129–151.

Painter, C., Martin, J.R. and Unsworth, L. (2013) *Reading Visual Narratives: Image Analysis of Children's Picture Books*. Sheffield: Equinox Publishing

Pallasmaa, J. (2005) Lived space: Embodied experience and sensory thought. *Encounters: Architectural Essays*. Hameenlinna, Finland: Rakennustieto Oy.

Pandya, V. (1993) *Above the Forest: Andamanese Ethnoanemology, Cosmology, and the Power of Ritual*. Bombay: Oxford University Press.

Pascoe, C.J. (2009) You have another world to create. In M. Ito, S. Baumer, M. Bittanti, D. Boyd, R. Cody, B. Herr, H.A. Horst, P. Lange, D. Mahendran, K. Martinez, C.J. Pascoe, D. Perkel, L. Robinson, C. Sims and L. Tripp (eds) *Hanging Out, Messing Around, Geeking Out: Living and Learning with New Media* (pp. 51–57). Cambridge, MA: MIT Press.

Paterson, M. (2007) *The Senses of Touch: Haptics, Affects and Technologies*. Oxford: Berg.

Pegg, J. and Panizzon, D. (2007) Inequities in student achievement for literacy: Metropolitan versus rural comparisons. *Australian Journal of Language and Literacy* 30 (3), 177–190.

Pels, D., Hetherington, K. and Vandenberghe, F. (2002) The status of the object: Performances, mediations and techniques. *Theory, Culture and Society* 19 (5/6), 1–21.

Pennycook, A. (2007) The myth of English as an International language. In S. Makoni and A. Pennycook (eds) *Disinventing and Reconstituting Languages* (pp. 90–115). Clevedon: Multilingual Matters.

Peppler, K.A. and Kafai, Y.B. (2007) From SuperGoo to Scratch: Exploring creative digital media production in informal learning. *Learning, Media, & Technology* 32 (2), 149–166.

Piaget, J. (1952a) *The Origins of Intelligence in Children*. New York: International Universities Press: International Universities Press.

Piaget, J. (1952b) *Play, Dreams and Imitation in Childhood*. New York: W.W Norton and Co. Inc.

Pickering, A. (1995) *The Mangle of Practice: Time, Agency and Science*. Chicago, IL: University of Chicago Press.

Pike, K. (1954) *Language in Relation to a Unified Theory of the Structure of Human Behaviour*. Glendale, CA: Summer Insitute of Linguistics.

Pink, G. (2007) Walking with video. *Visual Studies* 22 (3), 240–252.

Pink, S. (2005) Dirty laundry: Everyday practice, sensory engagement and the constitution of identity. *Social Anthropology* 13 (3), 275–290.

Pink, S. (2009) *Doing Sensory Ethnography*. London: SAGE.

Porteous, D. (1990) *Landscapes of the Mind: Worlds of Sense and Metaphor*. Toronto: University of Toronto Press.

Potter, J. (2010) Embodied memory and curatorship in children's digital video production. *English Teaching: Practice and Critique* 9 (1), 22–35.

Prain, V. (1997) Multi(national)literacies and globalising discourses. *Discourse: Studies in the cultural politics of education* 18 (3), 453–467.

Price, S., Jewitt, C. and Brown, B. (eds) (2013) *The SAGE Handbook of Digital Technology Research*. London: SAGE.

Prinsloo, M. and Snyder, S. (2008) Young people's engagement with digital literacies in marginal contexts in a globalised world. *Language and Education* 21 (3), 171–179.

Ranker, J. (2007) Designing meaning with multiple media sources: A case study of an eight-year-old student's writing processes. *Research in the Teaching of English* 41 (4), 402–434.

Ranker, J. and Mills, K.A. (2014) New directions for digital video creation in the classroom: Spatiality, embodiment, and creativity. *Journal of Adolescent and Adult Literacy* 57 (6), 440–443.

Reese, D. (2008) Indigenizing children's literature. *Journal of Language and Literacy Education* 4 (2), 59–72.

Reinking, D. and Pickle, M. (1993) Using a formative experiment to study how computers affect reading and writing in classrooms. In D.J. Leu and C.K. Kinzer (eds) *Examining Central Issues in Literacy Research, Theory, and Practice: 42nd Yearbook of the National Reading Conference* (pp. 263–270). Chicago National Reading Conference.

Reinking, D., McKenna, M., Labbo, L. and Kieffer, R. (eds) (1998) *Handbook of Literacy and Technology: Transformations In a Post-Typographic World*. Mahwah, NJ: Lawrence Erlbaum.

Resnick, M., Rusk, N. and Cooke, S. (1998) The Computer Clubhouse: Technological fluency in the inner city. In D. Schon, B. Sanyal and W. Mitchell (eds) *High Technology and Low-Income Communities*. Cambridge, MA: MIT Press.

Reyes, I. and Estebann-Guitart, M. (2013) Exploring multiple literacies from homes and communities: A cross-cultural comparative analysis. In K. Hall, T. Cremin, B. Comber and L. Moll (eds) *International Handbook of Research on Children's Literacy, Learning and Culture* (pp. 155–171). West Sussex: Wiley-Blackwell.

Rich, A. (1979) *On Lies, Secrets, and Silences*. New York: Norton.

Richardson, P. (1991) Language as personal resource and as social construct: Competent views of literacy pedagogy in Australia. *Educational Review* 43 (2), 171–190.

Riggins, S.H. (ed.) (1997) *The Language and Politics of Exclusion: Others in Discourse*. London: SAGE.

Robertson, S. and Dale, R. (2009) World Bank, IMF, and the possibilities of critical education. In M. A. Apple, W. Au and G. Armando (eds) *The Routledge International Handbook of Critical education* (pp. 23–35). New York Routledge.

Rodaway, P. (1994) *Sensuous Geographies: Body, Sense and Place*. London: Routledge.

Roe, M. (2012) Book Review: Pahl, K., and Rowsell, J. (2010). Artifactual Literacies: Every Object Tells a Story. New York, NY: Teachers College Press. *Journal of Educational Research* 105, 299–301.

Rojas-Drummond, S.M., Albarran, C.D. and Littleton, K.S. (2008) Collaboration, creativity and the co-construction of oral and written texts. *Thinking Skills and Creativity* 3, 177–191.

Rosowsky, A. (2008) *Heavenly Readings: Liturgical Literacy in a Multicultural Context*. Bristol: Multilingual Matters.

Rowsell, J. (2011) Carrying my family with me: Artifacts as emic perspective. *Qualitative Research* 11 (3), 331–346.

Rowsell, J. and Chen, L. (2014) English studies through a New Literacy Studies - multimodal lens. In C. Leung and B. Street (eds) *The Routledge Companion to English Studies* (pp. 464–474). London: Routledge.

Ruesh, J. and Kees, W. (1954) *Nonverbal Communication: Notes on the Visual Perceptions of Human Relations*. Berkeley, CA: University of California Press.

Ryokai, K. and Cassel, J. (1999) Computer support for children's collaborative fantasy play and story telling. Paper presented at the CSCL Standford, CA.

Sanford, K. and Maddil, L. (2006) Resistance through video game play: It's a boy thing. *Canadian Journal of Education* 29 (1), 287–345.

Sannino, A., Daniels, H. and Gutiérrez, K. (2009) Learning and Expanding with Activity Theory. New York: Cambridge University Press.

Schwartz, A. and Rubinstein-Ávila, E. (2006) Understanding the manga hype: Uncovering the multimodality of comic-book literacies. *Journal of Adolescent & Adult Literacy* 50 (1), 40–49.

Scollon, R. and Scollon, S.W. (2003) *Discourses in Place: Language in the Material World*. London: Routledge.

Scollon, R. and Scollon, S.W. (2009) Multimodality and language: a retrospective and prospective view. In C. Jewitt (ed.) *The Routledge Handbook of Multimodal Analysis* (pp. 170–180). London and New York: Routledge.

Scribner, S. and Cole, M. (1981) *The Psychology of Literacy*. Cambridge, MA: Harvard University Press.

Selfe, C.L. (1992) Preparing English teachers for the virtual age: The case for technology critics. In G.E. Hawisher and P. LeBlanc (eds) *Reimaging Computers and Composition: Teaching and Research in the Virtual Age* (pp. 24–42). Portsmouth, NH: Heinemann.

Semali, L.M. (2002) *Transmediation in the Classroom: A Semiotics-Based Media Literacy Framework* (Vol. 176). New York: Peter Lang

Semali, L.M. and Fueyo, J. (2001) Transmediation as a Metaphor for New Literacies in Multimedia Classrooms. *Reading Online* 5 (5).

Sensenbaugh, R. (1990) Multiplicities of Literacies in the 1990's, *ERIC Clearing House on Reading and Communication Skills (ED320138)*: Bloomington.

Sheehy, M. and Leander, K.M. (2004) Introduction. In *Spatialising Literacy Research and Practice* (pp. 1–14). New York: Peter Lang Publishing.

Shields, R. (2011) Henri Lefebvre. In P. Hubbard and R. Kitchin (eds) *Key Thinkers on Space and Place* (2nd edn, pp. 279–285). London: SAGE.

Shilling, C. (1991) *The Body and Social Theory*. London: SAGE.

Shor, I. (1999) What is critical literacy? *Journal of Pedagogy, Pluralism and Practice* 4 (1), 1–27.

Short, K.G., Kauffman, G. and Khann, L.H. (2000) I just need to draw: Responding to literature across multiple sign systems. *The Reading Teacher* 54 (2), 160–171.

Siegel, M. (1995) More than words: The generative power of transmediation for learning *Canadian Journal of Education* 20 (4), 455–475.

Siegel, M. (2006) Rereading the signs: Multimodal transformations in the field of literacy education. *Language Arts* 84 (1), 65.

Simmel, G. (1997 [1907]) Sociology of the senses. In D. Frisby and M. Featherstone (eds) *Simmel on Culture: Selected Writings*. London: Sage.

Simon, R. (2012) Rembering together: Social media and the formation of the historical present. In E. Giaccardi (ed.) *Heritage and Social Media: Understanding Heritage in a Participatory Culture* (pp. 89–106). London: Routledge.

Siu, K.W., Lam, M. and Seung, M. (2005) Early childhood technology education: A socio-cultural perspective. *Early Childhood Education Journal* 32 (6), 353–358.

Skerrett, A. (2014) Religious literacies in a secular literacy classroom. *Reading Research Quarterly* 49 (2), 233–250.

Smith, D. (1990) *Text, Facts and Femininity*. London: Routledge.

Smith, D. (1999) *Writing the Social: Critique, Theory and Investigation*. Toronto: University of Toronto Press.

Snyder, I. (1997) *Page to Screen: Taking Literacy into the Electronic Era*. London: Routledge.

Snyder, I. (1999) Using information technology in language and literacy education: An introduction. In J. Hancock (ed.) *Teaching Literacy Using Information Technology* (pp. 1–10). Carlton South, Australia: Australian Literacy Education Association.

Snyder, I. (2001) A new communication order: Researching literacy practices in the network society. *Language and Education* 15 (1 and 2), 117–131.

Snyder, I., Angus, L. and Sutherland-Smith, W. (2002) Building equitable literate futures: Home and school computer-mediated literacy practices and disadvantage. *Cambridge Journal of Education* 32 (3), 367–383.

Soja, E. (1996) *Thirdspace: Journeys to Los Angeles and Other Real-and-Imagined Places*. Oxford: Basil Blackwell.

Soja, E. and Hooper, B. (1993) The spaces that difference means: Some notes on the geographical margins of the new cultural politics. In M. Keith and S. Pile (eds) *Place and the Politics of Identity*. London: Routledge.

Soja, E.W. (1989) *Postmodern Geographies: The Reassertion of Space in Critical Social Theory*. Oxford: Verso.

Soja, E.W. (2004) Preface. In K.M. Leander and M. Sheehey (eds) *Spatialising Literacy Research and Practice* (pp. ix–xv). New York Peter Lang.

Soja, E.W. (2008) The city and spatial justice. Paper presented at the Spatial Justice Conference, March 12–14 Nanterre, Paris.

Somerville, M.J. (2007) Place literacies. *Australian Journal of Language and Literacy* 30 (2), 149–164.

Sorenson, E. (2009) *The Materiality of Learning: Technology and Knowledge of Educational Practice*. Cambridge: Cambridge University Press.

Spencer, M. (1986) Emergent literacies: A site for analysis. *Language Arts* 63 (5), 442–453.

Stanton, D., Bayon, V., Neale, H., Ahmed, G., Benford, S., Cobb, S., Ingram, R., O'Malley, C., Wilson, J. and Pridmore, T. (2001) Classroom collaboration in the design of tangible interfaces for storytelling. *CHI Letters* 3 (1), 482–489.

Stein, P. (2006) The Olifantsvlei fresh stories project: Multimodality, creativity, and fixing in the semiotic chain. In C. Jewitt and G. Kress (eds) *Multimodal Literacy* (pp. 123–138). New York: Peter Lang.

Stein, P. and Slonimsky, L. (2006) An eye on the text and an eye on the future: Multimodal literacy in three Johannesburg families. In K. Pahl and J. Rowsell (eds) *Travel Notes from the New Literacy Studies: Instances of Practice*. Clevedon: Multilingual Matters.

Steinkhuehler, C. (2007) Massively multiplayer online gaming as a constellation of literacy practices. *E-Learning* 4 (3), 297–318.

Stevens, L.P. and Bean, T.W. (2007) *Critical Literacy: Context, Research and Practice in the K-12 Classroom*. Thousand Oaks: SAGE.

Stoller, P. (1989) *The Taste of Ethnographic Things: The Sense in Ethnography*. Philadelphia, PA.

Stoller, P. (1997) *Sensuous Scholarship*. Philadelphia, PA: University of Pennsylvania Press.

Stoller, P. (2004) Sensuous ethnography, African persuasions, and social knowledge. *Qualitative Inquiry* 10 (6), 817–835.

Strassman, P. (1997) Information systems and literacy. In G. Hawisher and C. Selfe (eds) *Literacy, Technology and Society: Confronting the Issues* (pp. 134–141). Upper Saddle River, NJ: Prentice Hall.

Street, B. (1975) The Mullah, the Shahname and the Madrasseh. *Asian Affairs* 6 (3), 290–306.

Street, B. (1984) *Literacy in Theory and Practice*. Cambridge: Cambridge University Press.

Street, B. (1995) *Social literacies: Critical Approaches to Literacy in Development, Ethnography and Education*. London: Longman.

Street, B. (1997a) *Cross-Cultural Approaches to Literacy*. Melbourne: Cambridge University Press.

Street, B. (1997b) The implications of the new literacy studies for literacy education. *English in Education* 31 (3), 45–59.

Street, B. (1999) The meaning of literacy. In D. Wagner, R. Venezky and B. Street (eds) *Literacy: An International Handbook* (pp. 34–40). Boulder, CO: Westview Press.

Street, B. (2003) What's 'new' in New Literacy Studies? Critical approaches to literacy in theory and practice. *Current Issues in Comparative Education* 5 (2), 77–91.

Street, B. (2012) New Literacy Studies. In M. Grenfell, D. Bloome, C. Hardy, K. Pahl, J. Rowsell and B. Street (eds) *Language, Ethnography, and Education: Bridging New Literacy Studies and Bourdieu*. UK: Routledge.

Street, B. (ed.) (1993) *Cross Cultural Approaches to Literacy*. Cambridge: Cambridge University Press.

Street, B. and Street, J. (1991) The schooling of literacy. In D. Barton and I. R. (eds) *Writing In the Community* (pp. 143–166). London: Sage.

Street, B., Pahl, K. and Rowsell, J. (2009) Multimodality and the New Literacy Studies. In C. Jewitt (ed.) *The Routledge Handbook of Multimodal Analysis* (pp. 191–200). London: Routledge.

Suhor, C. (1984) Towards a semiotic-based curriculum. *Journal of Curriculum Studies* 16 (3), 247–257.

Sunderland, N., Bristed, H., Gudes, O., Boddy, J. and Da Silva, M. (2012) What does it feel like to live here? Exploring sensory ethnography as a collaborative methodology for investigating social determinants of health in place. *Health and Place* 18 (5), 1056–1067.

Sutton, R.E. (2006) Cooking skill, the senses, and memory: The fate of practical knowledge. In E. Edwards, C. Gosden and R.B. Phillips (eds) *Sensible Objects*. Oxford: Berg.

Thibault, P.J. (1993) Editorial: Social Semiotics. *The Semiotic Review of Books* 4 (3), 1.

Tilley, C. (2006) The sensory dimensions of gardening. *Senses and Society* 2 (3), 329–351.

Toledo Museum of Art (2013) *The Art of Seeing Art: A, B and See.* Toledo, OH: Toledo Museum of Art.

Tollefson, T. (2007) Language policy and the construction of national cultural identity. In A. Tsui and J. Tollefson (eds) *Language Policy, Culture and Identity in Asian Contexts* (pp. 1–20). Mahwah, New Jersey: Lawrence Erlbaum.

Trimbur, J. (2001) Review: Multiliteracies: Literacy learning and the design of social futures. *College Composition and Communication* 52 (4), 659.

Turkle, S. (2007) *Evocative Objects: Things We Think With.* Cambridge, MA: MIT Press.

Ulmer, G. (1989) *Teletheory: Grammatology in the Age of Video.* New York: Routledge.

Unsworth, L. (2001) *Teaching Multiliteracies Across the Curriculum: Changing Contexts of Text and Image in Classroom Practice.* Buckingham, United Kingdom: Open University Press.

Unsworth, L. (2002) Changing dimensions of school literacies. *The Australian Journal of Language and Literacy* 25 (1), 62–77.

Unsworth, L. (2006) *E-Literature for Children: Enhancing Digital Literacy Learning.* London: Routledge.

Unsworth, L. (2014) Multimodal reading comprehension: Curriculum expectations and large-scale literacy testing practices. *Pedagogies: An International Journal* 9 (1), 26–44.

Unsworth, L., Thomas, A., Simpson, A. and Asha, J. (2005) *Children's Literature and Computer Based Teaching.* New York: Open University Press.

Urry, J. (2000) *Sociology Beyond Societies: Mobilities For the Twenty-First Century.* London: Routledge.

Urry, J. (2007) *Mobilities.* Cambridge: Polity.

Valk, F.V. (2008) Identity, power, and representation in virtual environments. *Journal of Online Learning and Teaching* 4 (2), 201–211.

van Leeuwen, T. (1985) Rhythmic structure of the film text. In T. van Dijk (ed.) *Discourse and Communication* (pp. 216–232). Berlin: de Gruyter.

van Leeuwen, T. (1999) *Speech, Music, Sound.* London: Macmillan.

van Leeuwen, T. (2011) Parametric systems: The case of voice quality. In C. Jewitt (ed.) *The Routledge Handbook of Multimodal Analysis* (pp. 68–77). London: Routlege.

van Leeuwen, T. and Jewitt, C. (2001) *Handbook of Visual Analysis.* London: SAGE.

van Sluys, K., Fink, L.S. and Fisher, D. (2008) Engaging as ethnographers: Insights into the collaborative study of a literacy learning community. *Voices from the Middle* 16 (1), 15–22.

Varga-Dobai, K. (2014) Responding to literature through storytelling, artifacts and multigenre writing practices: Explorations of cultures and self. *Literacy* 49 (2), 57–59.

Vasudevan, L.M. (2014) Multimodal cosmopolitanism: Cultivating belonging in everyday moments with youth. *Curriculum Inquiry* 44 (1), 45–67.

Vaughn, M. (2012) Review: Artifactual literacies: Every object tells a story, by Kate Pahl and Jennifer Rowsell, New York, Teachers College Press, 2010, p. 176. *Community Development* 43 (5), 684–685.

Vygotsky, L. (1962) *Thought and Language.* Cambridge, MA: Massachusetts Institute of Technology.

Vygotsky, L. (1978) *Mind in Society: The Development of Higher Psychological Processes.* London: Harvard University Press.

Vygotsky, L. (1987) *The General Problems of General Psychology: Including the Volume Thinking and Speech* (Vol. One). New York: Plenum Press.

Wakkary, R., Desjardins, A., Muise, K., Tanenbaum, K. and Hatala, M. (2012) Situating the sociability of interactive museum guides. In E. Giaccardi (ed.) *Heritage and Social Media: Understanding Heritage in a Participatory Culture* (pp. 217–238). London: Routledge.

Wall, W. (2010) Literacy and the domestic arts. *The Huntington Library Quarterly* 73 (3), 383.

Walton, M. (2007) Cheating literacy: The limitations of simulated classroom discourse in educational software for children. *Language and Education* 21 (3), 197–215.

Warner, J.M. (2013) Mapping literacy in poverty: Rhizoanalysis of the multimodal digital literacy practices of low achieving, low income high school students. Paper presented at the Education and Poverty: Theory, Research, Policy and Praxis: Annual Meeting of the American Educational Research Association, April 27 - May 1 San Francisco, CA.

Warren, S. (2008) Empirical challenges in organizational aesthetics research: Towards a sensual methodology. *Organization Studies* 29 (4), 559–580.

Warschauer, M. (2004) *Technology and Social Inclusion: Rethinking the Digital Divide.* Cambridge, MA: MIT Press.

Warschauer, M. and Matuchniak, T. (2010) New Technology and digital worlds: Analysing the evidence. *Review of Research in Education* 34 (1), 179–225.

Waters, M. (1995) *Globalisation.* London: Routledge.

Weiner, E.J. (2002) Beyond remediation: Ideological literacies of learning in developmental classrooms. *Journal of Adolescent and Adult Literacy* 46 (2), 150–168.

Wellman, B. and Gulia, M. (1999) Net-Surfers don't ride alone: Virtual communities as communities. In B. Wellman (ed.) *Networks in the Global Village: Life in Contemporary Communities* (pp. 331–366). Boulder, CO: Westview Press.

Wenger, E. (1998) *Communities of Practice: Learning, Meaning and Identity.* Cambridge: Cambridge University Press.

West, A. (1992) Reading against the text: Developing critical literacy. *Changing English: Studies in Culture and Education* 1 (1), 82–101.

Wheeler, S. and Wheeler, D. (2009) Using wikis to promote quality learning in teacher training. *Learning, Media and Technology* 34 (1), 1–10.

White, S. (1998) Foreword. In M. Cole (ed.) *Cultural Psychology: A Once and Future Discipline* (pp. ix–xvi). Harvard: Harvard University Press.

Whitehead, A.N. (1967) *Adventures of Ideas.* New York: The Free Press.

Whitehead, A.N. (1978) Process and reality. In D.R. Griffin and D.W. Sherburne (eds) *An Essay In Cosmology.* New York: Free Press.

Wilf, E. (2010) Swinging within the iron cage: Modernity, creativity, and embodied practice in American postsecondary jazz education. *American Ethnologist* 37 (3), 563–582.

Williams, D. (1982) 'Semasiology': A semantic anthropologist's view of human movements and actions. In D. Parkin (ed.) *Semantic Anthropology* (pp. 161–182). London: Academic Press.

Wilson, A. (2000) There is no escape from third-space theory: Borderland disourse and the 'in-between' literacies of prison. In D. Barton, M. Hamilton and R. Ivanic (eds) *Situated Literacies: Reading and Writing in Context* (pp. 54–69). London: Routledge.

Wilson, A. (2008) Moving beyond the page in content area literacy: Comprehension instruction for multimodal texts in science. *The Reading Teacher* 62 (2), 153–156.

Wilson, J. (2004) Four days and breakfast: Time, space, and literacy/ies in the prison community. In K. Leander and M. Sheehy (eds) *Spatializing Literacy Research and Practice.* New York: Peter Lang Publishing.

Yi, Y. (2008) Relay writing in an adolescent online community. *Journal of Adolescent & Adult Literacy* 51 (8), 670–680.

Young, I.M. (1992) Five faces of oppression. In T.E. Wartenbergy (ed.) *Rethinking Power* (pp. 174–195). Albany: State University of New York Press.

Index